SUGARLAND TEX MAR 21 1913

Sugar Land, Texas
and
The Imperial Sugar Company

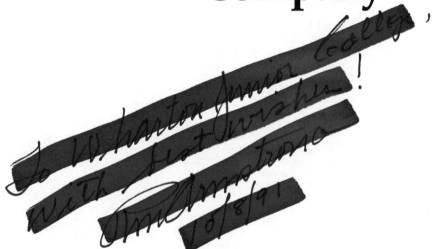

To Wharton Junior College,
with best wishes!
Wm Armstrong 10/8/91

75436

BY

R. M. ARMSTRONG

1 9 9 1

ISBN: 0-9629314-0-3
Library of Congress
Catalog Card Number: 91-091957

Typography and Printing by
D. Armstrong Co., Inc.
Houston, Texas

To my wife, Louise, for 55 years of
love, encouragement and tolerance.

Curtis Hall, 30 year part-time constable, on the lack of crime in the company town, "Busy
people with good jobs, security and nice homes just don't get into much trouble. They don't
have the time or the inclination. This was a family town. It's the loafers who commit the
crimes and we just don't have any of them and we never have had."

1932   The isolated company town of Sugar Land, with the Imperial Sugar refinery in the center. Farm lands shown in this photo include most of the 15,000 acres owned by Sugarland Industries.

1988   *Modern Sugar Land and suburban Houston.*

CONTENTS

PREFACE

There needed to be someone to preserve the story of a unique company-owned town and an unusual Texas industry, as well as the stories of those individuals who influenced the past and present. I seem to be the only one left with the memories, access to the information and the ready inclination to conserve the chronicle.

My father, O. R. Armstrong, began his employment by the Cunningham Sugar Company in 1908, five hours after I was born. He spent the rest of his long life working for either the successor Imperial Sugar Company or the short-lived Texas Sugar Refining Company at Texas City, and retired in 1947 as vice president and director of Imperial. During the last 14 years of his active business life he lived in Sugar Land.

He brought me up in the business. I worked in the Imperial and Texas City refineries prior to my graduation from Sugar Land High School in 1926. I was well acquainted with both Mr. W. T. Eldridge and Mr. I. H. Kempner, co-owners of the company town. I began full time employment with Imperial in 1938, and retired 35 years later as president, and director in 1973. I am currently director emeritus of the successor company, the Imperial Holly Corporation. From 1953, when I became executive vice president of Imperial, I shared the governance of the company-owned community with T. L. James, president of the sister company, Sugarland Industries, until the town was incorporated and turned over to elected officials in 1959.

During all those years, I was a ready receptacle for the many recollections of the older employees and citizens, some of whom had worked and lived in Sugar Land in the early 1900's, when the place was known as "The hell hole of the Brazos." Foremost among these was Gus Ulrich, who came to Sugar Land in

1906 to take charge of the building of a model community on the site and who managed everything in the company owned town and its surrounding 12,500 acres until his death in 1947. He was an inexhaustible source of Sugar Land fact and lore—he loved to talk about the good old days, which he defined as from 1900 to the beginning of World War II.

Another reliable source of information has been our resident historian and raconteur, T. C. Rozelle. T. C. was born in Sugar Land in 1915, and except for a tour of duty with the U. S. Navy, has spent his entire life in Sugar Land, retiring in 1980 as personnel manager of the Imperial Sugar Company. Betty Anheiser has also been most helpful and encouraging. I am particularly indebted to W. M. Von-Maszewski, who heads the Department of Genealogy and Local History at the George Memorial Library in Richmond, Texas, for his encouragement and professional assistance. Ed and Lea Eitelman, with their word processor, became my friendly collaborators in this effort.

References for the first seven chapters of this book are as shown at the end of each chapter.

The information contained in the remaining chapters, starting with chapter eight, is taken primarily from the historical and other files of the Imperial Sugar Company; including the minute books of Imperial, the Sugarland Industries, the Cunningham Sugar Company and other locally owned corporations, as well as financial statements, reports, correspondence, hand written letters or notes from former employees, etc. This information has not been indexed or collated and is not generally open to public inspection.

Sugar Land, Texas   R. M. A.
July 15, 1989

INTRODUCTION

The modern city of Sugar Land is located in the eastern portion of Fort Bend County, which places it in what has been described in the 1980's as the fastest growing portion of the fastest growing county in the United States. It is twenty-five miles southwest of Houston and for all practical purposes is a growing suburb of that city. It is seven miles east of the county seat at Richmond. At present, it has thirteen square miles within the city limits and an additional thirty-five square miles in its extra territorial jurisdiction.[1]

What once was a swampy, semi-tropical, partially wooded area seen only by small wandering bands of Indians is now an area of new homes, most of them built in the 1970's and 1980's. Among the homes have grown shopping centers, freeways, office buildings, parks, schools, hospitals, landscaped lakes, and streams. There is a modern airport capable of landing large corporate jet aircraft. There are three deluxe country clubs, two with twenty-seven hole golf courses and one with eighteen. One of the twenty-seven hole courses is being enlarged to thirty-six. An eighteen hole public course was completed in 1990.

The population of Sugar Land and its extra territorial jurisdiction in 1990 is approximately 50,000, and projections are for growth to 100,000 by the year 2,000.[2] The Sugar Land schools are part of the Fort Bend Independent School District, which now has four modern high schools, seven junior high schools, and twenty elementary schools, with a total school population of 34,000.[3]

The huge, modern Imperial Sugar Company refinery, which dominates the skyline for miles around, occupies a thirteen acre tract on the western edge of the city. It is the oldest business in Texas still operating on the same site and still manufacturing the same products, sugar and molasses. In 1988, it capped its long history by merging into what is now the Imperial Holly Corporation, the second largest publicly held manufacturer of refined sugar in the United States, with sales of $717,000,000 in fiscal 1990, placing it among the prestigious Fortune 500 leading companies in the country.

There have been a number of interesting histories written about Fort Bend County, but they concern themselves largely with the happenings around Richmond and the western portion of the county. This is understandable, since Richmond was the first settlement to be recognized as a city, and become the county seat and center of county government, as well as the home of many of the county's distinguished citizens and families.

In the eastern half of Fort Bend County, until the latter part of the twentieth century, there were only a few small communities, the largest of which was Sugar Land, and it was isolated from the rest of the county by the undeveloped roads. And Sugar Land was unique, a sort of 15,000 acre kingdom in itself, managed from an almost entirely self-sufficient company town. The only distinguished citizens or families were the owners, and they took little part or interest in what happened in Richmond or the western half of the county. As late as the 1950's, aside from electing precinct representatives, Sugar Land played almost no part in county activities.

The story of the city of Sugar Land, Texas, including that of the Imperial Sugar Company, is part of the history of Oyster Creek. This creek has its beginning about fifteen miles north and west of Sugar Land. It meanders through farm lands, through the center of the city, through the sugar refinery grounds and continues south and east to the Gulf of Mexico. Many well known farms and plantations in early Texas were located along its course.

The earliest reported visitors to the Oyster Creek area around Sugar Land were small groups of Indians, organized more by family than by tribe. Later, they would become known as the Karankawas. These groups were first reported in the early 1500's by Spanish explorers.[4] They represented the most primitive level of native culture in Texas.[5] These were not yet the horseback, bow and arrow Indians; their weapons were stones, sharpened sticks and clubs; some early reports said they were, at times, cannibalistic. They were nomadic, wandering among the strip of islands along the upper Texas coast and the mainland opposite, often up the fresh water rivers inland: seeking nothing more complicated than survival. They planted no crops and wore little or no clothing, covering themselves with rancid animal fats, fish oils and mud for protection from insects.[6] They liked to keep within range of fresh water. An early explorer reported that nuts were one of the most important food items of the Indians, who congregated in the river valleys in the fall to harvest pecans and persimmons. One of their most easily available foods was the black-shelled, gray-fleshed freshwater clams that abounded in shallow waters along the shores of Oyster Creek—which is named for them—and in the nearby muddy marshlands. These clams are still found in Oyster Creek and the connecting lakes.

The main contribution made by the early Indians to the future of Sugar Land as a home for sugar plantations and the Imperial Sugar Company was the discovery and frequent use of a low water point on Oyster Creek. This spot could be completely dry at low water, and wadable most of the rest of the time. It became a crossing point for a well-used Indian and game trail, which would develop into an important route across southeast Texas in later years. In 1990, the old low water crossing is marked by the two concrete bridges on Highway 90A spanning Oyster Creek just 50 yards from the corner of the Imperial Sugar Company grounds.

During the 200-year span between the early 1600s and the 1800s, Spanish rulers of Mexico made abortive attempts to colonize Texas by establishing missions and forts generally throughout the southeastern portions of the state. One of their main routes of travel ran from the Gulf Coast through what is now Houston, then along the old Indian trail across Oyster Creek at the low water point and on to the Spanish headquarters in San Antonio. It was still more of a trail than a road, but it was important because it provided a recognized pathway or route along which travelers and their wagons, carts and ox-drawn sleds could move without encountering and having to detour around unexpected forests, rivers, lakes and cane brakes. Thus, the low water crossing at Oyster Creek became an established point on a frequently used route which would later be

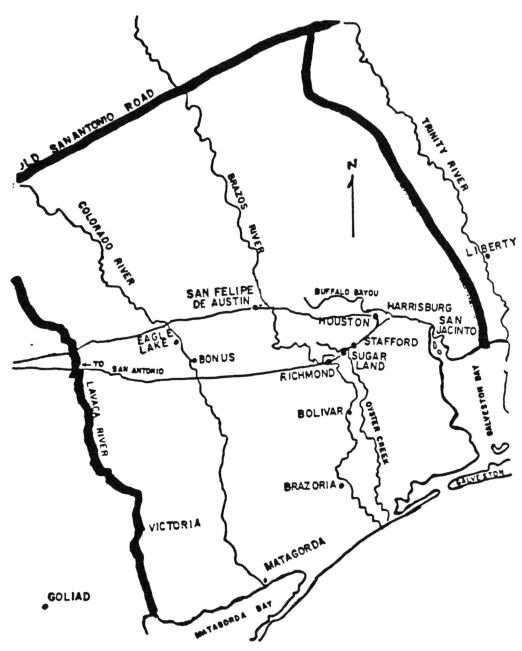

The area outlined by
the Austin Colony.

designated as Highway 90A from Beaumont through Houston and Sugar Land to San Antonio.

In the early 1800's, after some 200 years of failing in various attempts to civilize the local Indian population or to make colonists out of Mexican immigrants into the area, the Spanish finally gave up and turned to the American pioneers who had proven their abilities to convert wilderness into productive enterprise.

In 1823, the Mexican government, by then independent of Spain but concerned about the future of their Texas territory, granted Stephen F. Austin a charter to bring the first 300 American households into Texas to settle under Mexican rule on land grants from Mexico.[7] Austin's charter was outlined roughly by the Gulf Coast on the south, the Lavaca River on the west, the Old San Antonio Road on the north (this ran from San Antonio through what is now Bastrop and Nacagdoches) and on the east by the San Jacinto River.[8] It was, in those days of difficult transportation, a large piece of territory, about 125 miles deep and 120 miles wide.

Austin's choice of this part of Texas for his colony was, first, that it was near the Gulf Coast, since a great deal of the movement of people and supplies could be by ship from new Orleans and east; and second that the watersheds of the Colorado and Brazos Rivers and Oyster Creek provided some of the most fertile soil in Texas, as well as plenty of fresh water, lumber for building, grass for cattle, and game for meat. Also, passable transportation was already provided by the old trail from the coast through the center of the colony, as well as the Old San Antonio Road on the north.

News of the possibility of free land had spread through the South, and even before the charter became official, Austin was besieged with applications for the promised Mexican land grants. The attraction was that each household, if it qualified, could receive a "league" (4,428 acres) of grazing land and a "labor" (177 acres) of farm land.[9] The only qualifications were that each head of a household present certification from his neighbors in his home community that he was of good character, sober and industrious; and that he would accept the Roman Catholic Church. Although the latter requirement was seldom enforced, it became a source of irritation among some of the colonists. The land was to be free of charge except for the costs of clerical and surveying work—this was set at 12½ cents per acre—payable over a seven year period. Since cash was scarce among the pioneer immigrants, payment could be made either in cash or barter, using almost any commodity, including cattle or slaves.[10]

Many would-be settlers were drawn by the greater opportunities for a new life in a new land; some sought adventure. But the main attraction was the chance to acquire land on easy terms. The Panic of 1819 had left many people in difficulty, and some were quite willing to try something new and promising. Some had little to leave behind so they loaded up what belongings they had, chalked "GTT" (Gone To Texas) on the doorpost, and left on horseback or in carriages and wagons for Texas. Some walked. Some were wealthy enough to travel by ship; some brought slaves and household equipment and farm supplies. Jared Groce, a wealthy planter from Alabama, acquired a number of leagues near what is now Hempstead, and arrived with a train of livestock, fifty wagons and ninety slaves.[11] Most reached the promised land with a minimum of goods

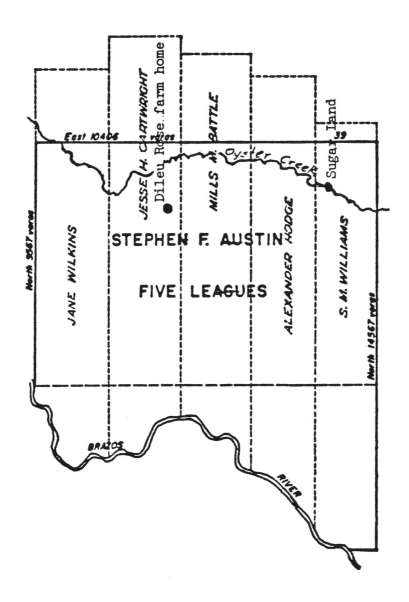

Wharton's History of Fort Bend County

and equipment but with plenty of pioneer determination.

People who moved into the Oyster Creek area around what is now Sugar Land found that the attraction was considerably more apparent than the hardships which might be encountered in moving into a strange and undeveloped land. The newcomers arriving at their chosen land grant, usually after a long, tiring and often hazardous journey overland or by sea, faced the pressing necessity of establishing some sort of living facilities. With a minimum of equipment, tools, food or supplies of any kind, they were forced to cut trees, build shelter, clear land and scratch out the beginnings of some sort of subsistence crops. But in general, the people who came to settle Texas at that time were venturesome and courageous people, and endured the hardships and dangers, building new lives for themselves and their families.

In the Oyster Creek area the settlers were fortunate to find an abundance of game. Those living in the area today find it hard to believe that not only were there smaller creatures such as rabbits, fox, wild pigs, turkeys, geese and ducks, fish, clams and frogs, but also deer, wild cattle, bear and occasionally buffalo available to the hunter. One early settler reported seeing a herd of an estimated 3,000 buffalo moving through what is now Sugar Land.[12]

Impatiently waiting for the first crop of corn and yams, the settler had to protect his crops, animals and belongings from predators, which included small wandering groups of Indians. The coastal Indians who often appeared seldom went farther than stealing. Even so, they were a source of concern to a lonely pioneer family often located miles from the nearest neighbor. It was, certainly at first, a difficult and occasionally dangerous existence. It does not seem at all strange that, in 1835, one old settler is reported to have advised a prospective Texan not to bring a wife with him, but to find one "already acclimated to Texas."

But they were a determined and hardy breed. Of the initial 300 land grants issued by Austin in his colony, only seven were forfeited. Fifty of the 300 were located in Fort Bend County, most of them near the Brazos River and Oyster Creek.

The first owner of the land grant on which the city of Sugar Land and the Imperial Sugar Company would later be established was Stephen F. Austin himself. For his services in leading this first successful colonization he would be known in the history books as the "Father of Texas." As compensation for acting as "empressario" in forming and managing the colony, Austin was allowed to award himself twenty-two leagues (over 97,000 acres) of land.[13] In 1824 he chose five adjoining leagues on Oyster Creek in what is now eastern Fort Bend County, for his homestead.[14] One of these leagues would become the site of the company-owned town of Sugar Land.

During the next four years after the issuance of the original 300 grants, Austin received permission to settle an additional 900 families.[15] By that time he was well into the many administrative duties which devolved upon the "empressario" of a rapidly growing and scattered group of independent settlers, with more on the way. He had no time to develop his own properties, and in 1828 he disposed of his five Oyster Creek land grants. The easternmost grant, which included the low water crossing of the old trail across the creek, he awarded to S. M. Williams for services to the colony.[16]

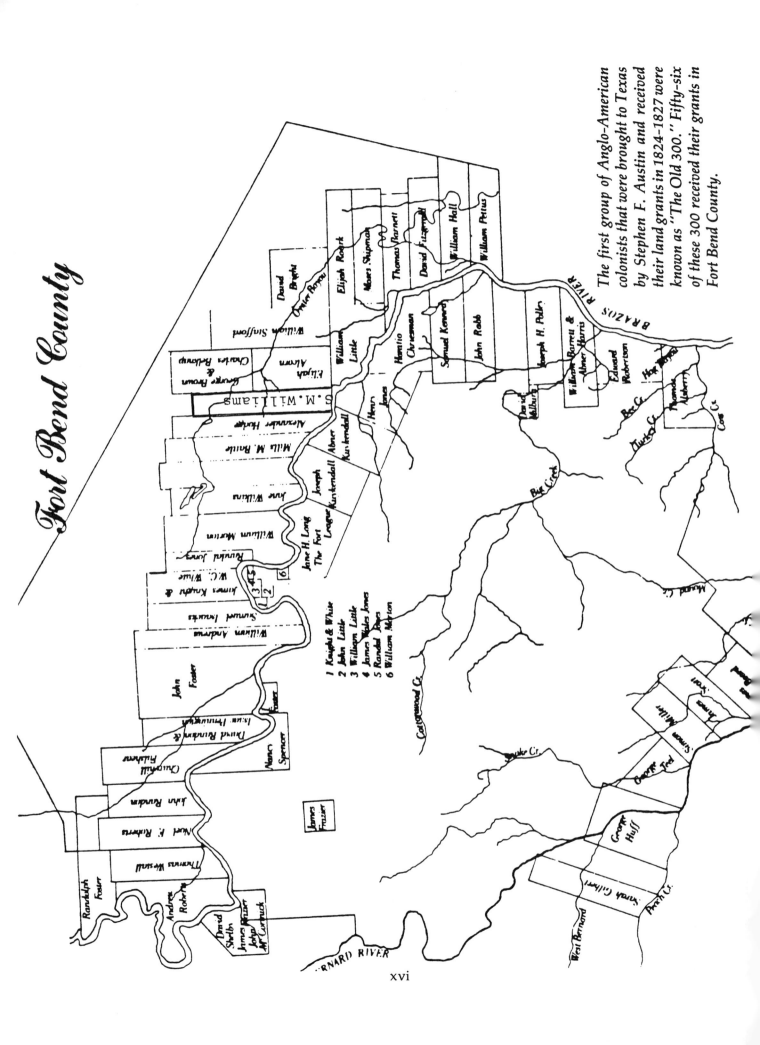

Fort Bend County

The first group of Anglo-American colonists that were brought to Texas by Stephen F. Austin and received their land grants in 1824-1827 were known as "The Old 300." Fifty-six of these 300 received their grants in Fort Bend County.

1 Knight & White
2 John Little
3 William Little
4 James Wales Jones
5 Randal Jones
6 William Morton

This transfer to Williams was the beginning of a series of ownerships, each owner playing an important part in the formation and growth of Sugar Land and the Imperial Sugar Company. Each successive owner was an interesting bit of Texas history in his own right.

[1]*Fort Bend, The Magazine of the Fort Bend Chamber of Commerce*, Spring/Summer, 1989, p.26.

[2]Interviews with Mayor Lee Dugan of Sugar Land, Texas, Tuesday, June 5, 1990.

[3]Interview with Frank Dzieranowski, Business Manager, Fort Bend Independent School District, Monday, May 7, 1990.

[4]Clarence W. Wharton, *History of Fort Bend County*, (Houston, Texas: The Anson Jones Press, 1950), p.33.

[5]*The Handbook of Texas* (Austin, Texas: The Texas State Historical Association, 1952) Vol. 1, p. 938.

[6]Wharton, loc. cit.

[7]*The Herald Coaster*, Sesquicentennial Edition, Rosenberg, Texas, June 1, 1972, Section VIII, p. 3.

[8]Ralph W. Steen, *The Texas Story* (Austin, Texas: The Steck Co. 1948), p. 69

[9]Ibid, p. 64.

[10]*The Herald Coaster*, op. cit. Section II, p. 3.

[11]T. R. Fehrehbach, *The Lone Star State* (New York, N. Y.: American Legacy Press, 1983) p. 138.

[12]Dilue Harris, *Reminiscences of Dilue Harris*, In the quarterly of the Texas State Historical Association (Austin, Texas: 1900) Vol. IV, No. 3, p. 161.

[13]Rupert Norval, Richardson, Texas, *The Lone Star State* (Englewood Cliffs, New Jersey: Prentice-Hall, Inc., 1958) p. 50.

[14]Wharton, op. cit. p. 40.

[15]*The Texas Almanac*, Sesquicentennial Edition (Dallas, Texas: The Dallas Morning News, 1985) p. 138.

[16]Wharton, op. cit. p. 40.

Samuel May Williams

SAMUEL MAY WILLIAMS — 1828-1853

Residents of a strip of land through Sugar Land are reminded annually of Samuel May Williams. Local tax notices received by property owners within this strip identify their land as being in the "S. M. Williams" league.

Born in Providence, Rhode Island in 1795, Samuel May Williams was twenty-seven years old when he came to Texas. He had first been apprenticed to his uncle in Baltimore as a clerk. Later he sailed to Buenos Aires as a supercargo and possibly found employment there in the service of an American firm. He stayed long enough to become fluent in both written and spoken Spanish and to develop an understanding of the Spanish business mentality, all of which would stand him in good stead in the new Texas colony.[1]

He returned to the United States, and in 1819 worked as a clerk in a merchant firm and later for a commission merchant. Here he enlarged his background of experience by setting up a household in New Orleans with a young lady named E. Eccleston. He lived beyond his means, and finally departed for Texas with her in May of 1822 using the name of "Mr. and Mrs. E. Eccleston" and leaving several unpaid debts, (which he paid at a later date). They traveled by schooner and arrived at Hawkins Landing near the mouth of the Colorado River in June 1822.[2] Probably because he had few belongings, and because of the difficulty of qualifying for a land grant under an assumed name, he set himself up as a schoolmaster and interpreter along the Colorado River, and as a clerk who understood and wrote both Spanish and French.

Meanwhile, Stephen F. Austin had constructed a log cabin office in San Felipe and embarked on a program of issuing the promised land grants. His most pressing need was a clerk who could read, write, and speak Spanish, as he was soon deluged with communications from Spanish headquarters, as well as from the settlers; and his greatest task was the surveying and written description of each individual's land grant.

Having heard of the talents of E. Eccleston along the Colorado River, in no time at all he had that young man and his lady ensconced in a log cabin in San Felipe; and Williams (for he immediately resumed his real name) became the right hand of Stephen F. Austin in the issuance of the prized land grants.[3]

Williams was a talented and hard worker, and he recognized an extraordinary opportunity. His knowledge of spoken and written Spanish, as well as his understanding of the customs of the Mexican governing classes, were invaluable to Austin. His duties required him to arrange for surveys of each land grant by engineers, locating the grant, writing all deeds and certificates of title both in English and Spanish, copying all documents into a permanent record book, and managing all financial transactions and collections.

His lady, E. Eccleston, apparently homesick for the more comfortable and cosmopolitan life to which she had been accustomed in New Orleans and caring little for frontier subsistence in a log cabin in San Felipe, left him in 1825 to

Sugar cane was grown in the area until 1928.

return to New Orleans. Three years later, in 1828, he married Sara Patterson Scott.[4]

By that time, Williams was well established as Austin's right-hand man in the development and governance of the colony. During Austin's many and often extended travels through the colony and into Mexico, he came to act as Austin's representative, not only in matters affecting the colony, but also in personal affairs.

Then in 1828, for services rendered Austin transferred one of his personal land grants to Williams,[5] this being the choice league on Oyster Creek which included the site of the old low water crossing. This 4,428 acre land grant, like the several adjoining grants, was long and narrow: seven miles long from south to north, with the south boundary being the Brazos River, the north about where the Covington Woods subdivision is located. It was one mile wide from east to west, with the east boundary where the Cullen Bank is now located, and the west line between the Nalco plant and Highway 6.[6]

But Williams was far too occupied with his activities at the colony headquarters and his frequent trips to the United States and Mexico on colony matters to manage the Oyster Creek farm personally. He named it "Oakland" (later owners would change the name to Sugar Land), had the land cleared, buildings constructed, accumulated a cadre of slaves and farm animals and hired an overseer to manage the farming operations. One of his early crops was sugar cane.

Originally, honey had been the only sweetener available to the pioneers,[7] but some of the early members of the Austin colony had brought sugar cane stalks with them for their own use; and it was discovered that this plant flourished in the rich soil around Oyster Creek and the Brazos as well as along the Colorado. A ship captain is reported to have brought a quantity of cane stalks from Cuba for distribution to the settlers in that area.

Sugar cane is a giant grass, sometimes twelve to fifteen feet tall. It flourishes in tropical and semi-tropical climates, generally throughout the world where warm temperatures, sunlight and rainfall are abundant. Several crops may be cut from cane once established, but each crop takes from one to two years to mature.

At first, families cultivated only a few stalks of sugar cane for their own use. It was hardly necessary for each family to provide its own sugar mill, as it became the custom for those who had mills to grind their neighbors' sugar during the short harvesting season. The sweetening they made from the cane stalks was crystallized cane sugar syrup, obtained by crushing the cane and boiling the resulting juice. The early crushers were small and primitive. Two short, round pieces of hardwood log, perhaps eighteen inches to two feet in length, were smoothed, then placed upright on a tree stump. Fastened tightly to cogwheels made from hardwood, they were clinched closely together, and rotated by a farm animal walking patiently around the mill in a circle. The cane stalks were fed between the rollers and the juice trickled down into pans. The juice was boiled in open iron kettles into brown, sticky crystals encased in a heavy, dark molasses. Dileu Rose Harris, in her recollections of daily life on a farm just two miles west of Oakland in the early 1830's and 1840's described the household sugar of that time.

Mule-powered cane sugar mill used in the 1830s.

This old newspaper engraving shows "a typical sugar boiling" in the 1830s, a scene enacted at Sugar Land during cane harvest a century and a half ago.

4

"The sugar was black as tar, had to be carried in a bucket. Father (Dr. Pleasant W. Rose) went to Mr. Stafford's to see a sick Negro, and mother gave him a bag to get sugar. He was going in his every-day clothes, but mother would have him put on his best suit, and when he got back he was holding the bag at arms length, his clothing covered with molasses. Mother hung the bag with a bucket underneath, and we had sugar and molasses."[8]

The first local venture into the commercial milling of sugar cane was at Stafford's point on Oyster Creek just four miles southeast of Oakland. In 1824, William Stafford had received a grant of one and one half leagues of land and established Stafford's Point, a short distance from what later became the city of Stafford. In 1834, Mr. Stafford built a cotton gin and a raw sugar mill near where Dulles High School stands today. But both the cotton gin and the raw sugar mill were to be short lived. Stafford, along with many of the neighboring plantations, including Oakland, would become victims of Santa Anna's vengeance in Texas' war with Mexico in 1836.[9]

After the brutal massacres at the Alamo and Goliad in March, 1836, as Sam Houston and his hastily recruited army retreated toward what became the San Jacinto battleground, word spread to the farms and plantations along the trail across the Colorado and Brazos Rivers and the Oyster Creek area that Santa Anna and his Mexican army were approaching. This news sparked a panic and marked the beginning of what would be known in Texas history as the "Runaway Scrape."

When word did come to the Oyster Creek neighborhood that the Mexicans were nearing the area and that the settlers would be wise to move, it was in considerable hurry and panic that they did so. Many of the able bodied men had joined the forces of Sam Houston and were to fight at the Battle of San Jacinto. Consequently the hasty exodus was made up mostly of women and children, a few men and a number of slaves. One of the participants in the Runaway Scrape was Dilue Harris, whose adventure started just two miles west of what is now Sugar Land, when her family and neighbors fled in panic. Her father kept a diary of the flight and she later supplemented this with her recollections.[10]

Comparable perhaps to some isolated incidents in the American Revolution and the Civil War, the Oakland area witnessed one of the rare occurrences in American history when families were forced to abandon their homes and flee in panic before the advance of a hostile army.

Some of the families and slaves around Oakland and along Oyster Creek managed to hide out in the woods until the Mexicans had straggled past, and they may have made the wiser choice, since their ordeal would be shorter. Most simply threw what belongings they thought they might need into whatever wagon, carriage, or sled was available and started east in fearful desperation. It was a season of heavy rains, and those who embarked on what was to be a long trek east encountered rain, mud, swollen streams, epidemics, jammed ferries, and lack of food, shelter, and clothing. There was a great deal of sickness among the fugitives; many persons died and were buried where they fell. Most of the Oyster Creek families fled nearly 100 miles, as far as Livingston, before word was received that Santa Anna had been defeated on April 21, 1836 at San Jacinto. They began the long and slow journey homeward, but in spite of the short

Cultivating the cane fields.

Harvesting the cane.

duration of the actual fighting in the Revolution, it was to be six weeks from the start of their flight until they managed to return to their homes on Oyster Creek. The misery and suffering they had experienced during their ordeal had been shocking.

In late April and early May, when the families finally returned, many in the Oyster Creek area found their properties looted and destroyed, their animals slaughtered and crops damaged. The Mexican army, some 600 strong,[11] with an inadequate supply train, one artillery piece and a cavalry troop, had swept across the countryside like a swarm of locusts, moving slowly and living off the land. Historians differ as to the route followed by Santa Anna after crossing the Brazos and continuing toward the Gulf Coast, but the supply wagons and sleds and most of the soldiers probably followed the path of the old trail across Oyster Creek at Oakland,[12] with part of the force foraging widely out to the sides. Santa Anna, desiring to teach the Americans a lesson they would not soon forget, encouraged his troops to carry off stored grains and wagons, slaughter the animals and burn the buildings along the routes.[13] The Rose farm, on the old trail just west of Oakland was looted and partially destroyed,[14] and it was logical to expect that the Williams farm at Oakland received the same treatment, although it was not reported. After leaving the Rose farm, the Mexican troops came through Oakland, crossed Oyster Creek at the old low water crossing and headed down the trail to the Stafford Plantation, where the raw sugar mill and the cotton gin were destroyed along with several buildings. The sugar mill was never rebuilt.[15]

Most of the settlers in the Oyster Creek and Brazos River areas simply buckled down to rebuild their properties with the same determination they had exhibited when they had first arrived at their land grants. A few became discouraged and left, but most, with the help of their neighbors, were able to restore their properties, and put their lives together again.

In September 1836, Texas became a republic, with its own constitution, its elected officials, and its laws. Restrictions under the Mexicans on ownership of land were no longer in effect, and the population around Oyster Creek, as well as that of the new state, was increasing. Under the laws of the new republic, counties and cities were officially recognized. At first, in early 1837, Oyster Creek and the Oakland area were included in Harris County, but later that year, Fort Bend County was formed to include what is now the eastern half of the county. Richmond was granted a charter and became the county seat.[16]

Samuel May Williams had played an active and important part in the Texas Revolution. Having been on the east coast of the United States prior to the start of hostilities, he remained there, making use of his business and political contacts in the procurement and financing of weapons, ammunition and supplies for the Texas forces. Three years later he was instrumental in securing ships for the Texas navy,[17] an undertaking which earned him the title of "Father of the Texas Navy."[18]

In 1837 he built a home in Galveston and in later years became quite prominent in local mercantile, banking and political circles.[19] He was elected to the Congress of the State of Texas in 1839, but was defeated in his bid for election to the Congress of the United States.[20]

A typical sugar cane mill of the 1840s is pictured in this old engraving. The one established by S. M. Williams on his plantation in Sugar Land in 1843—giving a start to the sugar industry in Texas—was similar to this.

After the cessation of hostilities, Williams continued his many activities in further developing the colony and in managing his own growing personal enterprises. In 1838, he transferred ownership of the Oakland property to his brother Nathaniel, who paid $13,284 for the plantation, buildings, farm animals and eight slaves.[21] Nathaniel, previously a successful commission agent in Baltimore and later in New Orleans, immediately turned the management of Oakland over to his younger brother, Matthew.

At the time Matthew took over at Oakland, cotton was the principal cash crop in the Oyster Creek area. However, in some parts of the Austin colony, it was soon to be challenged by a new crop, sugar cane, which had been a significant part of the farm economy of Louisiana since the early 1820's. When it was discovered that sugar cane flourished along the southern Colorado and Brazos Rivers and along Oyster Creek, and when the growing population of the colony created a market for the sweetener, local settlers began to look into the commercial possibilities of milling sugar cane.

By this time attempts had been made in various parts of Texas to grow sugar cane. In East Texas, a variety of cane which produced an acceptable syrup was grown in abundance, but the product was too low in saccharin content to produce crystallized sugar. In the Rio Grande Valley of Texas, sugar cane for home use was grown successfully as early as 1830, and the first commercial raw sugar mill was constructed in the Valley in 1858. Later, four more raw sugar mills were located in the Valley.[22]

But in the four county area of Fort Bend, Matagorda, Brazoria, and Wharton Counties, the growing and processing of sugar cane on a large and commercial basis became a dominant industry by the mid 1840's. This area had the proper combination of soil, climate, rainfall, temperature, and level land for the production of bounteous crops of sugar, and it was nearer the growing population of Texas. As Texas grew, so grew the sugar industry in these four counties, which became known as "The Sugar Bowl of Texas."[23] Predictions were made that "Texas will add the article of sugar to her staple productions and export immense amounts of it within the next twenty-five years."

As sugar crops increased, commercial grinding became quite profitable. The primitive mills were replaced with cast iron rolling and crushing units; the open fire pits with underground furnaces and flues and iron kettles for boiling. Horse drawn carts on small rails transported the cane stalks from the fields. Chemical treatment of the juice improved the color and quality of the sugar and the molasses. Steam power replaced animals as sources of power for the grinding.

In 1843, the Williams' sugar crop on Oakland and the crops of other nearby farms were large enough to justify the installation of a commercial raw sugar grinding mill on the property. Nathaniel and Matthew, probably with financial assistance from Samuel, built their mill within a stone's throw of the ford on Oyster Creek[24] and unknowingly established the site of the future Imperial Sugar Company.

By 1855, there were forty raw sugar mills[25] in the four county area, and on many plantations sugar cane had replaced cotton as the dominant crop. It was a crop which did not lend itself to planting and harvesting in small plots, and it required a good deal of labor and handling, so it was natural that most sugar plantations of that time tended to be large and well organized. A drawing made during that time depicts rows of sugar cane described as "two miles long."[26] In the 1850's Texas was producing more than enough sugar to satisfy its needs and the surplus was being shipped to Eastern and Southern cities, much of it through Galveston. In the Sugar Bowl of Texas, sugar growing and milling was becoming big business.

Sugar cane crops were planted in January, using cuttings from last year's crops, or the left over "ratoons" or stubble in the fields. By the fall of the year, the fields were closely covered with cane stalks as much as fifteen feet tall, "as high as a man on a horse." Grinding usually began about the middle of October, at the time when the sugar content of the cane was at its maximum, and it had to be completed before the first freeze might damage the cane. Once the time arrived and the cane was ready, the sugar plantations became beehives of activity for the three or four month grinding period. The field hands, equipped with large knives, cut each stalk off close to the ground, leaving the roots in the ground, and stripped off the leaves and top joints. The stalks were then loaded into wagons and carted to the mill.

As demand for the sweetener increased, sugar growers and millers were encouraged to increase their sugar acreage and to expand their mills. As the plantations grew more and more sugar, all being harvested between September and January, when the sugar content was at its peak, it required a substantial raw sugar mill to process so much cane within such a short period of time, only to be shut down for eight or nine months out of the year.

Particularly during the harvesting and grinding season, sugar cane was a very labor-intensive crop. As more land was cleared and planted, the demand for more slave labor intensified, and the larger plantations became dependent upon the slave trade. Slavery played an important part in the continuing growth of the farms and plantations, indeed became a basic factor in the development of the large plantations in the Oakland area and along Oyster Creek. On the larger plantations, the slave population far outnumbered the whites. It was a condition of life at the time, and the only good thing that could be said about it was the value of a slave was high enough that most owners felt the need to protect the health and general welfare of their investments.

As the individual plantations grew in area and population, they became self-sufficient communities. They needed not only the cotton, corn, yams, and sugar crops for commerce, but food and fiber, clothing and shelter for the labor population, feed for the animals, and equipment and maintenance of all types. Transportation was such that the labor force had to live on the plantation. Some of the larger plantations then became forerunners of company towns.

In the Sugar Bowl of Texas, growers were becoming uneasy over the growing sentiment for the annexation of Texas by the United States, although there was substantial opposition within Texas, along with resistance from some factions in the national government and in foreign countries which had special interests. Around Oyster Creek, there was concern among the planters that northern sentiment against slavery could become a problem. However the sugar growers quickly espoused the cause for annexation when they learned that the United States had a sugar tariff to protect the growers from increasing foreign competition,[27] and that there was talk in Congress of possible bounties for sugar growers. Annexation was completed in 1845, and Texas became a state.

In the early 1850's roads from coastal points to inland communities were becoming more usable, as was river transportation, which made the import of goods and the export of farm production more practical and economical. The old trail across the low water point at Oakland, often used by such notables as Austin, Bowie, Crockett, Lamar, Fannin and Wharton,[28] had become the route of a stage coach service from Harrisburg, across Oyster Creek at the Williams plantation and on to Richmond. There were rumors of a railroad between Harrisburg and Richmond, and of a plan to make the Brazos more navigable by boats.[29]

Matthew Williams died at Oakland on October 10th, 1852.[30] Neither of his brothers, Samuel and Nathaniel, had the time or the inclination to take over the growing activities at Oakland. In 1853, Nathaniel sold the entire property to a partnership of W. J. Kyle and B. F. Terry for what Nathaniel described as a considerable profit.[31]

Samuel May Williams died at his home in Galveston on September 13, 1858.[32] His home has been preserved as a historical site and a tourist attraction. Although infrequently mentioned as prominent in Texas history, he played an important part in the colonization of Texas and in the economic growth of the state. He and his family had founded what was to become a sugar empire.

[1]Margaret Swett Henson, *Samuel May Williams, An Early Texas Entrepreneur*, (College Station, Texas: Texas A&M University Press, 1976) pp. 5, 6.

[2]Ibid., pp. 1, 7, 8.

[3]*The Handbook of Texas*, (Austin, Texas: State Historical Association, 1952), Vol. II, p. 915.

[4]Ibid.

[5]Clarence W. Wharton, *History of Fort Bend County*, (Houston, Texas: The Anson Jones Press, 1950), p. 40.

[6] Ibid, two maps preceding preface. *The Herald Coaster*, Sesquicentennial Edition, Rosenberg, Texas, June 1, 1972, Section VII, p. 2.

[7]*The Herald Coaster*, Sesquicentennial Edition, Rosenberg, Texas, June 1, 1972, Section VII, page 2.

[8]Dilue Harris, *Reminiscences of Dilue Harris*, in the *Quarterly of the Texas State Historical Association*, (Austin, Texas: Texas State Historical Association, 1900) Vol. IV, No. 2, p 96.

[9]William R. Johnson, *A Short History of the Sugar Industry in Texas*, (Houston, Texas: The Gulf Coast Historical Association, 1961) Vol. V, No. 1, pp. 11, 12.

[10]Harris, op. cit. Vol. IV, No. 3, pp. 162-178.

[11]A. J. Sowell, *History of Fort Bend County*, (Waco, Texas: W. M. Morrison, 1964) p. 122.

[12]Ibid., Footnote.

[13]T. R. Fehrenbach, *Lone Star*, (New York, New York; American Legacy Press, 1983) p. 227.

[14]Harris, op. cit., 178.

[15]Johnson, op. cit., p. 12.

[16]Wharton, op. cit., pp. 86, 87.

[17]Henson, Preface, pp. xi, xii.

[18]Galveston Historical Foundation, printed information flyer.

[19]Ibid.

[20]Henson, op. cit., pp. 104, 105, 132-135.

[21]Deed, Samuel May Williams, Nathaniel Williams, *Fort Bend County Deed Book*, Vol. A, p. 251.

[22]*The Houston Post*, January 4, 1988, p. 13D.

[23]*The Handbook of Texas*, op. cit., p. 684.

[24]*The Herald Coaster*, op. cit. Section III, p. 15.

[25]Johnson, op. cit., p. 34.

[26]From a collection of sugar prints depicting production and manufacture of sugar in the 15th-19th centuries, Imperial Sugar Company, Sugar Land, Texas.

[27]Johnson, op. cit., pp. 15, 16.

[28]*The Herald Coaster*, Vol. VIII, p. 4.

[29]Wharton, op. cit., p. 149.

[30]Henson, op. cit., 150.

[31]Ibid., p. 114.

[32]Ibid,. p. 161

W. J. KYLE AND B. F. TERRY — 1853-1886

William Jefferson Kyle was born in November, 1803 in Hawkins County, Tennessee. Benjamin Franklin (Frank) Terry was born in 1821 in Kentucky. Both families moved to Brazoria County, Texas, where the two men became acquainted.[1]

In 1849, they joined an expedition of 40 Texans traveling by wagon train from Austin, Texas to the California gold fields. Enroute the party had several conflicts with Indians and lost two of their number.[2] Kyle and Terry were reported to have struck it rich in prospecting for gold, and this seems to have been born out by the amount of money they spent in buying and enlarging the Oakland plantation.[3]

Returning to Texas in 1852, they bought approximately 2,400 acres of the Oakland plantation from Nathaniel Williams for an undisclosed price. On January 1, 1853 they bought the remainder of the S. M. Williams land grant including some 2,000 acres, several buildings, 19 Negroes, 500 head of cattle, 30 mules and horses, 15 yoke of oxen, and a herd of hogs, paying $57,165.00.[4] The total of the two purchases under which the Oakland Plantation changed hands was probably in the neighborhood of $85,000. Included in the sale were field after field ready to produce sugar cane, corn and cotton, a large and well maintained raw sugar mill, a commissary, numerous outbuildings, houses for labor, and wagons for transporting cane stalks from the fields to the mill.

No sooner had they completed the purchase of Oakland, than they changed the name to Sugar Land,[5] and began buying up as many of the adjoining plantations as became available. In this they were aided by the weather. In 1853 a very wet spring was followed by a prolonged drought in the summer, and in 1854 a hurricane did considerable damage to crops, animals and buildings on the plantations around Sugar Land. While 1855 was a fairly good year, in 1855 and 1856 most of the seed cane was killed by frost, and in 1856 very little sugar was produced.[6] Some of the nearby planters became discouraged and sold out.

But it was apparent that Kyle and Terry had great faith in the long term prospects of the area, because they were willing buyers when others were selling. In the 5 years between 1853 and 1858, they acquired title to an additional 8,000 acres, all contiguous to the original Williams' plantation, including parts of the land grant leagues of William Little, George Brown, Charles Belknap, Alexander Hodge, J. Hodge, Elijah Alcorn, and the William Stafford league.[7] At that time, the 12,500 acre Kyle and Terry plantation at Sugar Land became one of the largest sugar plantations in the state.

During that period, Kyle and Terry completed a program of modernizing the harvesting and milling of the sugar cane and of upgrading the final product. The original, primitive processing of sugar cane into an edible sweetener had been considerably improved and mechanized, and the end product was lighter in color, more uniform in grain, containing fewer impurities and less molasses.

13

Col. Benjamin Franklin Terry

Mechanical handling of the cane had also been made more efficient. The cane stalks were brought in from the fields to the mill in tram cars drawn on rails by oxen, mules or horses. These small gauge rails, on light weight ties, could be moved in sections to different parts of the fields being harvested, so that the cars could be loaded within a short distance of the cutting activities. From the cars, the cane stalks were dumped on a conveyor which moved the stalks into a hopper above the crushers, which were turned by steam. The juice was screened to remove trash, then piped to a series of heated kettles over flues and furnaces. Slaked lime was added to the cane juice, causing most of the remaining impurities to form a scum on the top of the juice. The scum was skimmed off, and the juice was further concentrated by boiling. When it had thickened to the proper consistency, it was ladled into cooling tanks, where, after twelve or more hours of cooling, it went to grain and formed into sugar crystals. These crystals, afloat in a thick molasses, were dumped into hogsheads on platforms above the molasses tanks. In two or three weeks, when sufficient molasses had drained from the hogsheads, the final product, a sticky, light brown granulated sugar, was ready for consumption or shipment.

Later, centrifugal machines would be developed to spin the dark syrup off the crystals, much as a modern washing machine spins the water from damp clothing, and these further improved the quality of the raw sugar. Instead of in open kettles, the sugar syrup was partially evaporated, then boiled to a grain in enclosed vacuum pans at a lower temperature to avoid caramalizing the sugar. But it was still "raw sugar," as distinguished from refined sugar, which is pure white and free flowing. At Sugar Land, raw sugar from the raw sugar mills was the only sweetening product available in quantity for the next forty years.

A raw sugar mill could cost as much as $30,000,[8] but some of the wealthier planters felt they could afford to build two mills to be sure they could process the crops in case of a breakdown. Crops which could not be processed immediately after harvesting were often a total loss, so the practice may have been justified. Kyle and Terry may have built such an alternate mill, as an older resident of Sugar Land stated that there had been a second mill near where Brooks Lake is located, south of Sugar Land.

Kyle and Terry were probably spurred more quickly into their program of modernization and expansion by the success they had in bringing Texas' first railroad through the middle of Sugar Land, and in front of the raw sugar mill, during their first year of ownership of the property—something which immediately put Sugar Land on the map and opened up a new opportunity for profit in shipping the end product of the raw sugar mill, the cotton gin, and other produce of the plantation.

Larger crops and more commerce meant increased need for adequate transportation, and the Brazos and Oyster Creek trade was important to Galveston and to the growing town of Houston. There were plans for Houston to build an eighteen foot wagon road through Sugar Land to Richmond, which Galveston countered with a program to remove the snags and improve the channels in the Brazos River to make river freighting more reliable. Fort Bend planters also proposed to improve the navigation of the river and to put the steamboat, *S. M. Williams,* in regular freight service.[9]

But Andrew Briscoe of Houston had an ambitious plan to raise financing and build a railroad from Harrisburg to the Brazos River at Richmond. By July 1853, he had completed his railroad, the Buffalo Bayou, Brazos and Colorado Railroad, as far as Stafford, four miles east of Sugar Land, "where the timber met the prairie." A large celebration was held at Stafford on July 4 of that year to celebrate the opening of the track and the arrival of the first train.[10]

The original plans were for the railroad tracks to continue in a straight line from Stafford to Richmond, and it was here that Kyle and Terry took an historical step as far as Sugar Land and the future Imperial Sugar Company were concerned. They saw the value of the rail line to their plantations and their produce, and made a trade with the railroad in which the railroad agreed to place a large bend in the tracks to run through Sugar Land in front of the raw sugar mill and cotton gin. In return, Kyle and Terry agreed to provide 2,500 acres of land, apparently for use as right of way. This bend in the railroad still exists today.[11]

The thirty mile Buffalo Bayou, Brazos and Colorado Railway from Harrisburg to Richmond through Sugar Land was the first railway built in Texas. In 1870, it was taken over by the Galveston, Harrisburg and San Antonio Railway Company and in 1905 became part of the Southern Pacific main line from New Orleans to Los Angeles.[12]

The late 1850's was a period of consolidation among the raw sugar millers, as the larger and better financed mills continued to grow and the smaller mills closed. Most growers whose mills closed continued to grow sugar cane, but sent it to those larger mills which remained in operation. The larger plantations, particularly those with raw sugar mills, prospered materially.

A number of planters in the Sugar Land area had become quite wealthy, and the plantation system provided the larger and more successful plantation owners a lavish livelihood. During the Kyle and Terry ownership, Sugar Land and the Oyster Creek area became the site of several large, antebellum plantations and a life style reminiscent of "Gone with the Wind." A few reminders of the old plantation system still remain in Fort Bend and Brazoria Counties, chiefly in the ruins of old foundations, or gaunt chimneys in weed choked fields, brick curbings of abandoned cisterns or wells, remnants of small gauge rail track for hauling sugar cane to the mills.

Homes of successful planters were often quite elaborate. Most were built in the prosperous decade prior to the Civil War. Two in the Sugar Land area have been described as opulent social centers of the times. Terry built a large, two story, brick plantation home on the prairie about a mile north of the ford at Oyster Creek, in the area now known as the Covington Woods subdivision. Kyle, reportedly less socially inclined than Terry, built a smaller home nearby.

Like several others in the area, the Terry home featured large airy rooms, most of which had fireplaces for use in cooler weather. A circular staircase led to the second floor, which had a veranda on three sides, often used as a "sleeping porch" in hot weather. The building was said to have been lavishly furnished and well maintained by the house slaves.

The large kitchen area was semi-detached from the main house. In back, on the north side, were numerous outbuildings, including a carriage house, stables, a smoke house, a storehouse for foods and household items. Between the house and the raw sugar mill there was a race track for horse races. North and west of the mill was the slave quarters, with over a hundred dwellings of one to five rooms, the number of rooms depending on the size of the family. The slave quarters had its own food preparation facilities, and Oyster Creek curved around three sides of the area, providing plenty of fresh water.

Near the quarters were the cotton gin and a storage barn for the cotton seed, as well as a press for baling. There was a small sawmill to provide building lumber and firewood. Cribs for storage of corn and other crops were located just across the creek from the quarters, as were the animal pens for cattle, pigs, chickens, turkeys, and pigeons.

Large cattle and dairy herds occupied the land to the north and west, about where the new Kempner High School is located today. The southern portion of the plantation was extensively farmed in cotton, corn and sugar cane, with the latter occupying most of the acreage.

Because of its isolation, the plantation had to be as nearly self sufficient as possible. Vegetable gardens and fruit trees, as well as local crops of berries, pecans and persimmons supplemented the milk and meats provided by the animals. Overseers and especially trained slaves as well as contract labor provided the necessary skills for building and maintenance of the properties. Cloths were spun on the plantation and basic clothing was sewn by the ladies of the house and the house slaves.

Some items had to be imported; items such as salt, flour, tobacco, coffee, tea, wines and liquors, shoes, boots and the better items of clothing, as well as tools, hardware, machinery, weapons and ammunition. But once established, the Terry and Kyle plantation was largely self-reliant.[13]

Social life on the Sugar Land plantation became known throughout the area as outstanding, typical of that seemingly enjoyed by wealthy planters in the Old South. Frank Terry, who had lived in the plantation area since he was a small boy, had married the daughter of Sir Francis Bingham,[14] one of Austin's original 300 colonists and one of the first to locate his league on Oyster Creek. Soon the Terry plantation at Sugar Land became the social center of the area.[15] There were horseback rides and racing, hunting and fishing during the day, cards, games, and dances at night. Hospitality was a way of life. Some of the most famous people of the day, many of them from foreign countries, were entertained in its spacious rooms. It was reported that by 1861, Terry was commonly regarded as one of the two or three wealthiest men in the state.[16]

If ownership of slaves and lavish life style were the criteria, the speculation was probably correct. In 1860, the census showed some 20,000 slave owners in Texas, but only 54 of these owned over 100 slaves.[17] In that year Kyle and Terry reported owning 150 slaves, as well as $136,000 in real property, $210,000 in personal property, 8,000 bushels of corn, 300 bales of cotton and 250 hogsheads of sugar.

It was also reported that the average value of a slave was $672. The actual value of a really good slave could be from $1,200 to $2,000, and a good slave could be hired from his owner for $275 per month.[18] One planter advised his heirs that if a choice had to be made to sell the slaves or the land it would be better to keep the slaves as a superior investment.

The well known Walnut Grove Plantation on Oyster Creek, just three miles northwest of Sugar Land, was, like Terry's, typical of some of the more lavish. The plantation house was described as a two story brick building with fluted columns and a white veranda in the front. Flower gardens enclosed in a picket fence and a brick walk led to the entrance. There was a wide hall and a stairway through the center of the ten room house. All the rooms were spacious, with high ceilings and white plastered walls. The floor of the parlor was covered with Brussels carpet. There was a huge candelabra with crystal pendants and a great deal of upholstered mahogany furniture and expensive lace curtains.

On the north side of the plantation were quarters for the overseer and 100 Negro slaves, as well as the quarters of the house servants, the stables, poultry and pigeon houses, smokehouse and carriage house.

The Walnut Grove Plantation raised sugar cane, as did most of the plantations in the eastern half of Fort Bend County. It also had a commercial cotton gin. The lady of the house had one of the first sewing machines in Texas, as well as a loom for weaving cloth. Flour, salt and sugar were bought by the barrel, tea by the chest and rice and coffee by the sack; as on the Kyle and Terry plantation, almost everything else in the way of food was raised on the place.[19] [20]

Older Sugar Land residents will remember the Eldridge home, located in front of the refinery on the main street of Sugar Land until 1963. It had originally been the Ellis plantation home near Sartartia and was moved from there to Sugar Land in the early 1900's. Also, the old Imperial Inn on Oyster Creek had been the plantation home of the Thatcher family and was moved to Sugar Land. It burned in 1946.[21] While these two examples were not the most elaborate in the area, they were representative of many of the local planters' homes.

The 1860 census showed that Fort Bend County had reason to be called, at least for some of the free whites, a prosperous and contented community. There were then 2,016 whites and 4,127 negroes in the county. Tax assessments showed land at $3,250,000, slaves at $3,140,000, and horses and cattle at $670,000 for a total of $7,000,000.[22]

Few if any of those fortunate white planters who were enjoying the prosperity and serenity of the late 1850's and the early 1860's could have had any inkling that within a few years their pre-Civil War plantation life styles and values would be gone forever for most of them. Only the hardy and the fortunate would survive the shocks of the Civil War and the postwar years.

As far as the local planters were concerned, this was a war over slavery. The importance of slavery to the planters in Texas in 1860 is evident from the population figures for that year. These showed a white population of 430,891, and 182,566 blacks.[23] A disproportionately large portion of the black population was in the southern and eastern parts of the state, which was more intensely farmed than the northern and western areas. The plantations around Oyster Creek and at Sugar Land depended heavily on slave labor.

So it is understandable that in 1860 there was deep concern over the growing anti-slavery sentiment in the Northern United States. The Southern planters in general felt that they had treated their slaves fairly, albeit more as farm animals than as human beings, and they felt strongly that legislation against slavery should not be forced upon them. As the North increased its pressures against slavery, the opposition in Texas became pronounced. Plantation owners including Kyle and Terry were strong voices for secession if necessary to protect their rights to own slaves. There were other issues, real and imagined, in which southern states felt they were treated unfairly, but the overriding interest in the Sugar Land area was slavery.

When other southern states felt compelled to secede from the Union and form the Confederate States of America in order to protect what they felt were their rights, there was sufficient clamor among Texans for similar action that a Secessionist Convention of representatives from all areas of Texas was called in early 1861. Citizens of Fort Bend County elected Frank Terry,[24] who was active in local political affairs and a prominent man in the state, to be one of their two delegates at this convention.

The convention immediately initiated an ordinance of secession to be submitted to the voters of Texas on February 23, to take effect on March 2, 1861, twenty-five years to the day after Texas declared its independence from Mexico. The February 23 vote was overwhelmingly in favor of secession, 44,317 for and 13,020[25] against, with Fort Bend County citizens voting unanimously in favor.[26] The same day, the Convention voted to become a part of the Confederate States of America.

No one could have foreseen the devastating effect of the Civil War and of the postwar changes which were to come. The entire economic, agricultural, political and social systems which had grown up around Fort Bend County and the Oyster Creek area were to be in turmoil for some ten or more years after the war ended.

But in the early days of the Civil War, the patriotic fervor for what the Southerners felt was a just cause quickly made itself felt on the Fort Bend County sugar plantations by the departure of many of the white male population who took up arms for the Confederacy. After the firing on Fort Sumter in April 1861, young Texans flocked to the colors and by September of that year there were ten regiments of Texas troops. One of them was commanded by Frank Terry, who received a commission to form what became known as "Terry's Texas Rangers."[27] He was given the rank of colonel. He established a headquarters in Houston and issued commissions to ten captains, each of whom was authorized to recruit a company of 100 men. Each man was to supply his own equipment and arms and to report mounted.[28] H Company, commanded by Captain John M. Holt, was recruited in Fort Bend County,[29] assembled with the regiment in August, 1861, and departed immediately for the eastern battlegrounds. By the time they entered their first battle, they had grown to a regiment of 9 companies totalling 1,176 men.[30] Although the officers and men of the regiment were to fight with distinction throughout the war, Colonel Terry was killed leading his men in their first charge at Woodsonville, near Bowling Green, Kentucky, on December 17, 1861. He was forty years old.[31]

After a large funeral ceremony, attended by dignitaries from throughout the state, Terry's body was buried at Sugar Land. It was moved in 1880 to Glenwood

Cemetery in Houston with the bodies of others of his family.

His will (apparently written before the name of the plantation was changed from Oakland to Sugar Land, and before the partnership had acquired land in addition to the Williams League) stated: "I request Oakland Plantation be kept up at present under the direction and management of Colonel Kyle until he becomes weary of the trouble, and then to be disposed of by my executors as they may think advisable in the S. M. Williams League."[32] Terry's thought that Colonel Kyle might "become weary of the trouble" was to be prophetic of the events and problems that were to befall the Sugar Land plantation and others in the area in the calamitous years following the end of the Civil War.

During the war, William Kyle, now nearing sixty years of age, had continued to operate the Sugar Land plantation, apparently with the help of his brother, Robert Kyle, but with ever increasing difficulty. With most of the able-bodied young men either away in the army or engaged in war work, there was a severe shortage of overseers, craftsmen, and management personnel, presenting a serious problem to a plantation as large as Sugar Land. The problems of those attempting to continue the operation of the plantations during the four years of the war were further exacerbated by shortages of manufactured goods and equipment. Naval blockades and shortage of shipping interfered with transportation of both imports and exports. Demand for food crops increased and that for cotton declined.

In January 1864, William Kyle, sixty-one years old and no doubt worn by the difficulties of managing the decline of the once prosperous Sugar Land plantation, died at Sugar Land.[33] His brother, Robert Kyle, who had been with him in the California gold rush, took over the management, the Terry heirs being represented by A. J. Terry, the son of Frank Terry.

It was estimated that some seventy percent of the white males between seventeen and fifty years of age had been away from home during the long war, and that less than half of them returned. Many of the plantations had been gallantly operated by wives, daughters, and parents under the most trying circumstances; many were now owned by widows. After the war, under the conditions of the times, they found it difficult to continue.

In the Sugar Land and Fort Bend County areas, the difficulties experienced during the war were to become even more crippling when the war ended with the surrender of General Robert E. Lee at Appamattox on April 9, 1865. Two months later, on June 19, 1865, Federal troops landed at Galveston, and Texas came under the authority of the United States government. The slaves were freed as of that date, all acts of the Texas government since secession were declared illegal, and all Confederate troops were placed under parole. Texas was to be managed from Washington.

The new government in Fort Bend County was characterized by the arrival of the bureaucrats and carpetbaggers from the north, by disenfranchisement of many white voters, particularly those who had been in the position of leadership, and by the election of local officials by a predominance of Negro voters. In Fort Bend County in 1867 only 153 whites were registered to vote as compared to 1,334 Negroes.[34]

County officials elected under this system were often lacking in knowledge of, if not careless of, local needs. Many of them were far from honest. All were instructed by state and federal officials, some of whom were not only incompetent, but antagonistic to the plantations and the previous leaders in the community.

The 1865 cotton crop had been appropriated by the government and many of the planters were unable to raise a crop the following year. Productive work in the fields virtually came to a halt. When told that they were free, most slaves were unable to understand what freedom meant, except that they were no longer required to work. Having been provided with the necessities of life by their owners, and with no training in earning a living and little idea of what the outside world was like, many were encouraged by representatives of the new government to abandon their labors on the plantations. The fields which were once so productive were taken over by weeds; lack of maintenance and parts caused deterioration of buildings and machinery. Thousands of acres lay idle. Plantation values declined in some cases to 20 cents on the dollar. It was too much for many of the planters, some of whom abandoned their properties, or sold out for a pittance. Fortunately, the Kyle and Terry Plantation at Sugar Land was one of the survivors.

For the twenty-five years following the end of the war, conditions in Fort Bend County were to be chaotic. The white population of Fort Bend County was declining. At the same time, thousands of slaves had been brought into Texas from other southern states to escape the invasion of the northern armies. By 1870 the white population had decreased to 1,600 and the blacks had increased to 5,400. Property evaluations had fallen from $2,600,000 in 1866 to $700,000 in 1870. The Fort Bend cattle population dropped from 100,000 in 1860 to 56,000 in 1870.[35]

In Fort Bend County, the brunt of mismanagement of governmental and civic affairs was naturally felt most heavily in Richmond, the county seat and the location of the county offices. Sugar Land, some seven miles distant and having no local government officials on the plantation, was isolated from the daily aggravations experienced by those in and around Richmond.

During the postwar years, two local political factions had arisen, mainly in Richmond and the western part of Fort Bend County. One of the factions, known as the "Woodpeckers," was part of the old Republican Party through which the carpetbaggers and Negroes had monopolized the elections and controlled the politics in the county. The other faction was the "Jaybirds," the Democrats, later organized as the "Young Men's Democratic Club."[36] There was considerable friction between the two groups, leading to hatred and bloodshed, and culminating in a shoot-out at the Richmond courthouse in 1889 in which several citizens were killed or wounded.[37] The whole postwar climate of animosity and racial tension had provided a sad chapter on the human condition in the area.

In 1889, the Democratic group called a mass meeting in Richmond for the announced purpose of "continuing and uniting the white people for the advancement and prosperity of the county." From this meeting, the Jay Bird Democratic Organization of Fort Bend County was formed and managed to give the Democratic Party control of local elections for almost seventy years. It was finally disbanded in 1959 after the Supreme Court ruled against it.[38]

During the difficult 1870's and early 1880's, in spite of the "troubles" Frank Terry had so prophetically anticipated, the Kyle and Terry heirs had managed to hold the Sugar Land plantation together and keep it operating at an affordable level. They were aided by a stronger financial position and by the fact that sugar, which represented a large part of their activities, was much in demand and at a relatively high price, and by their ideal location directly on a functioning rail line.

They also seem to have been able to make better use of the freed labor than some of the others, possibly because they had the facilities for an almost self contained community on the plantation and thus were able to hire the former slaves on a day labor or contract basis and to provide better housing and living conditions. Also, during this period, share cropping became an important part of the larger farming operations. In this system, the land owner supplied the workers with housing and equipment and received one half to two thirds of the resulting crop.

In the Sugar Land area the labor shortage was also mitigated to a considerable extent by the reprehensible but growing practice of using convict labor on the farms. In 1871, a law had been passed by the Texas legislature which required the state to lease the state convicts to entrepreneurs.[39] It is recorded that in 1875 there were sixty convicts leased in Fort Bend County on two plantations, one of them probably being Sugar Land and the other the adjoining Ellis plantation.[40]

Even so, the Kyle and Terry families were having difficulties in their efforts to rebuild their rundown plantation. A number of the older and smaller raw sugar mills in the "sugar bowl" had closed, which should have improved the opportunities for those still operating, but it seemed that the heart had gone out of the Kyle and Terry heirs, and major repairs and maintenance loomed in the offing. Adding to their discouragement, the Terry and the Kyle plantation homes burned at the same time when a combination of a grass fire and a high wind swept through the area. In 1875, the plantation was partitioned equally among the heirs, with the Kyle heirs receiving the raw sugar mill and the farm lands immediately adjoining.

But it was not going to work out, and, starting in 1882, the heirs of both families began selling off portions of the plantation to Colonel Edward H. Cunningham.[41]

[1]*The Herald Coaster*, Sesquicentennial Edition, Rosenberg, Texas, June 1, 1972, Section VI, p. 3.

[2]Ibid.

[3]Ibid.

[4]*Fort Bend County Deed Records*, Book C, pp. 272, 333.

[5]*Herald Coaster*, loc. cit.

[6]William R. Johnson, *A Short History of the Sugar Industry in Texas* (Houston, Texas: The Gulf Coast Historical Association, 1961), Vol. V, No. 1, pp. 30-35.

[7]*Fort Bend County Deed Records*, Book D, pp. 748-750.

[8]J. Carlisle Sitterson, *Sugar Country*, (University of Kentucky Press, 1953) p. 160.

[9]Clarence R. Wharton, *History of Fort Bend County*, (Houston, Texas: The Anson Jones Press, 1950), pp. 148, 149.

[10]Ibid., pp. 149, 150.

[11]*The Herald Coaster*, op. cit., Section VI, p. 4.

[12]*The Handbook of Texas*, (Austin, Texas: The Texas State Historical Association, 1952), Vol. I. pp. 240, 665.

[13]Interviews with G. D. Ulrich of Sugar Land, who had accumulated his knowledge of the Terry plantation and its life style from descendants of the slaves and overseers who had worked on the place.

[14]*The Handbook of Texas*, op. cit., Vol. II, p. 727.

[15]Jesse A. Zeigler, *Wave of the Gulf*, (San Antonio, Texas: The Naylor Press, 1938, p. 326.

[16]James Day, et al., *Soldiers of Texas*, (Waco, Texas: The Texian Press, 1973), p. 75.

[17]T. R. Fehrenbach, *Lone Star*, (New York, New York: American Legacy Press, 1983) p. 309.

[18]Rupert Norval Richardson, *Texas, the Lone Star State* (Englewood Cliffs, New Jersey: Prentice-Hall, Inc. 1958), p. 162.

[19]Wharton, op. cit., pp. 132, 133, 166.

[20]*The Herald Coaster*, op. cit., Section VIII, p. 1, 11.

[21]Ibid., Section VI, p. 3.

[22]Wharton, op. cit., p. 153.

[23]Richardson, loc, sit.

[24]Wharton, op. cit., p. 169.

[25]*Handbook of Texas*, Vol. II, p. 588.

[26]Wharton, loc. cit.

[27]Wharton, op. cit., p. 170.

[28]Ibid.

[29]Day, et al., p. 80.

[30]Ibid., pp. 78, 79.

[31]*Herald Coaster*, Section VI, p. 4.

[32]Ibid.

[33]Ibid.

[34]Wharton, op. cit., p. 177.

[35]Ibid., p. 180.

[36]*The Herald Coaster*, op. cit., Vol. VIII, p. 8.

[37]Pauline Yelderman, The Jay Bird Democratic Association of Fort Bend County, (Waco, Texas: the Texian Press, 1979), pp. 95-99.

[38]Ibid., p. 276-277.

[39]Johnson, op. cit., p. 41.

[40]Ibid.

[41]Ibid., p. 61.

Edward H. Cunningham

COL. ED. H. CUNNINGHAM — 1886-1908

E. H. Cunningham was a native of Arkansas, born in 1834. When he was twenty-two years old, he moved to Bexar County, Texas, and organized a stock raising firm at Martinas Creek, near San Antonio.[1]

He apparently had considerable success, and at the start of the Civil War in 1861, he organized and helped equip a Texas regiment known as the "Mustang Greys."[2] It became a part of Hood's 4th Texas Brigade and participated in numerous battles during the Civil War. Cunningham also "received renown in Hood's brigade, and his hand-picked Mustang Greys were credited by General Lee with turning McClelland's flank and thereby saving Richmond, Virginia. At the great battle of Gaines Mill, 400 of the regiment were engaged, and out of this number 252 were killed or wounded. Colonel Cunningham himself was "slightly wounded fourteen times, the most serious in the foot." Before the war ended, he was appointed chief of staff and inspector-general of Hood's Brigade.[3]

Returning to Bexar County after the war, Cunningham added to his farming and ranching activities in that area and within the succeeding fourteen years became known as a very wealthy man. He had a large stone home within what is now the city of San Antonio with large, well-kept grounds. The home later became the Base Hospital at Camp Travis in San Antonio.[4]

Looking for favorable investments, Cunningham became interested in the sugar plantations in Fort Bend County, and in 1875, at age forty-one, he entered into a partnership with Col. Littleberry A. Ellis,[5] who had also been an officer in Hood's Brigade. Ellis had acquired some 2,000 acres 2 miles west of Sugar Land, and later bought an additional 3,300 acres adjoining. This brought the Ellis plantation up to 5,300 acres at that time. It became well known as the "Sartartia" Plantation, named after the first name of his eldest daughter.[6]

It appears that this partnership of Ellis and Cunningham was initially formed partly for the purpose of contracting with the state of Texas for the entire convict population, which they would then sublease to other plantation owners.[7] The partnership performed this service for nine years, until 1886, when the State decided to take over this leasing function.

In 1880, over half the convicts in the system were being used in Fort Bend and Brazoria counties.[8] In that year Ellis and Cunningham between them worked 365 convicts, and Cunningham had seven on his Bexar County ranch.[9] The Sugar Land country side in the late 1800's was described as, "a low, mosquito infested swamp and the sluggish bayous were habitats for alligators and noisome creepers. Convicts labored barelegged in wet sugar cane fields, dying like flies in the periodic epidemics of fevers. Civilian labor could not be kept on the place. In those days, a free man who stayed more than two weeks was suspected of hiding out from the sin of commission or omission."[10] By the end of the century, Cunningham would be operating a plantation at Sugar Land which would have the largest convict population in the state.[11] It is difficult to accept the fact that the peaceful town of Sugar Land had been the host of such an unfortunate practice, no more acceptable than the use of slave labor that had proceeded it.

The convict lease system continued with slight modifications into the twentieth century. From 1894 to 1889 planters paid $15 per convict per month when the prisoners were working in the sugar cane fields, $14.50 per month when they were used to grow cotton and cane; and $14 per month when they cultivated cotton alone. After 1889, the price advanced slightly to $19.50 per month, but the state then assumed the cost of furniture, bedding, clothing, medical attention, transportation and food. During all these years, the leased convict population numbered around 1,000 per year with the sugar plantations accounting for roughly one-half the number."[12]

In 1882, after bad crop years had lowered land values in the area, Cunningham began buying portions of the Kyle and Terry plantation from the heirs. He was in no hurry, as it took him several years[13] to complete the purchase of some 12,500 acres of the Sugar Land plantation, including the crops, raw sugar mill, farm buildings, and commissaries.

In 1883, he extended his partnership with Ellis. They put their acreages together and built a 600 ton raw sugar mill which they named the "Imperial Mill," located about one mile west of the Cunningham mill (the Cunningham mill was originally the Williams' mill built in 1843 and later enlarged by Kyle and Terry). A year later this partnership was dissolved, with Ellis retaining 5,300 acres and the Imperial Mill; Cunningham retained his raw sugar mill and 12,500 acres of land. He continued to increase his landholdings in the area until he controlled a total of 20,000 acres, some of which he leased from other land owners. His Sugar Land plantation was then one of the largest in the state, growing 7,000 acres of sugar cane as well as crops of cotton, corn, alfalfa, sorghum grain, and a variety of vegetables and fruits. He had several hundred head of cattle. There was also the large raw sugar mill with the necessary field help and transportation equipment for bringing the cane to the mill.

He converted some of the Kyle and Terry plantation buildings into a semblance of a company owned town, sufficient to provide the bare necessities for his labor force.[14] He made extensive use of convict labor in the fields, usually had over 300 living in barracks located on the southern part of the property. Workers in the raw sugar mill and elsewhere on the property were, with the exception of a few executives, largely transient, hired when work was to be done and let go when the particular crop was harvested and the particular project was completed. Cunningham ran a commissary to provide the bare necessities, but furnished few amenities for his workers, some of whom lived in the old abandoned slave quarters, some in jerry-built shacks, some under buildings or in the fields.

Like other large plantation owners of his time, in spite of the miserable condition of labor on his place, the Colonel intended to live as a wealthy southern planter felt he deserved. He maintained his family home in San Antonio and visited there often, but most of his time was spent in Sugar Land. He built a large one story frame house, just south of the Southern Pacific tracks, between Oyster Creek and Brooks Street, where the present Sugar Land Police

1890s   Ox-drawn carts haul cane stalks to the raw sugar mill.

Headquarters is now located. It was an attractive, rambling place, with numerous rooms and with open porches all around, a large dining room and ball room. The building was painted white, with clematis vines climbing on the front. There were large gardens, with banana trees fifteen feet high, on the grounds. His particular hobby was Tennessee walking horses, of which he had several, and he was proud of his herd of Texas longhorns. He raised Belgian hares, being particularly fond of these as a dinner course.[15]

He was a large man, well over 6 feet and 250 pounds. As Dan Guteleben (a prolific writer about people and events in the sugar industry of that time) reports, "After the War, he became a planter at Sugar Land. Dressed in black, with a wide brimmed hat to match, and a white ruffled shirt resplendent with a great diamond stud, the Colonel was an impressive sight as he towered above his cronies at the frequent conventions in the lobby of the old St. Charles hotel in New Orleans."[16]

Cunningham also became actively engaged in the transportation of the products of the Sugar Land plantation. By the early 1890's, he was originating a large volume of freight from his raw sugar mill, the paper mill, his cotton and corn crops and various other farm products, all shipped over the Galveston, Harrisburg, and San Antonio Railway. It was speculated then that he collected as much as twenty-five percent of the destination freight cost by originating the shipments. However, he felt that he needed to be able to ship over lines competing with the Galveston, Harrisburg, and San Antonio, possibly for a better rate but also for the wider choice of destinations.

He modernized and enlarged some seven miles of his privately owned rail line which brought cane to his mill from some of his southern neighbors. He finally completed fourteen miles of track and chartered it as the Sugar Land Railroad Company in 1893, forming connections with the Santa Fe at Duke and with the International and Great Northern (later to be the Missouri Pacific) at Arcola.[17] That allowed him to ship to most destinations in the central United States and to demand competitive prices and service from the long-haul railroads.

He also built a small gauge railroad some twelve miles west from Sugar Land to the bank of the Brazos north of Richmond, ending near what is now the Foster Farms. Its purpose was to haul sugar cane from that area to the mills at Sugar Land. In 1907, he received a charter for this line as the Imperial Valley Railroad,[18] and it was useful until the decline of cane growing in the early 1920's. In 1926, it was discontinued, the small amount of equipment was sold, and the tracks were abandoned.

In the early 1900's the two local short-line railroads were bringing in huge tonnages of raw sugar cane to the raw sugar mills on the Ellis and Sugar Land plantations from a number of farms located throughout eastern Fort Bend County, enough to tax the capacities of Ellis's Imperial mill as well as the Cunningham mill. The latter was old and in need of constant repair. Cunningham spent a great deal of money in repairing and modernizing the mill, adding an expensive diffusion process to increase the extraction from the sugar cane, but unfortunately giving rise to an unexpected increase in fuel costs. He formed a company named the Sugar Land Manufacturing Company to operate a paper

Early 1900s.   **Men in striped trousers were convict workers.**

Early 1900s.   **Cane stalks from the fields on the way to the raw sugar mill at Sugar Land.**

mill to make heavy brown wrapping paper from the crushed and dried cane stalks, and an acid plant for use in the paper making process.

Cunningham recognized the need to insure a larger and more dependable source of fresh water from Oyster Creek, because of the water requirements of his raw sugar mill and his paper plant. Along with Ellis, whose Imperial raw sugar mill was also on Oyster Creek, and who also faced shortages of water in dry periods, he installed a large pumping station on the Brazos River where his Imperial Valley Railroad met the river, dug a canal to Oyster Creek, and began pumping Brazos River water into Oyster Creek when necessary. He also set in place a series of small dams on Oyster Creek above and below Sugar Land, and these enabled him to control the water level in the creek as well as in the adjoining storage ponds. This system of pumping from the Brazos and damming below Sugar Land, much enlarged one hundred years later, is still the means of insuring adequate cooling water for the Imperial refinery year round.

As Cunningham and some of the other raw sugar processors enlarged and modernized their mills, smaller and less well-financed millers were closing. In the ten years from 1882 to 1892 the number of raw sugar mills declined from forty-six to fourteen and by 1909 to ten.[19]

But Cunningham was determined to be the largest and most modern sugar processor in the state. He spent lavishly for capital improvements and further enlarged the capacity of his mill. With the Ellis mill just a mile away, more and more local growers were increasing their crops and sending the cane to the Cunningham and Ellis mills. Sugar Land grew to be the center of sugar cane processing for most of eastern Fort Bend County. Cunningham became known as "The Texas Sugar King."

In the early 1890's, Cunningham recognized a significant and exciting trend in the sugar industry. Although the sugar consumed in the South and Midwest was still the customary sticky brown raw sugar, in the Eastern markets this product was being replaced by an improved white, free flowing refined sugar. Refined sugar was produced when the sticky, yellow raw sugar crystals were passed through a refining process whereby the raw sugar was melted, chemically treated, filtered several times, decolorized and boiled to a grain. The syrups were spun off the grains, which were then dried by warm air. The result was the pure, white, free flowing sugar in use today. Responding to the demand, several refineries had been built in Louisiana, and Cunningham could see the handwriting on the wall.

Anticipating a similar trend toward white refined sugar in his Texas and midwestern markets, he tested the market by shipping raw sugar to Louisiana to be refined and returned to Sugar Land for shipment to Cunningham customers. He quickly learned that the future of the business would be in the conversion of the raw sugar from his mills into sparkling white refined sugar.

In 1896, Cunningham embarked on his most ambitious step. He began construction of a cane sugar refinery at Sugar Land to manufacture 100,000 pounds per day of white refined sugar. The refinery was built next to the Cunningham raw sugar mill, some fifty yards north of the Galveston Harrisburg and San Antonio Railway tracks. This location placed it squarely on top of the foundations of parts of the old Williams raw sugar mill built in 1843. It would later become the Imperial Sugar Company. The investment required was huge for that time, over $1,500,000.[20] Nevertheless, he began the project in 1896 and it took several years to complete.

Early on, Cunningham began to run into difficulties. Part of his heavy machinery was lost on a ship which was sunk in a storm while coming from New York, and although insured, its loss delayed the construction. A bad flood from the Brazos in 1899 caused a sizeable loss in crops. In 1899, a new boiling house had just been completed, a building three stories high with a foundation about 100 ft. by 150 ft. On December 30, 1899, the building was destroyed by fire. Finally, just when it seemed that he had his new refinery in full scale operation, the 1900 hurricane which almost destroyed Galveston did considerable damage to the Sugar Land plantation and the new refinery. But he persisted, and in early 1901, the refinery was producing Cunningham Refined Sugar. (Different references give different dates for the "completion" of the refinery, but the truth probably is that one seldom gets a refinery "completed" because it is always found to need something else.)

Cunningham had invested a great deal of money in the Sugar Land property, much of it borrowed, some from relatives. Income from his farms and the raw sugar mill had gone into the completion of the refinery, and by 1901 his credit was being questioned. He had expected the opening of the refinery to solve his problems, but it seemed that his troubles were not over. In the early 1900's he had several bad crops due to weather; plant diseases and pests caused a loss of sugar content in his cane. Raw sugar prices were subject to the vagaries of Congress and sugar legislation.

By 1902, Cunningham was in trouble. He was getting along in years, and his son, on whom he had been depending, had not turned out well. But he thought he saw a way out by importing raw sugar from Cuba in burlap bags, in sufficient quantity to enable him to operate the refinery throughout the entire year, instead of the past practice of operating only several months per year to process the local sugar crops. He arranged to receive boat loads of 300 pound burlap bags of raw sugar from Cuba, to be unloaded at Galveston and transhipped by rail to the door of the refinery at Sugar Land.

He worked out a processing-in-transit arrangement with the railroads whereby, on all refined sugar shipments out-bound from Sugar Land by rail, he would be refunded a substantial part of the inbound rail freight costs on raw sugar from Galveston to Sugar Land. A similar processing-in-transit arrangement remained in effect for over eighty years, until the increased volume of truck shipments of refined sugar from Sugar Land to customers brought about a change.

His plans for importing raw sugar for the refinery were sound, and he might have survived had he been able to carry them through. He was able to buy a few cargoes of off-shore raws in 1902 and 1903, but he simply did not have the credit to finance the necessary continuous schedules of raw sugar arrivals to keep the refinery operating; and intermittent operation was no longer practical. He was reluctant to reduce his many activities at Sugar Land, although he did sell some of his less productive land, leaving roughly 12,000 acres under his ownership.

1906   Cunningham Raw Sugar Mill and Refinery.

32

THE CANE SUGAR REFINING PROCESS

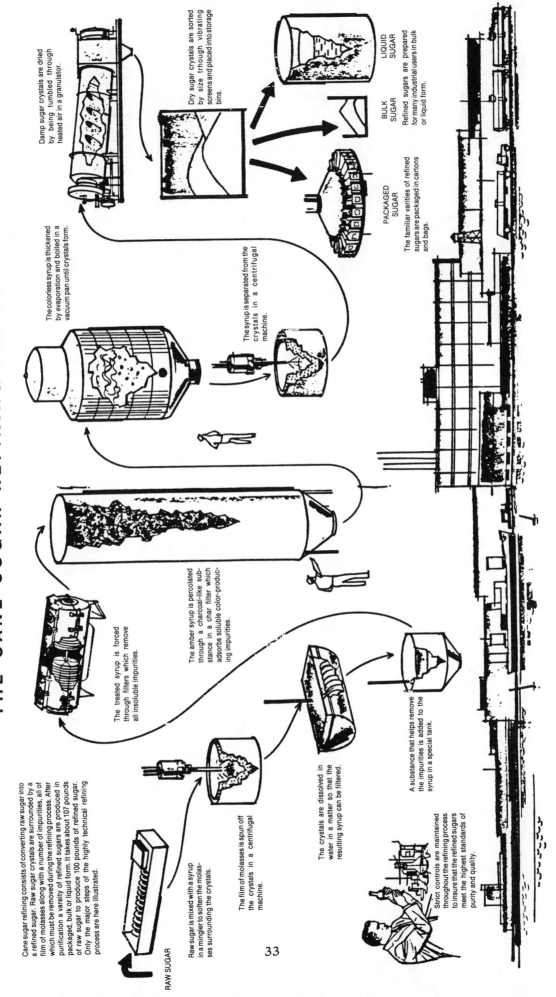

Cane sugar refining consists of converting raw sugar into a refined sugar. Raw sugar crystals are surrounded by a film of molasses along with a number of impurities, all of which must be removed during the refining process. After purification a variety of refined sugars are produced in packaged, bulk or liquid form. It takes about 107 pounds of raw sugar to produce 100 pounds of refined sugar. Only the major steps of the highly technical refining process are here illustrated.

RAW SUGAR

Raw sugar is mixed with a syrup in a mingler to soften the molasses surrounding the crystals.

The film of molasses is spun off the crystals in a centrifugal machine.

The crystals are dissolved in water in a matter so that the resulting syrup can be filtered.

A substance that helps remove the impurities is added to the syrup in a special tank.

Strict controls are maintained throughout the refining process to insure that the refined sugars meet the highest standards of purity and quality.

The treated syrup is forced through filters which remove all insoluble impurities.

The amber syrup is percolated through a charcoal-like substance in a char filter which adsorbs soluble color-producing impurities.

The colorless syrup is thickened by evaporation and boiled in a vacuum pan until crystals form.

The syrup is separated from the crystals in a centrifugal machine.

Damp sugar crystals are dried by being tumbled through heated air in a granulator.

Dry sugar crystals are sorted by size trhough vibrating screens and placed into storage bins.

LIQUID SUGAR

BULK SUGAR

Refined sugars are prepared for many industrial users in bulk or liquid form.

PACKAGED SUGAR

The familiar varities of refined sugars are packaged in cartons and bags.

Cunningham was not in good health, his refinery, mill, and farms were deteriorating, and he was having troubles with his creditors. In 1903, he was unable to make the required payments on $550,000 worth of bonds held by the San Antonio Loan and Trust Company and in that year, his company was placed in the hands of a receiver. The receiver was Ed C. Lassiter, a nephew of Cunningham. Twenty years earlier in 1883, Lassiter, then a young man of 23, had come to Cunningham and asked assistance in arranging a business loan from a San Antonio bank. Cunningham took Lassiter to his own banker and stated that, "I will endorse this young man for anything he wants."[21] By 1900, Lassiter had become quite wealthy, and when Cunningham was verging on bankruptcy, Lassiter provided Cunningham with an unsecured personal loan of $300,000.[22] He was probably the largest unsecured creditor and accepted the role of receiver. He appointed his brother-in-law, Garland Miller, as assistant receiver.

In spite of all his problems, Cunningham still expected that the importation of Cuban raw sugar, and the resulting opportunity to operate the Cunningham Sugar Refinery year round could provide a resurrection. The refinery was in the center of the sugar district; large enough to process all the raw sugar from the surrounding plantations. Although distressed, it still had a value approaching $1,000,000. The plantation itself was diversified, and his railroad provided a most favorable transportation opportunity.

The receivers appeared to share the Colonel's optimism. In 1905, they formed a "Plantation Club" in Sugar Land with thirty-three members, all employees of Cunningham Sugar Company, taking over the Cunningham mansion and moving the Colonel to smaller quarters. They installed tennis courts, a polo grounds, a gymnasium, with reading rooms, sleeping rooms, bathrooms, and a wide gallery.[23] There were beautiful lawns, a large lake, boating and fishing facilities. This investment may have inspired the employees, but apparently had no noticeable effect on the basic problems.

By then, neither Cunningham nor his son were capable of the effort and devotion required to pull it all together. The receivers did not have the experience necessary to manage such a large enterprise, particularly one in financial difficulties. Short of capital and with deteriorating credit, they were allowing the plantation and buildings, as well as the raw sugar mill and the refinery to deteriorate. Drainage ditches became clogged, floods and heavy rains altered the level of the fields, creating stagnant ponds and breeding mosquitoes.

In 1904, Sugar Land was reported to have a seasonal population of 700 people, of whom 400 were convicts living in barracks south of town and working on the farms, mostly in the cane fields. The other 300 people, mostly transients, were employed by the various other Cunningham activities in and around the town.

Field hands and workers in the various businesses, particularly in the refinery were almost all transients, and were, for the most part, a rough crowd. With no readily available transportation in or out of town, workers, out of necessity, had to live in the area. Some lived in the old slave quarters, many in tents, some in jerry-built shacks, some even slept in the various company buildings—late arrivals often slept in the open.

One such late arrival was hired at 75 cents per day, including bed and board,

This photo, found in Imperial's old files, was probably taken in the very early 1900s, during the time when Sugar Land was known as "The Hell Hole of the Brazos." It was captioned "A residence of Sugar Land in the early days."

Early 1900s.   Saloon and pool hall at Sugar Land.

and when he asked where he could sleep, was handed two blankets and told to, "try the cane brakes." He also reported that the town was all male, the only local entertainment being a saloon. The town contained five buildings—the sugar plant, three small hotels and a commissary. Each hotel had a Chinese cook and two helpers. "We ate a lot of fat bacon, navy beans and two-day old bread."[24]

Sugar Land was known as "The Hell Hole of the Brazos" and was no place to raise a family. A most graphic picture of conditions there in the early 1900's is presented by a lengthy, but well worth quoting, handwritten letter from L. H. Rayner, who came to Sugar Land in 1904 as assistant superintendent of the refinery, after both his father and his brother had worked there some years earlier.

"After dad had built the new plant of the American Sugar Refinery Co. in New Orleans, he went to Sugar Land upon the invitation of Col. Cunningham to help him with his refinery. It was about 1894. He remained to start it and left my brother to supervise its operation, my brother having been a chief chemist with the old Planters Refinery in New Orleans. Col. Cunningham offered my dad a 1/3 interest in Sugar Land if he would stay and manage the properties. But after my brother told me the lurid tales about Sugar Land, I understand why my dad did not accept the Colonel's offer, and I never dreamt that I would go there. My dad told me the Colonel would retire to his cottage and go on a binge for a month. He would have his man serve him a big plate of cheese and crackers and go back to the bottle. Sugar Land in those days had a terrible reputation. I went to Sugar Land in 1904, and the Colonel was about 74 then. Colonel Cunningham was a very large man, about 6'2" and weighed around 280. He was a typical Texan, rather slouchy in appearance, large jowled with a deep voice, and a commanding appearance. He was an omnivorous performer with a knife and fork. There were eight in our dining room with the Colonel at the head of the table, and we were served in courses. In strawberry time the Colonel would look at the large bowl of strawberries, look around and casually remark that there did not seem to be enough to go around, and polish off the whole bowl. He would get away with 4 or 5 cups of coffee, a quart of milk, half dozen eggs with ham, and a dozen plate sized pancakes. The old gentleman was a lusty trencherman.

"Ed, Jr. was a tall lanky redhead about 35 then, soft spoken, charming with impeccable manners. He had a M.E. degree from Cornell and a law degree from, I think, Harvard. He had a brilliant mind, speaking Spanish, and several other languages. When Ed, Jr. left college, he returned to Sugar Land and became manager for his father. He would go to Houston, collect a conglomerate entourage, and go on a binge for a week or two, and then one night the watchman would pick him up at the gate where the train conductor had tenderly dropped him. The gate was the junction of the Southern Pacific and Sugar Land Railway and according to law all trains had to stop there." (This was about 100 yards from the refinery.)

"Every once in a while Ed, Jr. would go on a binge and chase the Negroes out of the yard brandishing his two silver handled 45's. He lived on the hill near Cleveland Lake in the settlement where the residents were the families of the principal men.

"We had 11,000 acres under cultivation and raised our own truck gardens, even two acres of strawberries. While most of the labor were ex-convicts, even some white, the plantations were exclusively convict labor, with their own quarters, guards, and overseers. A Capt. Brooks was the head and a fine cultivator. Convicts were leased from the state penitentiary for $30 per month per convict. The guards were paid a higher wage, and Capt. Brooks got $2,500 per year. The state paid for the convicts' food, clothing, and medication, but I think Sugar Land paid for Capt. Brooks and the guards. If I remember correctly, we had 350 to 400 convicts. We furnished all housing and facilities for the convicts and the guards. A gang consisted of from 20 to 30 convicts, each having its own bloodhounds.

"The plantation railroad, cane cars, and repair shops were all operated by free men.

"The labor in the yards, railroad, and factories consisted of many ex-convicts and about every nationality anyone could mention. The skilled labor, such as sugar boilers, centrifugal operators, and other skilled were mostly from Louisiana. We never lacked for labor, and Sugar Land seemed to be the dump for deserters from ships in Galveston, hoboes needing a couple of bucks, and hikers. When a warship visited Galveston, I was sure to have a couple of men come up at 3 A.M. (when we started melting) salute and ask for a job. The salute gave them away.

"About a mile from Sugar Land there was a dump called 'Mexico.' Liquor was sold openly, dance and gambling places, and prostitution operated full blast. It was a cesspool . . . all nationalities, scum, drifters, and professional gamblers. I visited the place once in company with a couple of deputies. Every week we dreaded Monday coming because from 20 to 100 men and women would leave Sugar Land going to Rosenberg, the court house seat, these being witnesses, or arrested for stabbing, shooting, or killing. In order to obtain some semblance of order in Sugar Land proper, we employed deputy sheriffs as yard supervisors and timekeepers."[25]

Also in Imperial's files is a short article entitled "History of Sugar Land," undated, written by M. R. Wood. Wood had come to Sugar Land under Cunningham in 1901 as chief chemist at the refinery. He later became plant superintendent. He states, "At the time I was here we had but three white women in Sugar Land. They were the wives, whose husbands were employed in the plants. You are doubtless familiar with the name that Sugar Land had in those days; 'the Hell Hole of the Brazos,' and it was just like that. It was warm and over 90 degrees or more and our workers in the mill and refinery were either ex-convicts or convicts. I never attempted going out to the plant after sun-down that I did not have my artillery strapped to my side. Fortunately I never had any occasion to use it, although it did save me more than once getting a 'rap.'"[26]

With the properties and the work force in this condition, there seemed to be little hope for a continuing turnaround under the Cunningham management. In 1904, Mr. A. A. B. Woerheide of the Lincoln Trust and Title Company, the major creditor of the Cunningham properties and the receiver of the adjoining Ellis Plantation, decided he had had enough. He was looking for a way out—preferably for someone or some group with the capital and the management expertise to reverse the downward trend at both plantations.

In 1905, all creditors intervened. The courts adjudicated these claims,[27] and the company was reorganized. A new company was formed, named the Cunningham Sugar Company, which took over all the properties at Sugar Land, as well as the obligations. In doing so, it was necessary for the new company to refinance itself through a mortgage issued to the Lincoln Trust and Title Company of St. Louis secured by first mortgage bonds.[28]

The newly organized refinery did manage to make a profit of $34,000 in 1906, apparently realizing the Colonel's dream of operating on foreign raw sugars most of the year—but this was followed by a critical loss of $320,000 the following year.[29] It was a good try, but it only bought time. The Lincoln Trust and Title Company was anxious for a newer and more capable management. Although it appeared that there were sufficient assets to satisfy the creditors, the Title Company preferred that the receivers find a well financed and capable buyer.

[1]*The Herald Coaster*, Sesquicentennial Edition, Rosenberg, Texas, June 1, 1972, Section VIII, p. 4.

[2]A. J. Sowell, *History of Fort Bend County*, (Waco, Texas: W. M. Morrison, 1964), p.349.

[3]Ibid

[4]*Herald Coaster*, Ibid.

[5]William, R. Johnson, *A Short History of the Sugar Industry in Texas* (Houston, Texas; The Gulf Coast Historical Association, 1961), Vol. V., p.42.

[6]*Herald Coaster*, op. cit. Section I, p. 11.

[7]Dale Lasater, *Falfurrias* (College Station, Texas: The Texas A & M Press, 1985), p. 58.

[8]Johnson, op. cit., pp. 42, 43.

[9]Ibid.

[10]Undated newspaper clipping in Imperial Sugar Company files.

[11]Lasater, Ibid.

[12]Johnson, op sit, 44.

[13]*Herald Coaster*, Vol. VIII, p. 5.

[14]Lasater, loc. cit.

[15]*Herald Coaster*, op. cit., Vol. VIII, p. 5.

[16]Letter from Dan Guteleben, self styled sugar tramp, in files of Imperial Sugar Company.

[17]Lasater, loc., cit.

[18]*Handbook of Texas*, (Austin, Texas: The Texas State Historical Association, 1952), Vol. I, p. 875.

[19]Johnson, op. cit., p. 53.

[20]Lasater, op. cit., p. 58.

[21]Lasater, op. cit., pp. 27.

[22]Ibid., p. 59.

[23]Guteleben letter, loc.cit.

[24]Clipping from *Fort Bend Mirror,* dated November 1971, quoting a letter from H. F. Gordon who worked at Sugar Land for six months.

[25]Handwritten letter from L. H. Rayner, in files of Imperial Sugar Company at Sugar Land.

[26]Handwritten letter from M. R. Wood, in files of Imperial Sugar Company, Sugar Land, Texas.

[27]Letter from Dan Kempner to I. H. Kempner, Jr., 1947, in files of Imperial Sugar Company at Sugar Land, Texas.

[28]Johnson, op. cit., p.64.

[29]Ibid, p. 66.

The Old Ellis Plantation home was moved to the refinery yard in 1908. It became the home of W. T. Eldridge.

THE ELLIS PLANTATION

The Ellis Plantation played a minor but interesting part in the history of the Imperial Sugar Company and of Sugar Land. It was comprised of 5,300 acres located along the western boundary of the Cunningham plantation. The portion north of the Southern Pacific tracks is now in the Central Unit of the Texas prison system. The southern portion of about 2,000 acres south of the railroad to the Brazos, had become the Clayton farm, known locally as Sartartia. The Clayton farm was sold in 1984 and is now being developed into a large, upscale residential community known as "New Territory" just west of the Texas Department of Corrections Central Unit on Highway 90A.

Littleberry A. Ellis was born in September 1827, and in 1859 he moved to Jefferson, Texas where he formed a successful merchandising business.[1] He served in the Confederate army and rose to the rank of Colonel in Hood's Brigade, where it is likely that he became acquainted with Colonel Ed Cunningham. Ellis's grandfather, Ambrose Ellis, and his uncle, Richard Ellis, were signers of the Texas Declaration of Independence.[2]

In 1868, three years after the end of the Civil War, L. A. Ellis bought 2,000 acres of land out of the Mills Battle League and the Cartwright League, near Clodine Road. On the Southern Pacific tracks there was a station known as Walker Station, which had a two story building. Living quarters were upstairs with a post office and a general store down stairs. Ellis's purchase included this building, which he operated. He changed the name from Walker Station to Sartartia, after the first name of his oldest daughter.[3] He later added 3,300 acres north of the railroad, most of it in the Mills Battle League, but some in the Alexander Hodge League.

He built a large plantation home at Sartartia, a home which many years later was moved to Sugar Land where it was located next to the char house on the refinery grounds and became the home of W. T. Eldridge. It is said that it was originally constructed with wooden pegs instead of nails and was built entirely by convict labor.

Most of the Ellis plantation was planted in sugar cane, which he harvested and sent to the Kyle and Terry mill on the adjoining plantation. He used mule drawn cars on moveable rails to transport the cane from the fields to the mill.

In 1875, he entered into a partnership with Col. Cunningham, as previously described, initially for the leasing of convicts from the state of Texas.[4] In 1883, when Cunningham was buying up the lands previously owned by the Kyle and Terry heirs, Ellis and Cunningham extended the partnership to join their properties. Since the Cunningham raw sugar mill, previously owned by Kyle and Terry, could not process all the raw sugar available to it at that time, the partnership of Ellis and Cunningham built a new 600 ton raw sugar mill in 1883. It was located on the Ellis lands about a mile west of the Cunningham mill at

Sugar Land, at what is known as Cooks Dam, near what is now Highway 6.[5] They named this mill the "Imperial" mill, a name which would endure in the sugar history of the state of Texas, and indeed nationwide.

Less than a year later, the partnership was amicably dissolved, with Ellis retaining his original 5,300 acres and the Imperial Mill. Cunningham retained the Cunningham mill and some 12,500 acres of land, including the town of Sugar Land.

By 1884, Ellis was in bad health and felt he could no longer manage the plantation. He moved to Austin, Texas, turning the operation of the plantation over to his two sons, W. O. (Will) Ellis and C. G. Ellis. Their management was less than exemplary, and, in combination with some of the ill fortune which plagued the Cunningham properties, led to the demise of the Ellis plantation.

Among their unprincipled management practices was the use of a tenant contract containing small print which gave the landlord the power to dispossess the tenant for almost any reason, real or imagined. One provision was that if the tenant left the premises for more than a week he could be summarily discharged.

In August, 1896, a tenant named George Priddy, after harvesting his crop, took his family on a vacation for a few days, and when he returned was notified he had violated his contract and must leave immediately. Finding that Ellis men were already confiscating and loading his crop, he drove them away with his Winchester. Upon being informed of this, Will Ellis rounded up his bookkeeper and his overseer, provided them with pistols, and picked up his shotgun, which he had loaded the day before with buckshot. The three men set out for the Priddy farm in a buggy. Unknown to Ellis, the bookkeeper had, the day before, used Ellis' shotgun hunting rabbits and had reloaded the gun with small mustard seed birdshot by mistake. Neither Ellis or the bookkeeper knew that the shot gun contained a harmless shell.

Arriving at Priddy's place, they espied him standing in his horse lot, armed with his Winchester. Ellis stopped the buggy, ran forward till he was about seventy yards from Priddy, at which point he and Priddy fired almost at the same time. Will Ellis, mortally wounded by the rifle bullet, died within a few hours. Priddy, with his face peppered with birdshot, was not seriously injured. He was tried in the Richmond courthouse and was acquitted.[6]

Four months after Will's death, Colonel A. E. Ellis died on December 19, 1896, at age sixty-nine, and the ownership and management of the plantation fell on the shoulders of C. G. Ellis, Will's brother. But C. G. was beginning to run into the same problems of weather, bad crops, sugar legislation, and competition that were plaguing Colonel Cunningham, and by 1904, the Ellis plantation, like the adjoining Cunningham properties, was in the hands of a receiver. In 1905, A.A.B. Woerheide of the St. Louis Trust and Title Company secured an option on the Ellis properties from the receiver.

C. G. Ellis continued to operate the properties until 1906, when he was shot and mortally wounded in a gunfight with a sergeant of his convict guards.[7]

After the death of C. G. Ellis, the only heirs were his mother and his wife. Neither had any knowledge of the workings or the finances of the plantation and were horrified to discover that not only was there no money, but that the estate owed various creditors over $240,000. At that time the property was appraised by the receiver at $350,000.

As early as 1904, W. T. Eldridge was in Fort Bend County looking for bargains and saw the opportunity to acquire both the Cunningham and Ellis plantations, but it was beyond his financial capabilities at the time. It happened that I. H. Kempner of Galveston was also interested in the same properties.

The story of the purchase of the Ellis and Cunningham plantations by the partnership of W. T. Eldridge and the Kempner family is of primary interest and is told in a later chapter. First, it will be of benefit to look at the histories of the two improbable partners-to-be, Eldridge and Kempner. It would seem unlikely indeed that two prospective business partners with such marked contrasts in family, educational, personal and business backgrounds could be compatible.

[1]*Herald Coaster*, Sesquicentennial Edition, Rosenberg, Texas, June 1, 1972, Vol. I, p. 11.
[2]Ibid.
[3]Ibid.
[4]Dale Lassiter, *Ed Lasater and the Development of South Texas*, (College Station, Texas: The Texas A&M University Press, 1958), p. 58.
[5]Conversation with G. D. Ulrich, who managed the Ellis property in 1906 and 1907.
[6]Clarence R. Wharton, *History of Fort Bend County*, (Houston, Texas: The Anson Jones Press, 1950), pp. 229-231.
[7]Ulrich, loc. cit.

1904   W. T. Eldridge, Sr.

W. T. ELDRIDGE

The following early history of Eldridge is largely taken from the voluminous and detailed transcripts of his two trials for murder held in Richmond, Texas in 1904 and in Bellville, Texas in 1907. In his own testimony and that of others, his early life and business dealings are described in considerable detail. The testimony also provides an interesting portrayal of the life and customs of the time in a small isolated Texas town.[1]

To avoid the repetitious questions and responses, the testimony has been paraphrased by the author, but the general sense of the events has been preserved. Some of the testimony is in minor disagreement with opinions and reports of events by others in Eagle Lake, but since it was accepted under oath, it has been used herein.

William Thomas Eldridge was born September 8, 1862 in Washington County, near Independence, Texas. He never remembered his father, a Methodist minister named Alfred Buckner Eldridge, who died shortly after the Civil War of a disease contracted during the war. His mother was Epsie Randle, of an aristocratic Virginia family.[2] She was financially well off, but her second husband managed in a few years to put the family in difficult straits and to embitter young Eldridge by demanding money the boy had earned doing small jobs.

Eldridge stated that he never went to school, or as he put it, "never did a lesson in a schoolhouse." It is probable that his mother, an educated woman, had taught him at least the basics. It was said that at one time he made his own candles so that he could study and acquire enough education for the pursuit of a business career. It is apparent from his business correspondence and from his successes that he did indeed manage to educate himself adequately for his purpose.

He was seven years old when his mother married her second husband and moved the family to Childress Creek, about twelve miles north of Waco. He could not get along with his stepfather, and in 1874, at age twelve, he ran away from home. He never returned.

For a twelve year old, he was resourceful. The first night, he slept in a wagon yard in Cleburne and the following day hired on as a cotton picker with a family in Granbury. He stayed there about a year, doing odd jobs on the farm, then went to Caldwell County near San Marcos, where he again spent a year picking cotton and doing chores on a farm.

In the spring of 1878, when he was sixteen, he moved to Belton where he got a job carrying mail on horseback between Belton and Gatesville for room and board and $10 per month. During the summer in Gatesville, he opened a fruit stand, and this was his initial entry into operating his own business. He must have been favorably impressed because he never again worked for wages unless it was at a business in which he also had a substantial interest. At times in his future, he became owner or part owner of as many as thirty enterprises, small and large. He learned to manage people and to operate to the limit on borrowed money.

In 1879, having saved and borrowed enough money to buy a wagon and four mules, he began freighting from Waco, Brownwood, and other points. He bought hides, wool, cotton, pecans, anything he could "traffic in" to haul and backhaul, and soon became a competent trader in commodities.

His mother became destitute and left her husband. Eldridge moved her and her remaining belongings to the home of her sister (where he had been boarding) in Gatesville, but her husband followed her and persuaded her to return to their home in Weatherford. Eldridge, upset over his mother's condition, "sold what I had in Gatesville and for two years I knocked around not doing very much." During that time he traveled around south Texas, to Galveston, San Antonio, and into Mexico.

Soon, the money he had received from the sale of his Gatesville property began to run low. He invested $85.00 in a tent, a wagon, two mules and some fishing tackle and set out to catch fish to sell door to door and to restaurants. He fished along the San Saba River, down the Colorado, and arrived in Eagle Lake in January 1884. He was twenty-two years old. Eagle Lake at the time had a population estimated at 400 people.

He arrived at Eagle Lake with a "few hundred dollars" in cash, his tents, wagon, team, and fishing tackle, all worth, according to his estimate, about $1,200. He continued fishing and sold apples and freshly caught fish that spring, and in the fall of 1884, he opened a small grocery store and added a restaurant to the building, hiring a man to do his fishing for him. Three years later, in 1887, he sold the grocery and restaurant for $3,000 and made his first mistake in selling the business on credit.

He entered the "gents furnishing" business, but the buyers of his store and restaurant weren't paying him as fast as the bills for the gents furnishings came due, and after only a few months he was forced to close his business. Some of his creditors accepted assignments and eventually received their money; the others he finally paid off at seventy cents on the dollar.

In the fall of that same year, 1887, at age twenty-five, he went back to trading in commodities and freighting in and around Eagle Lake, buying and selling cotton, cotton seed, pecans, cattle, and dabbling in land, usually using the leverage of other people's money by cutting them in on the profits of his trades. In trading pecans, he found that access to quotations in other areas gave him a formidable advantage, and he built the first telephone line ever known in Wharton and Colorado Counties.[3]

In 1888, at age twenty-six, Eldridge was elected the first marshal of the newly incorporated city of Eagle Lake, a position which was described as the "unofficial chief of police." He also served as the tax assessor and collector, the combined salary being $20 per month and fees. It certainly enlarged his experience.[4]

In a 1905 pre-trial hearing he was compelled to tell of several of his more violent encounters with the citizenry, as follows:

Q. How many different shooting scrapes have you been in prior to this?
A. I have been in two prior to this one ... A darky whose name I cannot recall.

46

I shot him once. He was not shooting at me. He had a hoe drawn on me. While I was city marshall of Eagle lake about 15 years ago, a half breed Indian and Negro . . . shot at me with a .44 Winchester, I shot him but didn't kill him . . . he was 10 or 12 feet from me. I was shooting a .44 pistol.

Q. Isn't it a fact that you struck a man on the head with a pistol of some kind and that he died?

A. A man snapped a pistol in my face, and I took it away from him and hit him over the head with it, and he died. I was an officer at the time. His physicians testified that he died of erysipelas and not from the blow. He had another pistol and a dirk knife after I took the pistol from him.

Q. Did he attempt to use them?

A. He had sent me word in the evening to leave town, that he was coming to town and paint it red, and that if I didn't leave they would have a new marshall at Eagle Lake. I notified a young man who was acting deputy for me; there was quite a crowd of them in town, of his gang. H. H. Moore is the only one I can name who was with him. Just after supper myself and Sutton walked into the public square and as we got about middle ways in the square, I saw some man on a horse elevate his six-shooter in the air and emptied it, I mean fired it all around. I ran over as quickly as I could and they informed me that it was Judy Frick. I jumped on a horse that was standing there and followed him. About 300 yards I came to the Aransas Pass Crossing, that being a little elevation my horse slowed up at that point, the man hailed me and he asked, "Is that you Eldridge?" I answered, "Yes" and about the same time he threw a pistol in my face. I caught the pistol and got off my horse by some means, we had quite a scuffle over the pistol, he tried to persuade me to turn it loose, that there isn't a load in the pistol. I finally succeeded in wrenching his gun from him and about the same time the constable ran up. Mr. Frick being a little below where I was standing, the constable says, "Look out, Will, he's got a knife." He was coming toward me up this elevation, I reached over and hit him with his own pistol, he staggered back and fell . . . T. W. Davis of Eagle Lake ran up with a lantern. . .H. H. Moore was standing close to him with a pistol in his hand. I ordered him to throw up his hands and surrender his gun, he said he would not do it for a living man. At that time I leveled down on him and he says, "I'll surrender." I asked Mr. Stuart to take the gun and he did so. I was using Frick's pistol, I had lost mine in the scuffle with Frick. I examined Frick's pistol and found that it was loaded . . . Frick lived several days after the blow."[5]

This sort of activity could well put an end to his plans for the future. Although he had been elected for a two year term, he resigned at the end of the first year to run for the office of alderman and served one year in that capacity.

This move may have been providential, as his successor, City Marshall W. R. Kinard, who was elected in 1889 was killed in a bloody battle in the street, a gun fight in which three men died.[6]

In the next few years, Eldridge enlarged the scope of his business enterprises in and around Eagle Lake. He bought a butcher shop, went into cattle feeding. He bought and enlarged a local hotel, known as the "Drummer's Home," and built a home on the grounds of the hotel. He brought his aunt, Mrs. Wadkins, down from Gatesville to run the hotel for him.

In 1890, at age twenty-eight, Eldridge married "the Widow Gordon" as she was spoken of at the time. She lived in Eagle lake and had a daughter and a son by a previous marriage. Subsequently the couple had a son, W. T., Jr., born in 1891, a daughter, Ivy, born in 1893, and a daughter, Ethel, born in 1895. By 1895, when he was thirty-three years old, he had become a substantial citizen of Eagle Lake and estimated his net worth at $14,000.

Eldridge and a prominent local rancher and farmer, named Captain W. E. Dunovant, had engaged in numerous trades together, usually when Eldridge found a promising transaction and would ask Dunovant to put up the money for half the profit. The men became close friends.

Captain Dunovant, a Civil War veteran some sixteen years older than Eldridge, had inherited large land holdings adjoining Eagle Lake. He farmed a great deal of rice, some cotton and raised cattle. He was the first to farm rice in the area, built the first rice mill and a pumping plant for irrigation, and later built a substantial raw sugar mill. He made use of convict labor, usually had about eighty-five convicts in three camps on his land. He lived over a mercantile store he owned at Lakeside, a mile from Eagle Lake, where he also owned a recreation center with a pavilion, picnic grounds, canoes, and boats.

According to the trial testimony of numerous substantial citizens who had known Dunovant for many years, he was an honest man, well regarded in the area, but very opinionated and very proud, dangerous and violent when crossed and unforgiving of any real or imagined slight or wrongdoing. There were numerous stories, quoted by citizens of the area, in which Dunovant retaliated to various slights or insults by striking, beating, and whipping citizens, such as a salesman, a priest, and several Negroes. He was tall, slim but powerful, a one-armed man. He had lost his left arm near the shoulder but at times carried two guns on his right side, one an English derringer in his pants pocket, and a short barreled pistol in a canvas-lined coat pocket. This coat pocket was to be his nemesis. He spent most of his time managing his substantial farming and ranching properties, often in company with his convict guards. He was an out of doors man and had little interest in detail.

Eldridge, on the other hand, was a man with a single minded devotion to his goal of business success. He cared little what others said or thought and was not sidetracked by non-essentials. He liked to trade and build, and he was good at it. It seemed that after the violence he had experienced as marshall of Eagle Lake, he would go far out of his way to avoid trouble of any kind; and threats against him never seemed to divert him from the business activity at hand.

In 1895, Eldridge and Dunovant became partners in what would grow into a large and profitable venture, but which resulted in a personal vendetta between the two men. At that time Eldridge was thirty-three and Dunovant was forty-eight years old. The partnership was formed when Eldridge came across an opportunity to buy a relatively large farm enterprise eleven miles south of Eagle Lake on the Colorado River. The property consisted of some 4,000 acres of land, of which only 425 was in cultivation. There were also a few cabins, 1,500 head of animals, mules, horses, cattle, as well as the unharvested crops. The price was $9.00 per acre, all inclusive.

Eldridge saw this as a bargain, but as usual, he was using his cash and credit to

In 1897, Eldridge minted brass coins "D & E" for Dunovant & Eldridge, for use on the Bonus plantation, good only at Bonus.

In 1901, after the partnership with Dunovant had been dissolved, Eldridge minted several denominations of pewter "W. T. E." coins good only at Bonus. He exchanged his W. T. E. coins for any outstanding D & E coins.

Around 1915, Sugarland Industries had light weight metal coins, as well as paper money, good only in Sugar Land.

49

the limit in his other enterprises, so he went out to see Dunovant to discuss it. He offered Dunovant a half interest in the property, and Dunovant suggested that they form a partnership, with each putting up half the cost. Eldridge was to become the full time manager. They formed the firm of Dunovant & Eldridge and bought the property by assuming a $26,000 note outstanding against it and paying $5,500 each in cash. Eldridge turned the daily management of his other enterprises over to subordinates and took up the management of the farm. He apparently saw a challenging opportunity to build up the property.

And build it up he did. His attorney, Jonathan Lane, stated that by 1900 it was the best equipped farm he'd ever seen. In 5 years he had nearly 2,000 acres in cultivation, upgraded the animals and had 200 people working on the property. He built a cotton gin, a rice mill, and a corn mill. He added cabins for the help and a general commissary store, organized a wholly owned company town.

He called the town "Bonus" and had his own brass currency struck, coins of different shapes for different denominations, with "D & E" and "Bonus" printed on one side and the words "Good for merchandise" and the denomination on the other. He paid his employees in these coins, good only at his company store. In such an isolated community, the employees were constrained to do most of their buying at the local store anyway. He would, when some employee needed to purchase something elsewhere, pay in United States currency. His subsequent business record indicated that one reason for his successful management of so many diverse activities was his ability to choose and motivate employees and to develop an esprit among them. This was to be noticeably true in his long management of the numerous businesses into which he entered in Sugar Land.

He accomplished his improvements almost entirely on credit, borrowing on everything the partnership could call an asset, and by 1899 owed some $70,000. At various times he owned five mercantile stores, one each at Eagle Lake, Bonus, Eldridge, Strickland, and McNeal. In 1900, there was a mercantile store in Eagle Lake named Dunovant & Eldridge.

By now he was becoming accustomed to thinking in larger terms. Attracted by the government protection and bounties on the production of sugar cane, he refused to be intimidated by the fact that he had no raw sugar mill and no transportation from the isolated Bonus farm. In 1899, he and Dunovant began construction of a $400,000 raw sugar mill at Lakeside, on property owned by Dunovant. Today, there is a State of Texas historical marker at the site of this mill.

In order to transport the sugar cane the eleven miles from the fields at Bonus to the mill at Lakeside, the two men chartered the Cane Belt Railroad. They bought an abandoned rail line from the Southern Pacific for $800, took up the ties and tracks and moved them to Bonus. They used labor and equipment from the Bonus plantation to clear a right of way and made additional ties from lumber cut from the farm. At first, when the road was completed, the freight was moved by mule-drawn wagons on the tracks. They had twelve wagons, six mules to the wagon, on the tracks. They had a total of ninety mules which were kept in a mule lot called the "roundhouse," to use railroad jargon. Within a year they had improved this rather antiquated system of moving freight by buying a discarded and decrepit steam locomotive and several rail freight cars, paying

$800 for the locomotive and $200 for the rail cars.

The original financing of the railroad was a typical Eldridge maneuver. He testified at the trial that the Cane Belt was capitalized at $15,000, with ten percent paid in. The "paid in" portion was accomplished when he and Dunovant each wrote personal checks for $750 and deposited them in the company safe. This was the only direct financial contribution either of them made to the railroad (other than the capital expenses mentioned in the above paragraph), which after a great deal of trouble and bad feelings was eventually sold for $1,600,000.

Other landowners along the eleven mile rail line began clearing more fields, planting sugar cane and increasing their crops of cotton, rice and corn, using the Cane Belt for transportation to the main line of the Southern Pacific at Eagle Lake. According to Eldridge, the price of land along the rail line jumped from five cents to fifty cents per acre, an opportunity which he was quick to exploit. They upgraded the road and equipment until they had a viable railroad originating considerable tonnage.

The Cane Belt turned out to be a profitable venture from the start. By originating freight such as cotton, corn and rice along the line and delivering it to the long haul railroad at Eagle Lake, they were paid a disproportionate freight by the main line. In 1900 they began to extend the Cane Belt to Sealy, some thirty miles. Later it reached as far south as Bay City and Matagorda on the Gulf Coast, with 177 miles of track.

In the process of this venture they managed to accumulate a debt of $750,000 to the Lincoln Trust and Title Company of St. Louis on the railroad, in addition to the $154,000 they then owed on the Bonus Plantation. The president of the Lincoln Trust and Title, A. A. B. Woerheide, was represented by Jonathan Lane of Houston, an attorney who also had some business interests around Eagle Lake. Both men became close friends of Eldridge. They were to play a large part in his various enterprises, including his murder trials and his later ventures in Sugar Land.

The importance of railroads in the everyday life of the citizens of that time is worth a comment. There were no highways worthy of the name, only minor dirt roads which were poorly maintained at best. The movement of goods and people in any quantity or numbers was necessarily by rail, so that the towns grew up along the rail lines. It was difficult and at times impossible to move goods any great distance from the rail stops.

The railroad depot was an important center in the town, and it was common practice to meet the trains to see who or what might be coming in or going out. Business men traveled extensively on the few regular trains, spending much time on trains and in depots, and consequently became widely acquainted with their contemporaries. It does not seem too unusual, in the light of the customs of the day, that both of Eldridge's confrontations with his enemies took place on trains.

When the Cane Belt was formed in 1899, the original agreement was that Dunovant and Eldridge would each own fifty percent of the stock, but at the last minute, Dunovant demanded that he hold two thirds of the stock and Eldridge one third. Eldridge agreed to this, and when asked why, replied that he gave in just because Dunovant insisted. At that time, according to Lane's testimony, Eldridge and Dunovant were the best of friends. When they incorporated the Cane Belt, Eldridge asked that Dunovant draw up a will for him (Eldridge). The will, read at the trial, named Dunovant administrator of all Eldridge's property, to be "left wholly to the integrity and honor of said Dunovant to give to my wife and children such property as he may determine in his sense of justice is theirs."

Dunovant was named president, with Eldridge as vice president and general manager, the understanding being that Eldridge would manage all the details and operations of the road. They hired Jonathan Lane, as attorney for the railroad and also as personal attorney for each of them.

Dunovant had taken very little interest in the details of operations and management of the plantation or the railroad, preferring to work on his own pursuits, although Eldridge consulted with him on matters of importance. Lane and Eldridge worked out the various operating and financing problems, after talking them over with Dunovant. However, after five productive years, things fell apart.

Dunovant, although owning considerable property, also had some debts and felt pressed for money. The Dunovant and Eldridge partnership had made a great deal of money in 1886, 1887, and 1888 although the improvements did necessitate borrowing up to $154,000 on the Bonus property. There is no indication of the results of their operations between 1888 and 1900, although it could be speculated that they continued to enlarge their activities, borrowing heavily as they progressed. In any event Eldridge testified that in 1900 they had a very bad year, when a severe storm destroyed their crops, damaged their buildings, and drowned a good many animals.

Dunovant began to worry about the debt on the Bonus Plantation and the larger one on the Cane Belt Railroad. He began quarreling with Eldridge over minor details in management. In addition to his financial problems, Dunovant began to resent the stature to which Eldridge had grown in the community. Eldridge had become the largest businessman in the area, and it was naturally to Eldridge that people turned in matters affecting Bonus and the Cane Belt. Dunovant felt left out, and his pride was hurt on several occasions.

The first serious indication of the depth of Dunovant's dissatisfaction came in 1900, when he charged into the Cane Belt office in a rage and offered to blow Eldridge's heart out over a small item in a newspaper. At the trial, Eldridge stated that he had given an interview to a reporter, and the subsequent article had quoted Eldridge as saying something about "a couple of small farmers building a railroad." Dunovant told Eldridge that he, Dunovant, was not to be referred to as a small farmer, nor was he to be mentioned as an equal because "you are not my equal, and I am superior to you." He also claimed that he had taken Eldridge from a poor boy and brought him up to his present position. He demanded a retraction of the article, which Eldridge was unable to promise. Dunovant continued to threaten Eldridge and finally left in a rage.

For the next year, Dunovant became increasingly critical of Eldridge over minor details, frequently took affront when not consulted, imagined personal slights, and began to interfere with the operation of the railroad and the Bonus Plantation. Finally, as recriminations and threats became more bitter, Eldridge announced to Dunovant that he could no longer work with him and suggested the dissolution of the Bonus partnership of Dunovant & Eldridge. He offered to sell his interest in the partnership for $7,000 if Dunovant would take over all debts, or alternately, he would give Dunovant $7,000 and take over all debts, dissolving the partnership. After some argument, Dunovant agreed to take the $7,000 and turn the Bonus Plantation and its debts over to Eldridge.

So in June 1901, Eldridge became owner of the Bonus property and its debt. One of the first things he did was to replace the brass D & E coins with W. T. E. coins made of metal alloy.

Dunovant and Eldridge were still involved together in the Cane Belt Railroad. Dunovant was still president and Eldridge was vice president and general manager. In 1900, in negotiating with the Lincoln Trust and Title Company for the several bond issues which now totaled $750,000, they had to sign over fifty percent of their stock to the trust company, giving that company a strong voice in the management. The other half of the stock was divided two thirds to Dunovant and one third to Eldridge. Neither Eldridge or Dunovant had invested any significant amount of their own money in Cane Belt stock, although the partnership of Dunovant and Eldridge had advanced $60,000 worth of labor and materials in starting the road.

At this point, A. A. B. Woerheide of Lincoln Trust and Title Company, Eldridge and Lane, were running the railroad; a situation which did nothing to heal the growing rift between Dunovant and Eldridge. Their relations worsened. Dunovant began making demands, such as the firing of a railroad employee who had slighted him. He charged Eldridge with stealing. In a meeting with Eldridge, Woerheide, and Lane, he insisted that he and Eldridge lock themselves in the next room and shoot it out.

Finally, Eldridge announced that he could no longer work with Dunovant on railroad matters. Lane and Woerheide made efforts to reconcile the two, even drawing up detailed lists of the duties and responsibilities of each, reasoning with them, and making concessions to Dunovant on minor matters. But nothing worked, and, unable to reconcile the problems, Woerheide stepped in and bought Dunovant's stock for $9,400. He valued the stock at $32,000, but the road had advanced Dunovant some $7,000 in cash and had built a tap to his rice fields. Lane estimated that Dunovant had actually received about $41,000 in cash and services.

At that point, Dunovant entered into a serious and public personal feud with Eldridge. He told everyone who would listen that Eldridge had cheated him out of the Bonus Plantation and some $200,000 in the railroad. He publicly and privately spoke of Eldridge as a liar, a cheat, scoundrel, rascal, "dog-faced s.o.b.," and frequently claimed that he would kill Eldridge if he could just get him to fight. Finally, he was stating that if Eldridge wouldn't fight, he would have to shoot him down like a dog. Often in public, Dunovant spoke disparagingly of the morals of Eldridge's wife.

The situation was further exacerbated by local politics, which in a small, isolated town like Eagle Lake played an important part in the life of the community. Feelings could run high, everybody seemed to know who was supporting whom, and as a consequence the polling places attracted a considerable amount of attention at voting time. More often than not, Dunovant and Eldridge were supporting opposing candidates.

There was a local election on June 19, 1902; the voting place was a table across the door of a bakery on the main street, with three election judges seated behind the table. Witnesses testified that the day before the election Dunovant instructed several of his convict guards to accompany him to the polls and to wear their guns concealed under their coats, as he expected to confront Eldridge at the polling place.

It is interesting to note that the common conception of Texas men carrying their .45's in holsters on their hips did not seem to be all inclusive in this part of the state. Many of the witnesses, most of whom seemed to be average businessmen and farmers, stated that they frequently or habitually carried guns, usually small .38's, although some few were partial to .44's or .45's. When asked where they carried them, several replied, "in my pants pocket, or hip pocket or coat pocket," a practice which may have accounted for the popularity of suspenders at that time.

On the afternoon of the election there were several people around the polling place, including Dunovant and his men, when Eldridge approached the polls in company with a furniture salesman named Dobbins. Neither was armed. As they came within about fifteen feet of him, Dunovant began cursing Eldridge and drew his gun. Eldridge raised his hands in the air and shouted that he was not armed. The furniture man, trying to get out of the way, collided with Dunovant. Dunovant tried to reach around Dobbins to fire at Eldridge, but Dobbins, still trying to get out of the way, collided again, and Dunovant was unable to get a clear shot at Eldridge. Meanwhile, Eldridge managed to escape over the election table and through the back of the store, closely accompanied by the election judges, who were also trying to get out of the line of fire.

Up to that time, Eldridge had not carried a gun, even though several people had warned him of Dunovant's threats. He usually replied that he didn't think Dunovant really meant to do him physical harm. But after the fracas at the polls, he kept a rifle and a shot gun in the Cane Belt office, and started carrying a pistol regularly. To some of his friends he expressed a desire to sell out and move away. It is interesting that Eldridge, who as a combative twenty-six year old, had shot two men and pistol-whipped another in his one year service as marshall of Eagle Lake, now, at age 38 and a successful businessman, sidestepped such overt and embarrassing threats to his future.

For almost two months after the incident at the polls, Eldridge carefully avoided Dunovant. Then, on August 11, 1902, Eldridge left Eagle Lake alone on the Aransas Pass Railroad bound for Houston, a trip he made frequently. It was mid-afternoon. When the train stopped at Simonton, Dunovant boarded the same coach, unseen by Eldridge, who was seated three seats from the rear in the last coach. Dunovant entered the front compartment of the coach through a swinging door which separated the Negro section from the white section. Dunovant and Eldridge appeared to see each other at the same time.

There were several witnesses to what happened next. The train had just started to move slowly when Dunovant seemed to hesitate at the swinging door and then reached toward his coat pocket. For comfort Eldridge had placed his pistol in his valise on the seat beside him, and when he saw Dunovant, he immediately snatched the gun from the bag and went charging up the aisle toward Dunovant. He fired at close range as the men collided near the swinging door, the bullet striking Dunovant in the lower chest.

Although mortally wounded, Dunovant threw his right arm around Eldridge's neck. Eldridge attempted to cock his pistol and fire again, but a passenger, John P. Campbell, (who by the time of the trial had been elected Mayor of San Antonio) jumped on Eldridge's back, placing his finger in the trigger guard, and every time Eldridge cocked the pistol, Campbell pulled the trigger, firing into the side of the coach and the seats until the gun was empty. A priest also joined in the fray and tried to separate the two men. When the pistol was empty, Eldridge struck Dunovant twice in the face with the gun.

At the sound of the first shot, the conductor pulled the emergency cord to stop the train, which came to a halt about 100 yards from the station.

One witness was a young man on the way to his first year in college. He happened to be sitting in the second seat from the swinging door. He was turned around with his back to the aisle, talking to a lady in the seat behind him. He saw or heard nothing until Eldridge's pistol went off almost in his ear. He turned, saw the gun, and went out the open window "head first" but managed to get his arm around a window support and hang on till the train came to a halt.

One couple, a man and his wife who were sitting in the rear of the compartment near Eldridge, saw him start up the aisle with his gun. They quickly jumped into the toilet just behind them but could not close the door because of the small size of that facility. The woman who had been talking to the young man who went out the window, ran back, and tried to crowd into the toilet also, but there was not room and the gentleman seemed reluctant to offer his place.

The young man who went out the window seemed to have done exactly the right thing at the right time, as several of the shots, fired from Eldridge's pistol by the passenger on Eldridge's back during the struggle, struck the very area where he had been sitting.

As the train stopped, the antagonists were finally separated by the passengers and the conductor, and Dunovant collapsed on the seat. The fight was over.

Eldridge asked the conductor to take Dunovant's gun. When the conductor tried to remove it from the coat pocket, he found that it was hung in the pocket, and he had to use both hands to free it. It seemed apparent that Dunovant, with only one arm, had been unable to extricate the gun from the canvas lined pocket in time to get off a shot. Dunovant was fifty-six years old and Eldridge was forty.

A doctor was located in Simonton, and he stayed with Dunovant until the train arrived in Houston. Dunovant was taken to a hospital, where he died the same night.

Eldridge was tried in Richmond, Texas a little over two years after the shooting, the trial lasting from November 11 to November 21, 1904. The charge was murder, the defense pleaded "self-defense." and the verdict was "not guilty." It seemed that the prosecution presented a rather weak case. The defense, on the other hand, had such a preponderance of witnesses and legal talent that the verdict seemed obvious by the time the trial was half through.

But Eldridge's troubles with the Dunovant family were far from over. In spite of his financial difficulties, Dunovant's estate was appraised at $600,000. He left the estate to two sisters, who turned the management over to Dunovant's brother-in-law, an insurance man from Gainsville and Dallas. This man was W. E. Calhoun, who moved to Dunovant's place at Lakeside, and who had often been heard to say that he intended to kill Eldridge in revenge for the shooting of his wife's brother. (Incidentally, Dunovant's grave marker in Houston shows an avenging angel with the legend "I will be avenged.")

Less than two months after Dunovant's death, at about 10:45 P.M., on October 3, 1902, as Eldridge walked the short distance to his home from the Drummer's Home, where he had been meeting with Woerheide, he noticed two men near his house. He kept his eye on them and started up the steps looking backwards. He stumbled and fell just as two blasts from a double barreled shot gun went over his head into the front of his house.

He felt sure that one of the men who fired was named Cobb, a former employee and crony of Dunovant. Cobb had been heard to urge Dunovant to kill Eldridge during the incident at the polling place. Eldridge thought the other man had been Calhoun, but he could not be sure.

Although there was continuing animosity toward Eldridge by the family and friends of Dunovant and reports of threats by Calhoun, Eldridge continued to expand his interests in the community. In 1903, he bought a lot on which a bank was to be built, and became one of the founders of the First National Bank of Eagle Lake.

Then, on June 6, 1904, some five months before Eldridge was due to be tried for Dunovant's shooting, Eldridge was shot in the back by a high powered rifle as he stood on the platform at the depot waiting for the arrival of the train. The bullet penetrated his body from the back through the chest and hand, missing his heart by 3/16 of an inch, and went through seven inches of wood at the station building. The shot came from a second story window just forty-five feet away, and several people testified that it was fired by Calhoun. Calhoun was arrested as he left the building and jailed at Columbus, Texas, but for some obscure reason was soon freed. Eldridge, badly wounded, spent twenty-one days in a Houston hospital.

After his recovery, Eldridge went to extraordinary lengths to avoid Calhoun. He moved his "family and all his worldly goods" to San Antonio and bought an interest in the City National Bank in that city.

He still had to make business trips back to Eagle Lake, pending the settlement of his interests there, but when he did, he arranged to be let off the train on the prairie outside of town, to be picked up by a friend with a buggy and smuggled into town. When his train passed through Lakeside, where Calhoun was then living, he hid in the baggage compartment. He again began carrying a gun, as he had been warned repeatedly that Calhoun had stated that he would "hunt Eldridge down."

He sold his Bonus property, reportedly for $250,000, with the buyer to take over the debt. The Cane Belt Railroad was sold to the Santa Fe for $1,600,000, and one can speculate that Eldridge may have received as much as $340,000 for his share after all debts were paid. It is not known what he may have received for his other interests in the Eagle Lake area, but he was undoubtedly a wealthy man for those times.

Then, about a year after he had been wounded, on May 5, 1905, he boarded the Aransas Pass Railroad in San Antonio about 9:45 P.M. He had a sleeper berth to Houston, and he asked the porter to wake him before they got to Wallis, as he had property along the Brazos and had heard the river was flooding. He also remarked that he was looking at a deal for the Cunningham properties at Sugar Land.

When awakened, he dressed and went forward toward the chair car. As he came to the door of the smoking compartment at the rear of the chair car just ahead of his sleeper, he saw Calhoun sitting in the corner of the smoking compartment with several other passengers. Eldridge, as was his custom, had his pistol tucked inside the waistband of his trousers, under his suspenders. He and Calhoun appeared to see each other at the same time, but Eldridge fired first, killing Calhoun instantly and wounding another passenger who was in the smoking room.

The men in the smoking compartment testified that, as Calhoun saw Eldridge, he said, "Oh, my God" and grabbed for his gun, which was in his valise beside him on the seat. Eldridge pulled his gun from his waist band and began firing from the aisle. There were five other men in the compartment at the time. One of them was struck in the arm by one of the four shots fired by Eldridge. The wounded man was a hardy soul, who, though bleeding from a bullet which had passed through his arm near the elbow, seemed reluctant to miss any of the excitement. He waited till a doctor had boarded the train at Wallis, examined the dead man and was leaving before he asked the doctor to look at his arm.

The doctor who examined Calhoun's body testified that one of Eldridge's bullets struck Calhoun in the chest near the throat and completely severed the spinal cord, causing death to be instantaneous. He also testified that he found a special holster attached to a suspender button inside Calhoun's "pantaloons." Apparently, Calhoun had found it more comfortable on a long train ride to remove the pistol from the holster and place it in the valise, a decision which may have cost him his life. At the trial, when the doctor was asked if he had had much experience with gunshot wounds, he replied that "they are a good part of my practice."

Eldridge was tried for murder about eighteen months later, on January 14, 1907, in Bellville, Texas, and on January 17 was adjudged "not guilty." The plea had been "self-defense" and, like the 1904 trial in Richmond, the prosecution effort seemed as weak as the defense was massive. It was generally felt that Eldridge himself had requested the full scale trials in both cases to make sure his name and reputation were protected. It is of interest that in both murder trials the prosecution had strongly suggested that Eldridge, feeling that the threats from both Dunovant and Calhoun endangered not only his health but his business activities, had obtained advance information of their intentions to be aboard certain trains and had deliberately waylaid them. If this was indeed true, he had planned well and had conclusively avoided any evidence to that effect.

Once again, it is of interest to turn to a letter written by L. H. Rayner, the man who had written a description of Sugar Land under Colonel Cunningham. At this time he was working at the Lakeside sugar mill, and had the following to say about Eldridge at Eagle Lake.

> Mr. Eldridge owned the Bonus Plantation about nine miles south, and we hired the Negro and Mexican labor from him. They (Eldridge and Dunovant) built the Cane Belt Railroad which ended at Bonus, and the labor would come up from Bonus and go back each day. Captain Dunovant's mill had burned down, and the new one was financed by the Lincoln Trust and Title Co. of St. Louis, of which Mr. A. B. Woerheide was President.

> "While not what one would call an educated man, Mr. Eldridge was the shrewdest man I knew. He was a heavy set man, about 5'10" tall. He was quiet, poised, and gave one the impression on first sight of being an ordinary man. He spoke softly and slowly and let you do the talking. He would listen until you got through and then ask questions in an off-hand way. His grey eyes would look straight at you and anyone looking at those steady eyes knew that no liberties would be taken."

In 1905, relieved of the threat posed by Calhoun, and while awaiting trial, Eldridge had expressed a desire to get out of banking and back into farming. He bought a 4,700 acre farm near Bonus on the Colorado River, located on the old Cane Belt Railroad (by then it had become the Santa Fe). He developed this investment into a company town, which he named Eldridge. This property would later be sold to the Sugarland Industries.

He became increasingly interested in the Cunningham Plantation at Sugar Land, as he had mentioned on the train, and in the adjoining Ellis Plantation, both of which he had learned from his friend Woerheide were in financial difficulties. It was rumored that they might be bought for as little as twenty cents on the dollar.

[1]The State of Texas vs W. T. Eldridge, in District Court of Fort Bend County, Richmond, Texas. November term, 1904, Cause No. 3851, murder, Vol. N, p. 71. Transcript in files of the Imperial Sugar Company. The State of Texas vs. W. T. Eldridge, in District Court of Austin County, Bellville, Texas. January term, 1907, Cause No. 2646, Vol. R, p. 258; undated deposition by W. T. Eldridge; undated transcript of preliminary hearing, W. T. Eldridge; in files of Imperial Sugar Company.

[2]B. F. Johnson, *Biographical and Family History Sketch of William Thomas Eldridge* (Washington, D. C.: B. F. Johnson, Inc., 1921), "For Private Circulation Only," p. 11. In personal files of T. C. Rozelle, Sugar Land, Texas.

[3]Ibid., p. 15.

[4]Eagle Lake Historical Committee, et al, *A History of Eagle Lake, Texas* (Austin, Texas: Nortex Press, A Division of Eakin Publications, Inc., 1987), p. 66.

[5]Op. cit., Undated deposition by W. T. Eldridge.

[6]Op. cit., Eagle Lake Historical Committee, pp. 64, 66.

THE KEMPNER FAMILY

(Most of the following information concerning the Kempner family is taken from an article prepared by Barbara Cronholm for publication in the Imperial Crown, the house organ of the Imperial Sugar Company, in 1980;[1] from Mr. I. H. Kempner's "Recalled Recollections," written from his eightieth to his eighty-eighth year:[2] and from "H. Kempner," a publication of the Texas Gulf Coast Historical Association.)[3]

Eldridge was a loner, an individual—I. H. Kempner was a family man. Isaac Herbert Kempner who would become affectionately known in Sugar Land as "Mr. I. H." and who would be the partner of Eldridge in the purchase and renaissance of the Ellis and Cunningham properties, was the oldest son of Harris Kempner, who had immigrated to this country in 1853.

Harris Kempner had left his home in Poland to avoid conscription in the Russian army. He arrived in New York at age seventeen, after a three week voyage in a sailing vessel, with no knowledge of the English language and with only a few dollars in his pocket. The account of his climb to success in the business world is typical of that of many immigrants of the late 1880's.

He first found employment as a hod carrier for bricklayers and began an intense study of English. After four years of drudgery at manual labor, and of avidly saving every penny he could accumulate, he had acquired an understanding of written and spoken English sufficient for him to become a small contractor on his own account.

Learning of the opportunities in what was then still the frontier in Texas, he emigrated again, this time to Cold Springs, Texas. He invested in a small stock of household items, such as pots and pans, sewing materials and spices, and began calling door to door on the local residents and farm houses. He soon found that there was a need for a great variety of items, and began taking orders from his customers for whatever they required. He ordered the merchandise from suppliers and when the goods arrived he personally delivered them to the buyer. This led to an ever growing list of needs. In the process, he acquired a wide range of suppliers and considerable knowledge.

At first he walked from door to door, always wearing a dark suit and hat, a white shirt and a necktie; a costume which must have been distinctive in Cold Springs and the surrounding countryside. He bought a horse and began enlarging his circle of customers to outlying farms—this led to an expansion of his line of goods into farm tools, seeds, supplies of all kinds.

He gradually accumulated inventories of merchandise, and rented increasing storage space until he was operating a small general store. He was a well-known and well-regarded fixture in the town and the surrounding area, and some of his

Imperial Sugar Company

Harris Kempner

customers began asking him to perform banking functions for them. He became an informal private banker and adviser to his neighbors.

In 1861, four years after his arrival in Cold Springs, the Civil War broke out. Although he had been a fugitive from Russian military service, he volunteered with his friends and neighbors in the Confederate army, joining Captain Stokes' Company from Ellis County, a part of Parson's Brigade. He served throughout the long war. In one engagement his horse was shot out from under him and he was wounded and left for dead. But he recovered and served the rest of the war in the Quartermaster Corps.

When the Civil War ended in 1865, he returned to Cold Springs and resumed his various business activities where he had left off four years earlier. Again he prospered, and three years later, by 1868, he had accumulated what was a small fortune in those days, about $45,000. He was thirty-three years old, still single, and now eager to enter a larger business arena. At that time, the port of Galveston was a leading city in Texas, a center of merchandising and banking activities, and seemed to offer the greatest opportunity. He moved there in 1869 and entered into the wholesale grocery business in partnership with M. Marx.

In Galveston, the firm of Marx & Kempner soon became one of the largest wholesale grocery firms in Texas. The wholesale merchant at that time exercised a greater influence on the economy than perhaps any other period in American history because the wholesale grocer acted in many ways as banker to the community as well as supplier of grocery items. It was then a logical step from the wholesale trade to banking and investments.

Harris Kempner had an abiding faith in the rural economy of Texas. Consequently, much of his profits from Marx & Kempner went into rural banks and various land holdings. He was for many years the president of the Texas Land and Loan Company of Galveston, and was a director and major stockholder in ten national banks which he was instrumental in founding throughout the state: in Giddings, Cameron, Mexia, Ballinger, Athens, Groesbeck, Marble Falls, Gatesville, Velasco, and Hamilton. His son later related that these banks were opened when local farmers whose crops had been financed by H. Kempner asked him to set up banking facilities in nearby towns. He would do so. Generally, years later, these same farmers would ask him to sell his controlling interest to them and again he would abide by their wishes.

Intrigued by the potential profit value of credit lines in the cotton factoring business, he found a favorable borrowing source in his early acquaintance with a Mr. Fry, then president of the Bank of New York, who had been a fellow Confederate soldier in the Virginia campaigns. The banking connection he established with the Bank of New York has continued to this day by the Kempner family, and the H. Kempner account is the oldest continuous one on the books of that bank.

Although comparatively unknown in foreign banking circles, through the recommendations of other prominent Galvestonians he was extended credits totalling one-half million dollars through banks in London, Switzerland and Paris. He soon became the leading cotton broker and merchant in Galveston.

In 1872, Harris married Elizabeth Seinsheimer of Cincinnati, Ohio, whom he had met on an earlier trip to New York City. In 1873, Eliza returned to her mother's home in Cincinnati to give birth to their first son, Isaac Herbert (I. H.) Kempner. Ten more children were subsequently born to the family: Abe, 1874; Daniel, 1877; Sidney, 1879; Hattie, 1880; R. Lee, 1883; Stanley, 1885; Joe, 1886; Fannie, 1888; Sara, 1890; and Gladys 1893. Abe, Sidney, and Joe died in infancy or childhood.

Harris Kempner was described as "cool, calculating, full of ready resources ... wholly and entirely engrossed in his business affairs ... a man of few words, and those to the point. . .quick to see a change in the market and to take advantage of it ... pushing, driving and energetic." He took an active interest in efforts to improve port facilities and railroad transportation for the thriving city of Galveston, being an original member of the Deep Water Committee and a charter member and lifelong director of the Gulf, Colorado, and Santa Fe Railroad, which was eventually consolidated with the Atchison, Topeka, and Santa Fe.

During his long years of business activities, Kempner became an active investor in a list of Galveston enterprises: a shoe and hat company, a wholesale clothing enterprise, several exporting and importing activities; he and his partner Marx bought the Tremont Hotel, now renovated and named a historic site; a steamship and lighter company and a cotton compress, to name a few. It seemed that he became a willing participant in almost any opportunity to forward the business and civic affairs of his chosen city.

In 1885, the Island City Savings Bank of Galveston was about to fail. Harris Kempner, although he was neither a stockholder nor a depositor, was called upon to wind up the affairs of the bank and became its temporary president. Because of his business ability and integrity, the customers were satisfied and the bank remained in business.

In 1886, the firm of Marx & Kempner was dissolved and Harris Kempner expanded his activities in the cotton factorage business. This became one of the largest cotton enterprises in the south, with offices in the principal countries of Europe. He was also a large importer of salt, bagging and ties, coffee, and other commodities.

He was strong in his religious faith. His grandfather reportedly was a rabbi; and his parents had thoroughly, but frequently secretly, schooled him in the Old Testament, the Talmud, and synagogue ritual. He was strong in his own religious faith and very active in the affairs of the local synagogue, but freely granted to others the right to worship in accordance with their beliefs and training. Harris and Eliza Kempner would raise their large family in the Jewish religion, and this new generation would, like the parents, become pillars of that faith in Galveston during their lifetimes.

In 1886, the family's large home was destroyed by the fire that swept Galveston, and in the same year, his oldest child, Isaac Herbert, was sent to Bellevue High School in Virginia. (This was the son who was to become the leader of the family and the benefactor of Sugar Land until his death in 1967 at age 94.) In 1889, "Ikey" as he was affectionately called by his family, entered Washington & Lee University at Lexington, Virginia.

In 1889, the young "Ikey" visited New York City during the Christmas holidays to be treated for a throat infection. The seemingly insignificant visit to the old Imperial Hotel, one of the grand hotels of the day, left such an impression on the teenager that he was moved a decade later, to rename the family's newly acquired sugar business the Imperial Sugar Company, because the name "Imperial" was synonymous in his mind with high quality and excellent service.

For the next two years, I. H. engaged in the study of law, passing all his examinations and preparing for graduation. His brother, Dan, by this time was a student at Bellevue High School. Harris Kempner wrote to I. H. on January 10, 1894 ". . . you have good health now, and if you will take good care of yourself, avoid excesses, pursue the 'happy medium' in your enjoyments, it may be the pleasure of God, as we fervently hope, to preserve you for a 'ripe old age.'" A similar passage to Dan, who was then 17, four years younger than "Ikey" was sent on March 25, and was the last letter Harris Kempner wrote to his oldest sons.

Harris Kempner died on April 13, 1894 from his previously undiscovered Bright's disease. I. H. was called away from his studies at Washington and Lee to take the responsibility of managing the family's affairs at age 21. He never graduated from law school, but was admitted to the Bar of Texas the next fall. He was, as he said "an alumnus without a degree and a lawyer without a client or fee."

H. Kempner's death in the prime of his life marked not an end, but a continuation of the Kempner holdings which endures to this day. The firm of H. Kempner has survived intact, without substantial division, although it has evolved into a trust association holding interests for the benefit of the many members of the Kempner family. The financial investments of this nucleus set the stage for even greater accomplishments for the next generations of Kempners under the leadership of Mr. I. H.

Harris and Eliza Kempner had nurtured a remarkable family of capable, kind and erudite people, four sons and four daughters. It was a loving family which throughout their lives seemed to enjoy a sort of mutual admiration and companionship in each others company. As each completed his education and became of age, the brothers took over some of the responsibilities for the various family business enterprises, always led and guided by I. H.; the daughters became active in various civic, charitable religious and community activities.

At the unexpected death of Harris Kempner, his wife, Eliza, having been totally devoted to the care of her large family as well as to her civic and charitable activities, had almost no knowledge of her husband's many business interests. Daniel, four years younger than I. H. was in high school; Lee was only eleven years old; Stanley nine. The four young sisters had no business experience. The entire burden of taking over and continuing the diverse empire built by Harris Kempner fell on the shoulders of the twenty-one year old I. H. Kempner, as the oldest son.

Mr. I. H. recalled that,

> "On that night of my Father's death, about an hour after his passing away, I went, shaken with grief, out on the west porch of the second story of our then home on 16th Street. I looked into a sky of darkness, only a few stars visible. Alone and disconsolate, I talked aloud about how hopeless was the

1910   I. H. Kempner

future for my Mother and her eight children and made a vow that as I could not help the dead, I would always seek to help the living. I have never heretofore told of this incident to anyone. I recite it now because I realize how this resolution has helped me. The thorough cooperation of my brothers and sisters, to keep our family relations free from strife, the family fortune intact, has been our goal. Each and everyone of my brothers and sisters have kept our interests on an equal and equitable basis."

He faced an immediate complication in the fact that his father's will had not been signed. As Mr. I. H. stated in his "Recalled Recollections,"

"The result necessitated the cumbersome handling of the estate by my mother nominally as 'survivor in community,' requiring a tremendous bond, which was generously and without compensation signed by individual friends, acceptable to the court. In the present day of self interest, a group would be hard to find to give bond of over a million and a half dollars to cover an estate whose continued solvency or liquidation would be dependent on the integrity and ability of a twenty-one year old with no business experience beyond that gained by three or four summers casual work in his father's office."

He often expressed his gratitude to his father's friends and business associates, particularly in Galveston, who rallied to his assistance in his efforts to continue the Kempner enterprises. He was much encouraged when, in a relatively short time, they communicated their confidence in him by appointing or electing him to important civic, charitable and religious posts previously held by his father.

The estate's business interests were concentrated mainly in cotton, banking and ranching. For the next thirty years, he and his brothers devoted themselves to the task of strengthening and expanding those assets.

During the ensuing decade he traveled to Europe to expand the cotton factorage business into a full-fledged cotton export company with large cotton compresses and warehouses on the wharfs at Galveston and an extensive international cotton trade. He became the youngest director ever elected to the Galveston Cotton Exchange, and served as its president, vice-president, or director for half a century. He followed his father's example of financing irrigation projects around the state. In the elder Kempner's case it had been the Colorado and Comal Rivers in Central Texas' Hill Country. I. H. sponsored Lake Wichita on Halliday Creek at Wichita Falls.

Under his direction, the family purchased a large majority of the Island City Savings Bank of Galveston, changing the name to Texas Bank and Trust, then bought the Merchants National Bank in Houston. I. H. served as the bank's president for four years, commuting several days a week from Galveston. With W. L. Moody, Jr., he shared joint ownership of the new American National Insurance Company in 1903.

I. H. recalls a story illustrative of the caution and perhaps the prescience of successful bankers in the early 1900's.

"At our wedding, one of our married friends asked to bring a guest, described as a charming young lady named Miss Smith, whose family was well known in East Texas with private banks in Nacogdoches and Tyler. The young lady appeared in the first strapless gown ever seen in Galveston outside the bedroom. The women gasped with open mouths; the men with open eyes. The next day Mr. Adou, a seventy year old banker, asked his partner, Mr. Lobit, 'How much do the Smiths owe us?' Lobit replied, '$50,000.' 'Lobit, when the Smith indebtedness is due, I insist that you collect it.' 'What have you heard?' Lobit asked. 'Nothing,' said Adou, 'but if a father can't control his own daughters sense of decency, he can't control his business affairs.' Before the term of the note had expired, Mr. Smith decamped to Central America and the Smith bank closed its doors. To his dying day Mr. Lobit believed that Mr. Adou had some advance information which he had kept to himself."

I. H.'s civic endeavors were widespread, and the young man became a well-known and prominent Galveston citizen and city father. He was a member of the Deep Water Committee, as his father had been. After the fateful storm of 1900, when half the Island was washed away, Kempner was a member of the relief committee. He was named Commissioner of Finance by the Governor of Texas under the original Galveston Plan which became the forerunner of the commission form of city government throughout the U.S. He was instrumental in reducing the city's bonded indebtedness after the disaster and restoring its municipal credit rating within five years. He subscribed generously to the original seawall bonds. He was a member of the John Sealy Hospital Board and remained active in the hospital and medical school's affairs throughout his life.

The description of the 1900 storm written by I. H. was graphic.

"The storm struck about noon on September 8. The streets were flooded, rains continued all morning—then beginning about 2 P.M. the velocity of winds increased, reaching beyond any then measurement the government could record. The tide rose, naturally influenced by unusual atmospheric and oceanic impetus. The waters from the Gulf of Mexico and Galveston Bay soon met, covering all of Galveston Island with depths generally ten to twelve feet. All areas at the beach front also were becoming immersed up to the level of the porches (this was before the construction of the Galveston sea wall) sufficient by early afternoon to career or lift the homes nearest the Gulf and jam them together.

"Gradually water from the Gulf rose; invaded more areas and joined with the waters of the Bay. Its depth and surge of wave action caused the drowning of people trapped in their homes or seeking to escape to safety, lifting frame houses from their foundations; winds of destructive velocity (120 miles per hour when the gage broke) demolishing hundreds of homes, forming massed wrecked timbers into a floating battering ram, smashing not only frail, but also substantial homes . . . the area of destruction was wide; the time within which 7,500 lives were lost and extensive property damage effected was little over an hour."

In the early 1900's, I. H. Kempner began his own family life. In 1902, on December 17, he married Henrietta Leonora Blum, daughter of a prominent

Galveston family of dry goods importers, and in 1903, their first child, Harris Leon Kempner, was born. In 1906, a second son, I. H. Kempner, Jr., who would be called "Herbert" rather than "Junior," was born. He was followed by three sisters, Cecile, Lyda and Leonora.

During this period, Ike Kempner's brothers, Dan, Lee and Stanley, were finishing their studies and stepping into the various phases of the business in which they had the most interest. Dan, who graduated from the University of Virginia and was four years younger that I. H., took an active interest in the international cotton business as well as the agricultural and real estate enterprises of the firm. Lee joined Texas Bank & Trust in 1902 and was named Cashier by 1904. Stanley became associated with the insurance company in 1903.

In 1905, I. H., and his brothers had taken swift advantage of the new State Banking Law and established state banks in Texas City, Rusk, Corrigan, Groveton, Huntsville, Willis, San Augustine, Nacogdoches, Alvin, and their father's original Texas home, Cold Springs.

In 1906, I. H., was elected a director of the Gulf, Colorado, and Santa Fe Railroad, in which capacity he served for over 50 years. The Gulf, Colorado, and Santa Fe had been built to Lampasas County in 1882 and the town of Kempner, Texas named for Ike's father. At one time or another, the Kempners had interest in the Velasco, Brazos and Northern; the Uvalde and Northern; the San Antonio, Uvalde and Gulf; the Asherton and Gulf; three Wichita Falls-based railroads; and the Rio Grande City Railway. All were sold.

By 1906, twelve years after the death of Harris Kempner, I. H. had indeed proved himself capable of sustaining and expanding the family empire begun by his father. He had also cultivated the education and interest in the family enterprises of his young brothers as they grew up. Each of the Kempner brothers, Mr. I. H., Dan, Lee and Stanley supervised sizeable parts of the various Kempner family enterprises, and, along with their sisters, gave generously of their time and money in service to Galveston and the State. The brothers worked together as a team, always led by I. H. It was said that differences of opinion were usually settled by the vote of the majority, although at times it seemed that the vote of I. H. might have carried a bit of extra weight. They had an agreement that once a course of action was determined no one would later say, in hindsight, "I told you so." It is noteworthy that the brothers took as salary from the businesses only enough to provide a comfortable life style for each; the ownership of all the business enterprises was held in a trust which was equally owned by the four brothers, the four sisters, and Eliza Kempner during her lifetime. Before Eliza died in 1947 at age 98 her one-ninth share was distributed equally among the eight children.

I. H.'s many activities in securing financing for the family ventures and his civic, religious and charitable activities had brought him into contact with state and national financial leaders, and with various political and judicial bodies. He was very well known throughout Texas, and the measure of his national reputation was manifested when he became a founding member of the first board of directors of the United States Chamber of Commerce.

By 1905, the family had acquired rather extensive land holdings in Brazoria and Fort Bend Counties; the Darrington and Chenango Plantations in Brazoria; and the Rice Farm on Smithers Lake, the Belvedere Plantation at De Walt and the Palo Alto and Riddick Plantations in Fort Bend County. It was at this point that they became aware of the opportunity to acquire the adjoining Ellis and Cunningham Plantations at Sugar Land. These two properties totalled 18,500 acres and included a sugar refinery, two raw sugar mills, a company town, two railroads and various other business enterprises.

Their interest in the latter two properties would lead to a partnership with W. T. Eldridge of Eagle Lake and San Antonio. Over the next eighty years, this investment would become one of the most important of the Kempner family interests, and one which sons and grandsons of I. H. would continue into present times.

[1]Barbara Cronholm, *The Kempners: First Family of Imperial,* appeared serially in four issues of the Imperial Crown in 1980.

[2]I. H. Kempner, *Recalled Recollections,* written by Mr. I. H. Kempner between his 80th and 88th birthdays, completed in 1961, unpublished, limited circulation, Rosenberg Library, Galveston.

[3]I. H. Kempner, *H. Kempner, the First 100 Years,* Texas Gulf Coast Historical Association, Volume II, Number 1, March, 1959. An address by I. H. Kempner at the second annual meeting of the Association, January 29, 1958.

KEMPNER AND ELDRIDGE — 1906-1930

It seems clear that the peripatetic Mr. A. A. B. Woerheide, president of the Lincoln Trust & Title Company of St. Louis, and Mr. Jonathan Lane set the Kempner-Eldridge partnership process in motion. It will be remembered that Woerheide and Lane had been the financial and legal, as well as business advisors to Eldridge during all of his successes and troubles at Eagle Lake, and they had worked well together.

Now, in the early 1900's, Woerheide and Lane were engaged in several transactions in Fort Bend County. In 1905, Woerheide had secured an option on the Ellis Plantation from the receiver, was deeply involved in the adjoining Cunningham Plantation through loans from Lincoln Trust and Title, and was having difficulty keeping that enterprise afloat. He needed to find some person or persons who could finance and manage both the Ellis and Cunningham properties back into profitability.

He knew of Eldridge's desire to get back into the farming business. Both Woerheide and Lane were acquainted with Mr. I. H. Kempner and had heard that he had expressed an interest in the Cunningham properties but had stated that his family did not have the personnel to take over such an extensive and run-down enterprise. When Woerheide reorganized the Cunningham Corporation in 1905, he had no difficulty in persuading both Eldridge and Kempner to serve on the new board of directors.

In 1904 the receiver had arranged for a sugar expert to examine the properties and recommend the steps needed for improvement. He found that much of the raw mills and the refinery were in need of replacement and repair, some of the cane-handling equipment was outmoded; the lakes adjoining Oyster Creek needed to be deepened to provide additional water storage; communications were bad between the refinery offices, the refinery, and the laboratory; and finally, that living conditions were inadequate and that it was difficult to keep good employees.

Before the year ended, Kempner resigned from the board because he did not think the company was sufficiently dedicated to cleaning up and reorganizing the properties. Shortly thereafter, Eldridge approached Mr. Kempner and his brother, Dan Kempner, with a partnership proposal in which he outlined a long range program for rebuilding both the Ellis and Cunningham plantations.

Kempner and Eldridge were to be equal owners of the properties—a 50-50 partnership. The Kempner family was to provide financing. Eldridge was to dispose of his San Antonio banking interests and move his family to Sugar Land. He would devote full time to the management of the properties there, except that he could continue to oversee his plantation and company town at Eldridge, Texas, as long as that did not interfere with his Sugar Land activities. He was to receive a salary of $5,000 per year and five percent of the profits of the partnership. One extra concession made by Kempner was that Eldridge was allowed to buy the Sugar Land Railroad as his personal investment and given a period of time to pay for it out of his share of the partnership profits. This was to amount to a generous concession within a very few years. Profits from the sugar company and the farms were to be plowed back into the sugar industries, the company town, and the land improvements. No dividends would be paid the owners until the program was established and working.

It appears that the Kempners had financed the purchase of the plantations by the sale of their interests in the Riddick, Darrington and Chenango properties— the extent of Eldridge's financial participation, if any, in the purchase price is not known. In any event, the partnership began its existence free of debt, and it was fortunate that it did, because the program for rehabilitating the properties was to be a long and expensive one. Eldridge was to borrow against the assets at Sugar Land to finance the building of the town, the improvements to the farms and the repairs and improvements to the raw sugar mills and the sugar refinery, always subject to Mr. Kempner's advance approval. There were also to be times when the Kempner family credit was needed to buttress the Sugar Land collateral. Any additional ventures Eldridge wanted to enter on behalf of the partnership had to have the agreement of the Kempners. If the Kempners disapproved, Eldridge could nevertheless go ahead on his own, provided such venture would not interfere with his management activities at Sugar Land.

So the two men joined forces to turn the properties around; Eldridge, the driving, rough and tumble loner with a reputation of violence, single mindedly intent on the acquisition of power, recognition and fortune; Kempner, the quiet erudite family man who already had all these things coveted by Eldridge, and whose sole interest was the welfare and good fortune of his family members. And Eldridge was ready to go; it was up to I. H. Kempner and his family to make the partnership decision. At this point, about all they seemed to have in common was a recognition of what could be done with the Sugar Land properties if they were cleaned up, properly managed and adequately financed.

Mr. Kempner, in his book "Recalled Recollections"[1] written fifty years later, mentioned that his mother advised against any partnership with Eldridge because of the latter's reputation. Mr. Kempner said that "She feared Eldridge would shoot one of us, but we had no troubles or serious difficulties in our business affairs and attendant personal problems." He also stated that he had doubts that Eldridge had given his two enemies, Dunovant and Calhoun, fair chances to defend themselves. (The prosecution at the two murder trials had expressed these same doubts.) Nevertheless, Kempner probably felt some sympathy with the problems Eldridge had endured through the many threats and attacks against him, and had been impressed by the considerable management abilities Eldridge had exhibited in developing his Colorado River company towns and farms at Bonus and Eldridge, Texas.

Once the partnership arrangements were finalized, the first step in the program was the acquisition of the Ellis Plantation, a relatively simple course of action. In 1905, Woerheide and Lane arranged for Eldridge to acquire the option held by Woerheide, and in April of 1906 Eldridge settled with the receiver by paying the Ellis widows $10,000 in cash, and the creditors approximately $150,000 for their $240,000 worth of claims. Apparently Kempner advanced part, if not all, the money. At one time, the receiver had valued the Ellis properties at $350,000. A few days after he received title to the Ellis Plantation, Eldridge transferred the title to the Imperial Sugar Company.

The Imperial Sugar Company was a private company which had been formed in 1905 by the Kempner family and Eldridge for the express purpose of taking title, first to the Ellis Plantation and later the Cunningham properties. In April of 1907 Imperial was incorporated with a capital stock of $500,000 with over ten percent paid in. Seven years later, in 1914, the capitalization was increased to $1,000,000.

The name "Imperial" arose from the fact that the Ellis raw sugar mill had been known as the "Imperial Mill" for many years. Mr. Kempner liked the name, as he had long been an admirer of the Imperial Hotel in New York and associated the name with quality and excellence. It was a prescient choice, as the Imperial Sugar Company in future years would embody the image he had in mind and would become known as the Cadillac of sugar refiners in the United States.

Mr. Dan W. Kempner, a younger brother of I. H. Kempner, was named the first president of Imperial. Eldridge was made general manager, to receive a salary of $5,000 per year and five percent of the profits of the Ellis operation. Eldridge moved his family from San Antonio into the Ellis Plantation home, a large three story building located at Sartartia, two miles west of Sugar Land and just south of the Southern Pacific tracks.

The Ellis purchase included everything on the 5,300 acre farm, including the Imperial raw sugar mill, the crops in the fields, the farm equipment and buildings, tenant housing, housing for the 250 convicts and guards leased from the State, numerous farm animals, horses, mules, hogs, and cattle, and the large Ellis Plantation home. It also included the tracks and rail equipment for hauling the cane to the mill, a commissary store, and a warehouse. The Imperial raw sugar mill, commissary, and the warehouse were located near the west boundary of the Cunningham Plantation, near where Highway 6 crosses Oyster Creek at present.

Also included in the Ellis purchase was title to the pumping station on the Brazos River, some twelve miles northwest of Sugar Land, and the rights-of-way along the canal and along Oyster Creek, bringing water from the Brazos to Sugar Land. The pumping station and the canal had been constructed by Ellis and Cunningham to insure an adequate year-round supply of water to the Ellis Imperial raw sugar mill, the Cunningham raw sugar mill, and the Cunningham sugar refinery; however, the title had been a part of the Ellis estate.

While Kempner and Eldridge were taking the Ellis Plantation off his hands, Woerheide was busy with his program for turning over the Cunningham properties also. But this took a bit more maneuvering. In 1905, he had incorporated the Cunningham Sugar Company to take over all the assets of Ed H. Cunningham, including 12,500 acres of land and everything on it. The corporation issued $850,000 worth of capital stock, divided into 8,500 shares of $100 par value. Eight thousand, four hundred eighty-eight shares were issued to Ed Cunningham. Each of the twelve remaining shares went to the twelve directors, with both Eldridge and Kempner, who had been elected directors of the new corporation, receiving one share each.

Daniel W. Kempner

Cunningham Sugar Company then issued $850,000 worth of twenty year first mortgage bonds to mature in 1925, at 6 percent interest, to Woerheide's Lincoln Trust and Title Company. Later, to provide operating funds and to liquidate several smaller Cunningham debts to St. Louis investors, Cunningham Sugar Company also issued new bonds totaling $280,000 by giving a second mortgage to Conway Elder of St. Louis.

Cunningham was elected president of the company, Woerheide first vice president, and Jonathan Lane second vice president. However, it was made clear in the minutes that Cunningham was president in name only, with Woerheide and Lane calling all the shots.

Corporate minutes were sketchy in those days, and there are no indications in the Cunningham minutes as to how Kempner and Eldridge finally took over. However, a summary included in a 1922 appraisal states that Kempner and Eldridge secured an option on the Cunningham properties in 1908, and Eldridge was suddenly appointed general manager of the Cunningham Sugar Company, "not to be under the supervision of anyone except the Board of Directors." Both Cunningham and Eldridge were to be paid $5,000 and 5 percent of the profits per year, but Cunningham obviously had no authority in the operations of the company.

There is no indication as to when Cunningham left the company. According to the minutes, he last appeared as a director and officer of the company at a directors meeting in March 1909. At the stockholders meeting in June of that same year, he did not appear as a stockholder and was not elected a director. At the directors' meeting immediately following the stockholders' meeting he was not elected to office. In fact, his name was never mentioned again in the records, and it can only be speculated that he may have returned to the property he owned in Bexar County.

It appears that Cunningham and the other stockholders turned over to Kempner and Eldridge the 8,500 shares of common stock in the Cunningham Sugar Company, and that Kempner and Eldridge assumed the liabilities, including the $850,000 first mortgage, the $280,000 second mortgage, and some $300,000 of miscellaneous debts. The receiver had placed a value of $1,500,000 on the Cunningham properties. An appraiser stated, in 1922, that Eldridge and Kempner paid a total of $1,476,000.

The Cunningham properties were much larger than those of Ellis; some 12,500 acres, with a variety of crops, mostly sugar cane. There was the usual farm equipment, numerous outbuildings, a blacksmith shop, cotton gin, and barracks for 400 convicts and guards. There were cane carts and tracks, farm animals, horses, mules, and cattle, the sugar mill, the refinery, the Sugar Land Railroad, the Imperial Valley Railway and the Sugar Land Manufacturing Company which operated the paper mill and the acid plant. Cunningham had provided a small commissary, two small restaurants, a boarding house and two small hotels.

At this point Kempner and Eldridge had formal control of the Ellis and Cunningham Plantations. They owned the Ellis Plantation under the name of Imperial Sugar Company, and the Cunningham Plantation under the name of Cunningham Sugar Company.

Having served on the board of directors of the Cunningham Sugar Company, Eldridge and Kempner had had ample opportunity to familiarize themselves with every detail of the company, the town, the labor force, the financing, the problems and the prospects for the enterprise.

Both men had a vision of a large and well run sugar refinery operating year round, with a steady and reliable labor force, and diversified and productive farm crops grown on properly drained and protected lands. In late 1908 they embarked on a long range program to accomplish the following:

1. Provide working and living conditions of a quality to attract young, stable families who would become capable and permanent employees.
2. Renovate the refinery so that it could operate year round, utilizing foreign grown raw sugar for the several months when it would have normally been shut down after the harvesting of the local crops of sugar cane were completed each year.
3. Drain and level the farm and grazing lands and provide a system of levees to protect the lands from flooding by the Brazos, enable irrigation of crops, and to provide larger lakes for storage of water near the refinery.
4. Attract sufficient farming and industrial activities to Sugar Land to further diversify the income of the community.

[1]I. H. Kempner, *Recalled Recollections*, written by Mr. I. H. Kempner between his 80th and 88th birthdays, completed in 1961, unpublished, limited circulation. Rosenberg Library, Galveston, Texas.

THE COMPANY TOWN — 1906-1930

Now Kempner and Eldridge owned literally everything in the 18,500 acre property except the Southern Pacific right of way which crossed their lands from east to west; and they were well aware of what was going to be needed in the way of capital, credit, planning and hard work in order to build the kind of community they envisioned.

First, the partners had to clean up the "Hell hole of the Brazos." They closed the bar and brothel at "Mexico." Then they turned their attention to the convict population.

Their initial plans had to include replacement of the 400 man convict labor force on the farms. By 1906, the public outcry against the brutality of a system by which, on some occasions, convicts were literally treated worse than slaves, had risen to the point where the handwriting was on the wall for this particular abuse. After several years of wrangling over a replacement system, in 1909 the legislature abolished the convict lease program entirely as of January 1, 1914, giving those who made use of the system ample time to phase out their involvement.

Eldridge had previously used convict labor on at least one of the farms he had owned, and probably would have continued their use at Sugar Land until the state abolished their use as leased labor. But apparently Mr. Kempner had flatly refused to be associated with the practice, insisting instead on the creation of a permanent well-chosen work force as quickly as possible.

They attacked the convict program in a hurry. Even before they finalized the Cunningham transaction in 1908, they had moved the entire convict population from the Cunningham farms over to the Ellis plantation, where they had previously constructed new housing facilities for the inmates. The new convict barracks, were large enough to house 416 convicts and guards, with a modern kitchen and with "pure artesian water." A newspaper clipping headlined Richmond, Texas and dated 1907 states that

> "Eldridge has in the course of construction what he proposes will be the best building in Texas for the housing of the convicts on the place. A well-appointed hospital will be connected with the building, and two concrete natatoriums arranged for hot and cold plunges will be built. In fact, the attempt will be made to make this plantation (Ellis) and its improvements model in every respect."

The partners began replacing convict labor on the farms as quickly as tenant and contract labor would accommodate. Long before the 1914 deadline they had discontinued the use of convict labor entirely. In 1914 they sold the entire 5,300 acre Ellis property (with the exception of the Imperial raw sugar mill) to the state of Texas. This property is still operated as a prison farm by the Texas Department of Corrections.

G. D. "Gus" Ulrich

They also began phasing out the use of itinerant labor as quickly as they could accommodate permanent employes. This meant the rapid construction of a complete permanent community to house and supply the type of workers they knew they could attract with steady work along with good living and working conditions. And they needed a lot of people to rebuild and operate the raw sugar mills and the refinery, to levee and drain the farm lands and to diversify and irrigate the crops.

To attract dependable, family type workers, Kempner and Eldridge set up a program which could be described as the capitalization of a company town. They gave first priority to the financing and construction of the town and its facilities in order to bring in and keep a work force of permanent employees.

This was not the first time Eldridge had taken over a run-down property, nor was it the first time he had built and manned a company town—he knew exactly what to do and he went about it with speed and determination. One of the opening moves was to hire several young men of solid background and training. The first was Gus Ulrich, twenty-six years old, from Schulenberg, Texas. In 1906 Eldridge put him in charge of the Ellis Plantation. At 26, it may seem that Gus was young for the job, but Eldridge had a history of placing young men in responsible positions in the several businesses he had operated before coming to Sugar Land. He believed in training very young men to do things his way, and then leaving it up to them to carry out his plans, a program he had previously followed in the management of his many and varied interests in Eagle Lake.

Within two years, Eldridge brought Ulrich over into the Cunningham program. In another year, Ulrich was made assistant manager of all the Ellis and Cunningham properties, and in 1917, Eldridge would write a letter to all the various businesses in Sugar Land to the effect that Ulrich was his personal assistant and that anything ordered by Ulrich was to be accepted as having come from Eldridge himself. It was a wise choice.

Ulrich brought in a steady stream of people as fast as he could build houses for them. Many were friends or relatives from the Schulenberg-Flatonia area of Texas, to the extent that Sugar Land soon became known as "Little Schulenberg." Many were of German and Czech background, the Guenthers, the Stablers, the Schindlers, Herders, Schultzes, Saegers, Hrncirs, Hruskas and many more. All were the solid, conservative, hard-working people he needed. It seemed that in no time at all he had a nucleus of craftsmen and storekeepers who could build and maintain the houses, streets, sidewalks, water and sewage disposal systems, and who could operate the new stores and various other businesses as the community grew.

From the start, like other small Texas towns of the time, this was to be a segregated community. Within a few years the population had stabilized at about fifty percent white, twenty-five percent black and twenty-five percent Hispanic. The tent city and shacks were replaced by hundreds of new houses; on the white-only, east side of town these were one, two and three bedroom frame buildings with baths, with metered water, electricity and gas connections, and with septic tanks. Each home had a yard large enough for a garden. Rooms were small by today's standards, but working people in those days simply did not accumulate the stocks of furniture, appliances and clothing which now seem so

1926   *The Company Town of Sugar Land*

necessary. There were no central heating or cooling units, no dishwasher or garbage disposals, no wall-to-wall carpets, no draperies. The buildings were built to last, of good lumber, with metal roofs; almost all of these houses, built between 1908 and 1930, are still occupied in 1990.

On the west side of town, in the bend of Oyster Creek where the old slave quarters had been located in pre-Civil War times, a separate community of houses was built for blacks and Hispanics. Here, the two and three bedroom houses were liveable, but in the beginning were without electricity, gas or indoor plumbing, furnished only with a single water faucet on the back porch. In later years the companies brought electric, gas and telephone connections to the houses. Rents on the houses in the quarters were set at less than half the level applied to those on the east side, although wage rates for labor were the same for blacks and Hispanics as for white employees. In the early 1950's as part of a general improvement program for the community, all the houses in the Quarters would be replaced with modern brick and frame buildings with all the modern conveniences.

Company homes were maintained by company personnel. There was a crew made up of a carpenter, a painter, a plumber, an electrician, and two laborers. The orders were to keep all company property in tip-top condition. Anything like a broken front door screen or a faulty water heater was repaired quickly. Otis Enquist, the tall Swede who was in charge of the maintenance of the company houses, prided himself on the speed of response by his crew. He loved to turn in his daily work sheets with notations such as, "Sheppard house, 114 Third St., leaking faucet, called 8:31 AM, fixed 8:53 AM."

Occupants of company homes were encouraged to plant trees, shrubbery and flowers to beautify the property. Each year, prizes were given to the most attractive decorative gardening and landscaping. Within a few years, the once barren lots on which the homes had been built were a source of pride to the tenants as well as the community. A local garden club was formed, and in one of its projects, watermelon-pink crepe myrtle bushes were planted lavishly along both sides of the streets in the town, between the sidewalks and gutters. They also beautified the creek banks in parts of the town.

As the houses were built, the streets were paved with gravel and crushed shell, concrete curbs and gutters lined the streets, and concrete sidewalks were installed along both sides of all streets. The layout of the townsite was such that, with the refinery and the various offices and stores in the center, everyone could conveniently walk to work on the new concrete sidewalks. It was only a mile from one end of town to the other. Many houses were within a block or two of the refinery, and the farthest were little over a half mile away. An added convenience was the location of the various retail and service establishments providing goods and services to the townsfolk. All were located in a two-block long row in front of the refinery, making shopping also within easy walking distance of the houses. In these days of backed up freeways it is difficult not to regard the more simple life of the 1920's with at least some degree of nostalgia.

As the first 10 houses for workers were finished, then 50, then 100, then 400, it became necessary to enlarge the local stores which provided the necessities for the citizens. One example was the Imperial Mercantile Company, the general

1926 *Company homes on Oyster Creek, and part of the farms lands of Sugarland Industries. By 1986 the entire open spaces as far as the horizon in this photo were solidly covered with homes, commercial and office buildings, shopping centers, schools, parks, churches, country clubs and freeways.*

store. When Kempner and Eldridge took over from Cunningham, this small, one-story structure of corrugated iron with its floor some four feet above the ground to avoid flood water, soon became inadequate. The ground floor space was quadrupled and a second and then a third floor and an elevator were added. Soon filled with a wide variety of goods, it was said to be the largest general store between Houston and San Antonio.

Immediately inside the entrance, to the right was a well-stocked grocery department, to the left a clothing and dry goods inventory, then a shoe store. Further into the building were household appliances and utensils, then general hardware. Then came the farm and ranch supplies, everything from wagon wheels, harnesses, saddles, tools, barbed wire, to sporting goods, and ammunition. In the back of the first floor were the sack goods, chicken and animal feed, cotton seed, fertilizer, etc. The second floor displayed the furniture and heavy household goods. The third floor was reserved for all sorts of miscellaneous inventory, from baby buggies to caskets.

A block west was a lumber yard with building supplies, paint, cement and building hardware. In between were corrugated iron buildings housing a meat market, a fresh vegetable market, a bakery, restaurant, barber shop, a small hotel, a shoe repair shop. A separate building housed a drug store, a pharmaceutical shop and soda fountain including an ice cream machine; the second floor of this building housed the telephone company switchboard and a doctor's office. Judge Pike, the local Justice of the Peace, operated a bakery, a restaurant and a barber shop in a separate building leased from the owners. One or two local ladies offered beauty parlor services from their homes.

There were two rooming houses, and in 1909, the pre-Civil War Thatcher Plantation house had been moved to Sugar Land to serve as a hotel and boarding house. It was located on the east bank of Oyster Creek, about where the dental offices are at present. The Thatcher house was a large building, to which numerous rooms and facilities were added, with a dance floor and dining room. Named The Imperial Inn, it served the community well until it burned in 1946.

The dairy made daily deliveries to the front door step. Before the electric refrigerator came in vogue, blocks of ice were delivered to the ice box on the back porch if people left a card in the window, indicating the number of pounds wanted. The vegetable and fruit man drove his cart down the streets ringing his bell. Garbage was picked up daily at the back door by a man driving a mule drawn wagon with flowers tied to the mules' bridles.

There was a loud steam whistle at the power plant in the refinery, a whistle which could be heard clearly throughout the town. It blew at 6 A.M., at 12 noon, at 1 P.M., and at 6 P.M. In those days the refinery operated on two twelve hour shifts, and the whistle indicated the shift changes and the noon hour. The whistle was also used to announce fires and to call out the volunteer firemen with a different number of blasts indicating different parts of town.

The general office building, also constructed four feet above the ground, housed all office personnel, a bank, the post office, and a Western Union office.

After three years, it must have been obvious to the Kempners that Eldridge was demonstrating the necessary management abilities. In 1909, the Imperial Sugar Company entered into a three year contract employing him as general

1929   *"Downtown" Sugar Land.*

The Imperial Inn. Formerly the Thatcher Plantation home. Destroyed by fire in 1946.

manager at a salary of $12,000 per year, to be paid by the various companies he was managing in Sugar Land, such as Imperial Sugar, Cunningham Sugar, Imperial Mercantile, the Sugar Land Manufacturing Company and other activities. This was to be in addition to his fifty percent ownership of everything in the area and his incentive bonus of five percent of the profits of the many business and farming activities of the partnership. He was also to have the use of the large Ellis plantation home, which he had moved into the refinery yard at Sugar Land, free of charge. The house was to be furnished to his satisfaction. He was to be given all the expense of its maintenance, including "provisions and supplies." The minutes stated that "it being the purpose of the resolution that said Eldridge shall receive all his personal expenses at Sugar Land in addition to his salary, in consideration for his services as general manager." He was also to be allowed to devote a reasonable amount of time to overseeing the management of his 4,700 acre farm and company town named "Eldridge," on the Colorado River south of Eagle Lake, and to oversee the management of his increasingly profitable Sugar Land Railroad. Kempner knew how to motivate his partner and was obviously impressed with the dedication and abilities being exhibited by Eldridge thus far.

Although the first priority of the partnership program was the homes, stores and townsite, Eldridge and Kempner proceeded at once with their planned improvements to the farm lands, the sugar mills and the refinery as quickly as the necessary workers moved into the town.

The most obvious and the most serious problem on the farms was the sporadic damage from flooding from the Brazos, often accompanied by heavy rains. At times, such as in 1913, water from the river and the rains had flooded over the entire southern and western portion of the seven mile long plantation, and up to the very door of the refinery in Sugar Land. Losses in crops and animals were serious. Even occasional heavy rains could result in the flooding of a portion of the lands. Kempner and Eldridge set about a long range program to build levees and drainage ditches, and to level the land along Oyster Creek for irrigation. This work was started in 1913 and was completed in 1929.

Eight and one-half miles of levees, from two to fourteen feet high, depending on the elevation of the land, and forty feet wide at the bottom were to be laboriously constructed along the southern, eastern and western sides of the Cunningham property, and the slow work of construction began with primitive tools. At first, mules, and wagons moved the earth from the farms to the levees, leveling the farm lands, draining and filling the many ponds and swamps in the process. Later, as mechanical earth moving equipment became available, it was substituted for the slow, back breaking labor of the earlier days of the program. When the levees were completed in 1922, the farm lands were leveled to fill in the ponds and swamps; twenty miles of ditches drained the newly leveled lands. Irrigation of farm crops on company lands along the banks of Oyster Creek became a reality, accomplished by constructing electric power lines along the banks of the creek, then mounting electric motors and pumps on barges for pumping irrigation water onto the fields. Engineers estimated that the construction of the levee, the drainage ditches, and the leveling of the lands required the moving of 5,000,000 cubic yards of dirt at a cost of over $700,000.

Imperial Sugar Company

1913   On December 10, 1913, the Brazos River flooded all the way to Sugar Land. This was not an
unusual occurrence. Levees completed in the early 1920s corrected the problem.

Imperial Sugar Company

Oyster Creek, the source of cooling water for the sugar refinery, was still a shallow, meandering, swampy stream, even when supplemented by pumping from the Brazos. It was an unreliable source at times and needed to be supplemented by lakes which could hold sufficient water in storage. In 1917, a dredge was brought in to experiment in what is now Cleveland Lake. It was found to be practical to increase the maximum depth of the lake to seventeen feet, and to enlarge the lake to cover forty acres, providing a large reservoir for the Imperial refinery and for the irrigation program on the farms. Another, even larger lake, known then for its animal population as Alligator Lake, was dredged to seventeen feet and the name changed to Alkire Lake. Brooks Lake was also dredged. These lakes, connected to Oyster Creek, acted as reservoirs and provided some 100 acres of water storage with an average depth of ten feet.

By means of the Brazos River pumping station and the dams built during the Cunningham regime and renovated during this improvement program, it was now possible to maintain the water in Oyster Creek and its tributary lakes at a reasonably constant level (within a couple of feet) throughout the year, despite dry spells and heavy rains. This system, little changed since the 1920's, continues in use in the 1990's.

By 1928, the levees were preventing the frequent floods of the Brazos from reaching the farm lands. The deepening of Oyster Creek and the adjoining lakes, supplemented by the pumping station on the Brazos, insured an adequate supply of fresh water for the refinery and the farms even during the worst drouth. The banks of the creek and the lakes had been cleared and shaped, and in some places near the town, landscaped.

After representatives of the American Society of Chemical Engineers visited Sugar Land on May 1, 1921, several reports were written about the drainage and irrigation programs there. Some excerpts provide an outsider's view of the progress which was being made.

"Levees now protect against the menace of overflow from the Brazos River. Dams conserve the waters of Oyster Creek. Drainage and irrigation, both vital to the operations here, have been provided. Unrelated waterways have been coordinated.

"Irregularities in contour have been leveled into harmony, and unsightly shorelines are being converted into parks and driveways, to be shaded in the years to come by thousands of Royal Walnut trees, imported from California.

"It has taken three years of constant pumping and digging by hydraulic and dipper dredges to achieve these results. The program is not nearly complete but has progressed sufficiently to completely change the topographical appearance of the Sugar Land section.

"The engineer and his allies, the dredge, the steam shovel and the pile driver, and his auxiliary aids, the electric light and the gasoline and electric driven motor have worked a transformation that is already exciting the wonder and admiration of those who knew the landscape under former conditions.

"The mosquito has been driven from his happy hunting grounds."

Like the construction of the houses and city facilities, the enormous cost of the land reclamation was all out-of-pocket expense to the partnership up to this point. They had also been spending a lot of money on the building of their raw sugar mills and the sugar refinery. And thus far, no dividends had been paid the owners, although they could see a lot of progress in the right direction.

By 1917, some 400 houses had been completed, occupied by a population of 1,200, counting tenant farmers, and the town was just about as self-sufficient as the partners could make it.

In the eastern half of Fort Bend County, which meant everything west of the Brazos River, and up to the outskirts of Houston, there was simply no place else of any consequence. And an isolated community of 1,200 people in those days of less than reliable transportation, needed to be self-sufficient. Until 1927 brought at least a semblance of paved roads, Sugar Land was, to a considerable extent, an isolated community. Citizens could travel the twenty-eight miles to Houston or the seven miles to Richmond in a passenger coach often attached to a freight train; travel by buggy was slow but sure; and the automobiles of the 1920's often had difficulties with the roads available at the time. Sugar Land was connected to Houston by a narrow, high-centered two lane road made of crushed shell and it was generally passable if a bit rough by today's standards. Going the other way, to Richmond, was seven miles of dirt road, rough but passable in dry weather. However, during wet weather it could be slick and doubtful or muddy and even more doubtful, made passable only by local entrepreneurial farmers who waited by the deep mud holes with mule teams and hand lettered signs quoting the 25 cent price for being pulled through. Many of the model T drivers would plunge in, get bogged down and signal for help. It could happen several times to a driver determined to complete the trip. In Sugar Land, contemplating a trip to Richmond during wet weather, a driver could call the telephone operator, who kept posted on such matters, to ask about the condition of the road, often to be told, "You can make it if you've got a pocket full of quarters."

In the early days, plantation owners, many of whom had little or no education and who wanted their children to be educated, simply set up a school on the plantation. They often brought in a teacher, provided a place to meet, and invited the neighbors' children. The earliest date on which a school was mentioned in Sugar Land was 1834. Dilue Rose remembered that it was held in a blacksmith shop about a mile south of Sugar Land. In later years, Kyle and Terry had a school on the Sugar Land plantation. In 1908, when Kempner and Eldridge took over, school classes were held in a small one room frame building with one teacher and five pupils. The new owners first enlarged the building and made it suitable to serve during the week as a school and on Saturdays and Sundays as a church facility.

In 1916, it was evident that larger and better school facilities were needed to replace the enlarged combination school and church building on Wood Street. Kempner and Eldridge instructed their chief engineer, M. R. Wood, to go to California and inspect a school plant which was reported to be one of the finest in the nation at that time and to draw up plans for a similar school plant in Sugar Land.

1918   The Sugar Land School—10 classrooms with a central auditorium and office building.

1918   Company houses on 2nd Street with new sidewalks, curbs and gutters, and graveled streets.

Wood copied the layout. Construction was started in early 1916, and completed in 1918. Located on the north bank of Cleveland Lake, the plant consisted of eleven individual buildings arranged in a semi-circle, with a large and airy auditorium at the center. All buildings were finished in white stucco on the outside, with a flat roof and large windows. The buildings were connected by paved and covered walkways and each contained a classroom and a restroom. In cold weather they were heated from a central system; the large windows provided cooling breezes in warmer weather. The auditorium seated 500 people, adequate for civic meetings and gatherings. It had a raised stage, complete with curtains and backdrops and a moving picture screen, a projector room at the back and a piano. Occasionally, the community was treated to silent movies twice a week at minimum charge.

The new school hired excellent teachers, provided a first class basic education, and was soon accredited to all state colleges. Graduates of the Sugar Land High School had no trouble competing in college with the graduates of big city high schools. The owners built a "teacherage," as it became known, to house some of the unmarried women teachers; other teachers rented rooms from employees of the companies. The "teacherage" was a large frame building located across Oyster Creek from the Imperial Inn. It operated as a boarding house, under the supervision of one of the older women who monitored the social activities of the younger teachers.

Initially, the new school plant was much larger than necessary, but it was built for the growing number of young people in the community. There were only ten grades at first, and the senior class of 1919 had only one graduate.

There were two separate segregated schools in the Quarters, one for blacks and one for Hispanics; and again, as in many Texas communities, the facilities were considerably below those available to whites, and the quality of education was less than adequate. Although there were improvements over the years, it was not until these schools were integrated with the white facilities in the early 1960's that equal educational opportunities were available to this neighborhood.

In 1923, in a speech to the Kiwanis Club in Houston, M. R. Wood stated that the cost of the school system was $100,000, another measure of the dedication of Kempner and Eldridge to the welfare of the community. It is interesting to note that the local cost of building and maintaining the schools, as well as paying the staff, was borne by Kempner and Eldridge almost entirely, there being no other substantial taxable entity in the area.

The old wooden school building, previously in use as a school facility five days per week, had also been used for church activities on weekends. There was no full-time minister, so various traveling preachers provided sermons. Church services were often supplemented by evangelical services conducted by traveling religious groups. Ladies taught the Bible to children and organized hymn singing. After the new school facilities were built, the old school building was donated to the community for use as a Union Church. The owners further enlarged the structure and refinished the interior, providing pews and seats for 200 people.

With little distraction from other activities, such as TV, organized sports, or frequent movies, much of the social life of the community centered around

1923   *The Laura Eldridge Memorial Hospital at the corner of Wood and Lakeview.*

1921   *First Presbyterian Church at 4th and Wood streets.*

church-related activities. In response to an expressed desire that the congregation divide itself into denominations, in 1918 the owners donated four sites at the corners of the block between 4th and 5th Streets and Main and Wood Streets. One corner went to the Catholics, one to the Baptists, one to the Methodists, and one to the Presbyterians. By 1921, all four churches had built their sanctuaries, with help from various sources. For example, the Presbyterians received a $1,000 donation from the First Presbyterian Church in Houston, an unspecified amount from the Board of Home Missions and from the General Assembly, a building fund of $500 and a loan from the Imperial Sugar Company for the balance. Total cost was about $10,000, and the loan was paid off in 1929. Other churches received similar assistance, including loans from the owners.

In 1921, Kempner and Eldridge turned their attention to the need for more and better medical facilities in Sugar Land. In 1909, workers could only receive adequate treatment by going to Houston or Richmond, not an easy journey in those times. In 1914, when the state prison system bought the Ellis Plantation from Kempner and Eldridge, the state had installed a Dr. Wells as prison doctor on the Ellis Plantation, and he agreed to accept outside patients. Dr. Wells was shortly succeeded by a Dr. Deatherage, who was also allowed to treat Sugar Land residents. In 1917, Deatherage moved his office to Sugar Land on the second floor of the drug store building. Deatherage was later joined by a Dr. Blackwell.

But seriously ill people were still having to be treated in their homes or moved to Houston or Richmond. So, in 1921, Kempner and Eldridge drew up a medical plan for employees which was years ahead of its time. They founded and funded the Laura Eldridge Hospital Association, a non-profit organization, to provide hospital and health care for all employees. The association was named after Eldridge's second wife, who had died only a few months after their marriage. The original endowments came from Sugarland Industries and the Sugar Land Railroad, and amounted to $165,000 in cash and land valued at $10,000. The purpose was to build a hospital and to finance an ongoing needed benefits program for employees.

In 1922, they constructed a complete, modern hospital at the corner of Wood and Lakeview, furnished with the latest in technical, laboratory, and operating equipment and staffed by two full-time doctors, Dr. Blackwell and Dr. Deatherage. They were joined shortly by a young physician, Dr. Carlos A. Slaughter, who, except for a brief period when he was forced to leave for health reasons, continued to minister to Sugar Land's health needs until his death in 1981. (It was suggested that with two doctors named Deatherage and Slaughter it would have been appropriate to find a third named Lazarus.) A registered nurse, Nema Sheppard, known affectionately and respectfully as "Miss Nema," quickly took over the management of the hospital. Until her death 47 years later, she ran the establishment, including the doctors, with a velvet hand, to the general benefit of the community.

Cost of the hospital was approximately $15,000. They were able to invest the remaining $150,000, because in the years when the hospital operated at a deficit, the Imperial Sugar Company and the Sugarland Industries covered the deficiency with donations. The $15,000 cost for a hospital may seem low by todays standards, but it was a well-built frame building and since the many advanced and expensive systems for diagnosis and treatment had not yet been invented, the initial outlay was not as great as might be expected. It served the community well and provided a range of immediate care not available to many Texas towns of the same size at that time.

In 1923, the owners established a program under the Laura Eldridge Hospital Association whereby any employee of the various Sugar Land enterprises could, for $1.50 deducted from his or her monthly pay, have complete medical and surgical treatment, outpatient services at the doctor's office, all medication, eye glasses, artificial limbs, and one year of hospital confinement. Workers' families were treated at modest cost. Standard fees were charged by the doctors and the hospital to treat citizens of the surrounding areas not part of the Sugar Land businesses, and considerable charity work was also done.

For the first eighteen years, from 1906 to 1924, the partners paid no dividends on their growing investment in the Sugar Land activities, preferring to invest their earnings in improving and enlarging the refinery, and to increase the productivity of the farms and local businesses. When it came to buying and selling of properties, goods and services for their industries, and in the selling and transportation of their products, they were shrewd and hard fisted traders indeed. They were constant proponents of the old adage that "a penny saved is a penny earned."

It was well known to the employees that Eldridge and Ulrich, who watched every detail, were intolerant of any form of waste. It was understood that there would be no discarding of bent or used nails, bolts, pipe, lumber or worn out machinery; nails and bolts would be straightened and used again, worn machinery was a source of parts or might possibly be used in some other less demanding purpose later. One executive was reprimanded personally by Eldridge for nervously bending paper clips. Eldridge also reproved a crew, who were shoveling sand through a screen to remove foreign particles, for not putting a tarpaulin on the ground so that no screened sand would be lost. Many of the retired employees living in Sugar Land today report that he made a practice of walking through the refinery late at night to be sure everyone was wide awake, on the job, and saving every grain of sugar.

Some of the stories may have been apocryphal; such as the one about the signs in the restrooms placing a maximum on the number of sheets of toilet paper per use. But the effect was to establish among the employees that saving was a requisite of their employment, and this saving spirit was passed on from employee to successor. Many employees who had worked under Eldridge and Ulrich were still employed by the companies in the 1970's, and they were still saving nuts and bolts.

Living next door to the sugar refinery, Eldridge loved to roam through the plant, the offices and business establishments, taking a detailed interest in everything that went on—and he was kept well posted by Gus Ulrich and the managers of the various enterprises. He knew most of the people in the town, as well as what they did. He always seemed to know what was happening and he wanted the people to know that he knew. No detail seemed too small to warrant his attention.

He took Tom James, a male typist, to task for roller skating on the concrete sidewalk, "If you break one of your arms, we aren't going to have much use for a one-armed stenographer."

One Monday morning in the summer of 1926, he summoned two recent high school graduates to his office from their summertime jobs in the sugar refinery. One had a black eye, the other a swollen nose. After an uncomfortable silence, Eldridge asked, "What started that fight in Richmond Saturday night?"

The spokesman explained, "We took two Sugar Land girls to a dance over there, and at an intermission a couple of Richmond boys tried to get one of our girls into the back seat of his car—and we stopped them" (proudly).

But Eldridge wasn't impressed, as his next question indicated, "Where did you boys get that whiskey?"

"From a farmer just off the road, he kept it in his hen house."

"How much did you pay for it?"

"A dollar a bottle."

Eldridge swiveled his chair around and looked out the window long enough for the boys to wonder if they were excused, and then made what, for him, was a rather long statement. "You know, I gave you boys a job because I heard you were going to college in the fall. There has only been one other graduate of our high school who had gone to college, and that is Merle Horn, who went to A&M last year. I thought it would give you a chance to earn some money to help you out." Then, after a pause, "How much are we paying you boys?"

"Twenty cents an hour."

Again that long pause while Eldridge turned around to look out the window, and then he pronounced, "If you boys can spend a dollar for a bottle of whiskey, then we must be paying you more than you need to help with your education. So I am going to cut you back to 10 cents an hour."

One of the boys said, "Mr. Eldridge, we can't do that kind of work for only 10 cents an hour."

Eldridge, of course, had the last word, "Well, you go down to the time keeper and tell him to pay you through 9 o'clock this morning. We're going to get along without you. And I'm going to give you some free advice—both of you are too young to drink and you're not big enough to fight." Since every job in town was controlled by Eldridge, the two young men perforce spent the rest of the summer among the unemployed. Before the sun set, the story was all over town, with a sobering effect on the rest of the population.

In the early days, with the use of wood, coal, and kerosene stoves in the wooden homes, stores, and buildings, fire was a constant hazard. Fires were fought by a bucket brigade consisting of every able-bodied citizen in the vicinity. Water mains and fire hydrants were installed throughout the town in 1918, and the companies purchased a Ford Model T hose truck. A Sugar Land Volunteer Fire Department was organized. All volunteers were employees of the local companies, and in later years, as fire fighting became more of a science, the companies regularly sent the volunteers to Texas A&M for training in the latest techniques.

Crime was almost non-existent. It was not deemed necessary to lock doors, and keys could be left in automobiles. The labor boss acted as local constable, but his police activities consisted mostly in assisting hoboes out of town. The population of Sugar Land and the quiet, conservative lifestyle did not attract the fast movers or the idle. There were homes only for the workers.

One isolated aberration was the discovery by Ulrich of some petty larceny going on among several employees, in spite of his careful screening of his work force. When a drug store clerk confessed that he had traded cigarettes from the store inventory for gasoline from the filling station, the clerk also implicated six other employees of various local businesses in similar small-scale activities. They were all known in the community as good, upstanding citizens and employees, so Ulrich's treatment of the disclosures was to call them all into his office. After a severe dressing down, he had each man write and sign a detailed confession ending with a statement that he understood that any future peccadillo would result in criminal prosecution. Ulrich kept the letters in some files which remained undiscovered for forty years. The men, without exception, continued as excellent employees and citizens, some of them became department heads, and all retired or died with unblemished records many years later.

Rents were reasonable, and there was an interesting rule that no rent would be raised as long as an employee remained in the same house. When one employee moved, it meant a chain reaction of several families moving, and the company felt it was easier and cheaper to persuade people to stay put. As a further incentive to stability in renting, if a family outgrew its current quarters, arrangements could be made with the company to add a room or enlarge the building in some way for an additional $5.00 per month rent. Later, as more employees bought automobiles, a garage could be added for $5.00 per month. These customs prevailed into the 1950's.

Unlike the stereotype of a company town, this one did not attempt to gouge its employees at the retail level. Kempner and Eldridge had spent too much capital in providing good living conditions and attracting good employees to attempt to profiteer at their expense just because the community was isolated by poor roads and it was difficult indeed for citizens to buy elsewhere. The stores attempted to price their merchandise at the same level as the Houston stores. In an aberrant bookkeeping program, it seemed the rule rather than the exception to transfer profits around from the profitable to the unprofitable among the various retail or service stores at the end of each year, so that all remained solvent. Often part of the farm income was used as a Band-Aid for the retail stores. Although it was known that the companies preferred that employees shop in Sugar Land, there were no penalties for shopping in Houston. It was not unusual for ladies to take the morning train to Houston to shop and return on the evening train.

Their program was based on making little or no profit on the operation of the company town facilities, the homes, the stores and the services. These were to be simply capitalized tools in the development of the industrial and farming activities of the partnership at Sugar Land. Mr. Kempner later stated that it wouldn't have made much sense to spend millions to build a company town, or to provide good living conditions for the people, only to take an unfair advantage on the price of a five cent can of beans.

One added convenience of life in the company town was the almost complete

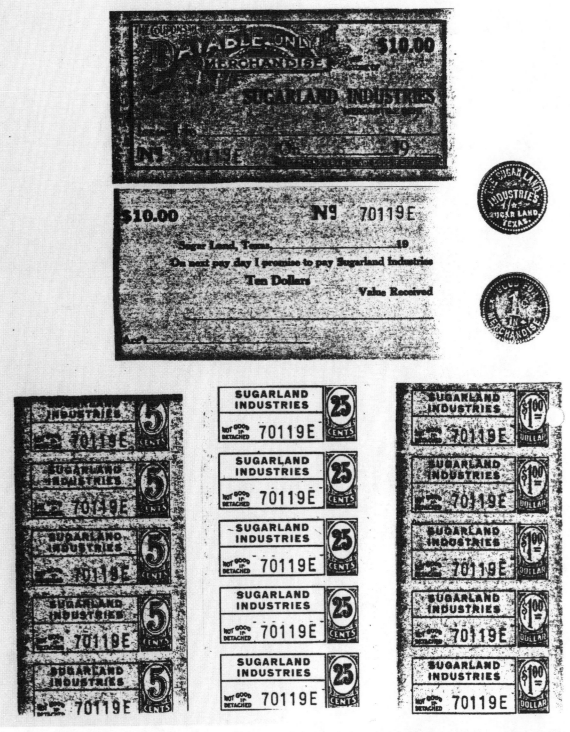

A ten dollar book of coupons, ranging in value from five cents to one dollar, good only for merchandise at the mercantile department of Sugarland Industries. It is interesting that the first page inside the book requires the borrowers signature and his promise to repay Sugarland Industries on his next pay day.

1912 Saturday afternoon in front of the company stores and office buildings in Sugar Land. People from nearby farms came into town to shop and visit. The sign on the large refinery building reads, ''Cunningham Sugar operated by Imperial Sugar.''

credit made available to the occupant of each company house. Long before the advent of American Express or Master Card, a Sugar Land resident was allowed to charge nearly everything to his monthly account; his rent, utilities, groceries, drugs, fuel, gasoline for his car, purchases at the general store; all were included in one monthly bill. Collections were no problem; everyone knew that if he wanted to keep his job he had to pay his bills—not a bad doctrine in any society, company town or not. Gus Ulrich was always ready to extend a helping hand to any employee with an unusual problem.

In addition the companies made available books of coupons and aluminum coins which were good only at the company store, but there was no attempt to force them upon employees. The most common use was when an employee asked for an advance in wages; these were issued in coupons or local coins. Apparently the companies felt that if a man wanted to borrow an advance on his wages at no interest, the money should rightly be spent at the local stores. The companies were unfailingly repaid for the coupon books, because before an employee was issued coupons he first signed page 2, on which he agreed that the company could deduct the value of the book from his next wages.

With the many advantages of living and working in the company town of Sugar Land, there is little reason to be surprised at the quality of employees the companies were able to attract and hold. Today, there have been many families on the payroll for three generations. Kempner and Eldridge were far ahead of their times in realizing the benefit to be derived from caring for loyal employees.

Life in this company town was good. Houses were comfortable and the cost of living was undoubtedly at least as low, if not lower than in most small towns in Texas. Health care was excellent for the times, as were the school and church facilities. This was a workers' town, and since everybody worked for the same owners and in the same small community, everybody knew what everybody else did, with the usual lack of privacy that life in isolated small towns implies, but also engendering a mutuality of interest and respect. Everyone had an identity known by the whole community—everybody was somebody and could see and appreciate his neighbors contribution. It was a far cry from today's neighborhoods where few even know much about the folks next door. The owners and managers were close enough to their enterprises to know and appreciate the efforts of employees.

It was a quiet, sleepy town six days of the week, but on Saturdays it was a beehive. Being an almost completely self-contained community, it provided just about everything needed in the way of goods and services, and on Saturdays farmers and farm workers in a five mile radius walked, or rode horses, buggies or wagons to that two block shopping area in the center of Sugar Land. In the fall, when cotton crops were being brought to the gin at the end of the street, the traffic was prophetic of what might happen later in Houston in the freeway-days to come.

There was little entertainment, but this could be said of just about every other small town in Texas in the early twentieth century. After the stores closed at 6 o'clock, there was simply nothing open. People listened to the radio, played cards or danced at home, sat on the screened porch and discussed the weather and the town gossip. Later, there were regular silent movies at the school auditorium, accompanied by local pianists supplying mood music, and dances at Imperial Inn.

Once established in Sugar Land, few people ever left. The companies almost never discharged an employee. If a business was discontinued, the employees were used in another activity. If efficiencies in the refinery, for example, eliminated the need for certain jobs, the men were used elsewhere in the town until a vacancy was created by death or retirement. Since Eldridge preferred to hand-raise his own talent, almost all executive positions in the companies were filled from within. Advancement was slow because nobody left, but there was a sense of security in the community.

In Imperial's files there is a copy of a letter written in 1926 by the company to Ed McCown in Itasca offering him a job at Sugar Land. It was described as a night job, working twelve hours per night, six nights per week for one week, followed by seven nights per week the following week. This gave him one night off every two weeks. The pay was $3.00 per night, and the added inducement was that "you can save almost all your pay, as there is nothing much in Sugar Land to spend money on." McCown took the job, worked his way up to the position of shift superintendent and retired after forty-six years with the company.

Young people, lacking the easy transportation to other towns, even to Houston and Richmond, tended to socialize together within the town. Most seemed to expect that, upon graduation from high school, they would go to work for the Imperial Sugar Company or the Sugarland Industries and marry a fellow graduate of Sugar Land High School. Very few went away to college in the 1920's and 1930's.

There was a great deal of intermarrying among Sugar Land families, to the extent that in later years it seemed that nearly everybody was related to everybody else in some manner. It was not safe to be critical of someone, because you might be talking to a relative. But the morale was high, and the end product was a work force which appreciated the efforts of the owners to provide comfortable living and working conditions.

In spite of the satisfaction he must have gained from his many accomplishments at Sugar Land, Eldridge had experienced a less than successful family life. Since his youth, he had been a man of single purpose, and he devoted all the hours in the day to his businesses. He had experienced an unhappy family relationship in his youth, and he had family problems in the later years of his life.

In 1918, after twenty-eight years of marriage, Mrs. Eldridge (the former "Widow Gordon" of Eagle Lake), obtained a divorce and moved to San Antonio, taking with her the two children of her first marriage. The two daughters Eldridge had in this marriage, Ivy and Ethel, soon married and moved away. Ivy Eldridge married R. J. Bauereisen and moved to the Rio Grande Valley; Ethel became the bride of Walter Woodul, a prominent Houston lawyer and politician who later became lieutenant governor of Texas. This left Eldridge with only his son, W. T., Jr., living in Sugar Land.

In July 1919, two years after his first marriage ended in a divorce, Eldridge had married Laura Steinman, who was a telephone operator for the Sugar Land telephone system, and who had moved to Sugar Land from Schulenberg. The Texas Commercial News printed a special edition for the occasion, with glowing tributes and with the entire front page taken up with copies of the many telegrams and letters received by the couple. Sadly, a little over six months later, while on a trip with her husband to new York, Laura was taken ill and died within a few days, in February 1920. Eldridge arranged for a special train to transport 300 passengers from Houston, Galveston, Eagle Lake and various other South Texas cities to Schulenberg for the funeral. The train displayed black flags on the engine and the cars. The Texas Commercial News again printed a special edition, this time on beautiful white silk cloth instead of on paper, with a black border; listing the names of all those who expressed their sympathies, and including many eulogies. Two years later, in 1922, at age sixty, Eldridge married a young school teacher in Sugar Land, Mildred Masterson, and in 1924 the couple had a son, William Randle Eldridge.

Eldridge had great hopes that W. T. Eldridge, Jr., his older son by his first marriage, known in Sugar Land as "Bill," would succeed him. He trained Bill as well as he could in all aspects of the Sugar Land activities, and as early as 1914, made Bill, at the age of twenty-three, a vice-president and director of Imperial Sugar and president of Imperial Bank. In 1919 Bill was named one of the original trustees of Sugarland Industries, which at that time owned and controlled everything in Sugar Land, including Imperial. He was twenty-eight years old.

Perhaps one of the great disappointments in Eldridge's life was that Bill was unable to adapt to his father's single-minded dedication. In 1929, Eldridge was forced to take away most of Bill's titles except for those of vice-president of Imperial and Sugarland Industries, a considerable blow to the pride of both men. Bill committed suicide in 1931, leaving his wife, the former Dorcas Allison and one child, W. T. Eldridge III, known locally as "T."

In 1928, Eldridge built a large white stuccoed Spanish style house with red tile roof on the north shore of Cleveland Lake, reputedly at a cost of $125,000. By Sugar Land standards it was a palace, fifteen rooms and five baths and 17,000 square feet of floor space. It is still an attractive residence, just south of Lakeview Drive; over the years it has been bought and sold a number of times and is currently owned by the Wm. E. Dinkins family. The old Eldridge home in the refinery yard became a rooming and boarding house, later a tea room, and finally was torn down in the 1960's. It was in need of extensive repairs, and the refinery needed the space for a building.

Mr. Kempner had taken very little part in the daily operations of the various enterprises. However, in spite of his many other business interests elsewhere, he remained in constant touch with Eldridge by mail and telegram and every week or so made a trip from Galveston to Sugar Land, often bringing his oldest son, Harris, with him. Roads and automobiles being what they were in those days, they came by train, necessitating a change of railroads in Houston and spending a night or two in the Eldridge home in Sugar Land. According to Mr. Kempner, the business and personal relationships between the two men were very good. The men used these meetings and their frequent correspondence to set the program and the tone for the town and the businesses, as well as in discussion of the various new enterprises they might consider. It was the consensus of the townspeople that it was Mr. Kempner's innate kindness and appreciation that provided financing for such amenities as the school, the

1932   The W. T. Eldridge home on Lakeview Drive, built in 1928.

hospital, the churches, the comfortable homes, well stocked stores at reasonable prices, and low rents. Although Eldridge may well have felt the same kindness and appreciation toward the employees and their families, he was by nature a gruff and withdrawn personality; and charged with the daily discipline of direct hands-on management, was less inclined to exhibit his consideration.

By 1923 late-comers would hardly believe that this community, probably one of the best planned and equipped in Texas for its size, had once been the "hell hole of the Brazos." A community of 1,200 people could not possibly have provided by taxation the facilities made available at Sugar Land by the owners of the town. And as yet, no dividends had been paid the owners, although at this point they could see a log of progress in the right direction.

It is interesting to read an observation in a 1928 issue of the *Southern Pacific Farm News* stating that:

> "Just a quarter of a century ago, Sugar Land consisted of a sugar mill on a swampy sugar plantation worked with convict labor—just a convict camp full of fever and disease in a country full of reptiles and insect pests."

By 1926, the population of Sugar Land had grown to 1,500 people living in 465 company homes. An editorial in the *Galveston Tribune* said of Sugar Land,

> "On the theory that it is possible to have contentment among workers who are comfortably housed, who are enabled to care for their families, and whose children are given the best privileges of childhood, recreation, education and religious training adequate provision for the homelife of the community has been made. This has been accomplished by the erection of handsome cottages and bungalows, situated on spacious grounds. The residences are unusual for an industrial center for the reason that there has been no monotonous uniformity of design or coloring. Rather, the effort has been toward the individuality of each home. They are modern, too, being equipped with electric lights, water and bathroom facilities, and in some instances with electric heating. These homes are rented to the workers at moderate charges. They are comfortable, attractive and well kept."

A year later, a similar article in the same paper commented that,

> "Making an investment in humanity as well as getting financial returns on investments and operations of industries is the unusual and outstanding situation at Sugar Land, Texas, one of the most unique industrial establishments in the United States."

During the first few years of the Kempner-Eldridge ownership, while they were building the company town and the stores, reclaiming the farm lands and modernizing the sugar plants, their various businesses were managed as departments of either the Imperial Sugar Company or the Cunningham Sugar Company.

But, as the two enterprises grew in size and complexity, these two entities were to be superseded by two more formal structures; Sugarland Industries, a trust estate, and the Imperial Sugar Company, a separate corporation. Both continued to be owned jointly by Eldridge and the Kempner family.

For clarity, the two companies will be discussed separately in the following two chapters.

SUGARLAND INDUSTRIES — 1906-1930

Sugarland Industries (often referred to just as "Industries") was to be the catch-all company through which Kempner and Eldridge managed the conglomeration of large and small businesses they established in Sugar Land over the years—some as departments, some as separate subsidiary corporations. No one remembers why the name of the town was compressed into one word in the corporate logo.

As soon as he had houses, employees, city services and the necessary company stores, Eldridge began adding new businesses, operating them as departments of one of the two companies. He had followed a similar pattern in the many and diverse enterprises he had entered in Eagle Lake as a younger man—a grocery, a restaurant, a clothing store, a general store; trading in cotton, hides, cattle and pecans; buying land and setting up two company towns; starting a bank and finally building a railroad. It seemed that he had a penchant for initiating an enterprise, small or large, turning it over to a young man to operate, always watching it closely; then looking for the next opportunity.

In Sugar Land he was particularly abetted by his ability to use the collateral of the properties as credit. Kempner usually acquiesced without much apprehension if the project was a fairly small one such as an ice cream plant or a telephone switchboard, but he entered into serious discussions indeed when it might be a large addition to the refinery, or a feed mill, a cotton gin, or the expensive clearing of a new farming area. So it was not long after the town began to take shape, more and more houses were built and people became available, that the partners began adding new services and enterprises.

They established a privately owned bank in Sugar Land in 1907, named the Imperial State Bank. Two years later, the name would be changed to the Imperial Bank & Trust Company. Its first statement of condition, dated November, 1909, showed capital of $10,000, deposits of $20,589 and earnings of $258.00. W. T. Eldridge, Jr. was named first president of the new bank.

They built a feed mill with a capacity of fifty tons per day, producing a full line of animal and poultry feeds, including an assortment of mixed feeds on which Eldridge held a personal patent. In 1917, this plant sold $2,000,000 worth of feeds. Later, as the demand for alfalfa feeds grew, they built a plant to dehydrate alfalfa and grind it into meal for feed.

They built a cotton gin which did a booming business in the late summer, processing and baling cotton grown on the Sugar Land acreage and the surrounding individual farms. They also purchased cotton on a large scale from farmers for resale to cotton merchants, shippers, and spinners, most of the cotton being sold in Houston and Galveston. The cotton seed purchased from the farmers who brought their cotton to the gin was sold to cotton seed oil mills;

later, the company built its own mill. They also began producing and selling registered cotton seed, which was classed as State Certified Seed, grown and processed under the rules and regulations of the Texas Department of Agriculture.

Most business communication in those days was by mail and by Western Union or Postal telegraph. Western Union maintained an office in the building which housed the Imperial and the Sugarland Industries staff, and was locally operated as a part of the telephone company.

The Sugar Land telephone company originated in 1908 when Mr. Eldridge demanded a phone line from his home and his office to the plant superintendent in the sugar refinery. It soon grew to three, then to ten, phones with one operator seated at a switchboard located in a corner of the corrugated iron building which housed the general offices. Additional lines were added from time to time to offices and to executive homes, but it was a limited system with only one operator on each shift until the early 1920's. It normally took nearly all day to complete a telephone call to New York City. In one instance, when the operator had managed to complete an executive call from the sugar company to New York in a record-breaking four hours, Mr. Eldridge presented the operator with a box of candy as a special reward.

In 1922, the telephone offices were relocated to the second floor of the corrugated iron building housing the drug store and soda fountain. By 1929 there were 221 telephones in service and the company was extending its lines generally throughout Eastern Fort Bend County and into parts of Harris County. In 1931, the company was organized as the Harris-Fort Bend Telephone Company, owned by the Sugarland Industries, G. D. Ulrich was elected president, and served in that capacity until his death in 1947, at which time T. L. James (who had been reproved by Eldridge for roller skating) became president.

In the early days of the partnership, the Sugar Land Manufacturing Company, which, under Cunningham had operated a paper mill and an acid plant, was used as a vehicle for the management of several miscellaneous enterprises. Eldridge enlarged the acid plant to produce all grades of sulfuric, picric, and muriatic acids, with a capacity of fifty tons per day. Much of their sulfuric acid was sold to battery manufacturers, and the picric acid to manufacturers of ammunition. Eldridge further enlarged this plant to produce vinegar and pickles. By 1917, it was producing $4,000,000 in sales.

In 1911, Sugar Land Manufacturing Company built a large four story building on the east bank of Oyster Creek at what is now the intersection of Kempner and Main Streets, for the Sealy Mattress Company. The Sealy Mattress was a nationally known product, with five plants located in Oklahoma City, St. Louis, Chicago, Kansas City, and Sugar Land with a combined output of over 500 mattresses per day. Sugar Land Manufacturing Company owned the building and machinery and made the mattresses under contract with Sealy. In 1922 this arrangement was discontinued and the building was used for various purposes in later years.

In 1917, Eldridge set up and operated a printing plant from which the printers published a monthly journal named the *Texas Farm and Industrial News*, with a statewide circulation at $1.00 per year. In 1922 they changed the name to *Texas Commercial News*, published weekly. They were distributing about 1,500 copies per week, with most of the advertisers being suppliers of goods and services to the various Sugar Land enterprises, and with a goodly amount of copy being devoted to the products and activities at Sugar Land.

There were thousands of native pecan trees on the lands, and in the early 1920's over 10,000 were grafted by a firm of tree experts. A large pecan orchard of various varieties was planted on the forty acre tract on the south bank of Cleveland Lake. These trees still provide bounteous crops.

Until 1918, the partners had been able to finance the townsite and the houses, the expensive rehabilitation of the raw sugar mill and the refinery, the flood levee and the land drainage, as well as the several industrial and commercial activities by borrowing against the Sugar Land assets. But the sugar refinery was growing; and as the farming of sugar in the "Sugar Bowl" of Texas declined, to be replaced by other crops, the sugar company was buying more and more of the cheaper foreign raw sugar year round. This required a different kind of financing since the imported raw sugars had to be paid for long before the refinery received payment for its refined sugar sales. Consequently, Mr. Kempner felt that they needed a more formal structure for the partnership at Sugar Land. In late 1918, they merged the Imperial Sugar Company and the Cunningham Sugar Company, the surviving entity being the Imperial Sugar Company. Then, on January 1, 1919, the Sugarland Industries was organized as a trust estate to own and operate all the various activities at Sugar Land as one unit, including the farms, the town, the various businesses, and the Imperial Sugar Company. Reflecting the original 50-50 agreement between Kempner and Eldridge, there were 80,000 shares of beneficial interest in Sugarland Industries, of which 40,000 shares were owned by I. H. Kempner for the benefit of his family; the other 40,000 were owned by Eldridge and held for him by the Kempner owned Texas Bank and Trust Company in Galveston.

The reorganization was a timely move, as the Sugar Land activities were becoming too large and diversified, and it was fairly obvious that Eldridge planned to continue his search for new opportunities. In 1921, an advertisement in the *Texas Commercial News* shows that the invested captial at Sugar Land was in excess of $10,000,000. Principal advertised products were Imperial Crown Sugar, Sealy Mattresses, Electrolite Battery Acid, Eldridge Mxtrite Feeds, Imperial Vinegar and Imperial Blackstrap Molasses. Principal agriculture included sugar cane, cotton, corn, alfalfa, cucumbers, celery, potatoes, spinach and cabbage.

In 1922, Industries added a new processing plant to dehydrate sweet potatoes. Sweet potato growing, like sugar cane growing, had always been well adapted to the soils around Oyster Creek, and the quality of the yams was superior. With equipment to remove the excess water, they could be preserved indefinitely without losing their texture and flavor. The dehydrating plant was built at a cost of $25,000 and was large enough to process yams from other nearby farms, including those grown on the prison system farms.

Before Prohibition in 1918, Sugar Land sported a large bar and a wholesale warehouse for alcoholic beverages. The floor in this old bar and warehouse building was about three feet above the ground, and under it was a solid concrete block. One of the old timers remembers that the concrete was poured under the wooden floor when it was discovered that someone had crawled under the building with a drill and drilled into the bottom of the liquor kegs. This story was replicated when the old Eldridge home was demolished in the 1960's, and it was discovered that the floor under the raised porch at the rear of the house, also about three feet above ground, was reinforced with steel plate to keep the contents of his wine stock safe from any potential driller.

In a large, two-story, brick building east of the Sealy Mattress plant, the Sugar Land Railroad set up a railroad roundhouse and repair shop. In one end of the ground floor, Sugarland Industries installed a meat packing and canning plant to process the output of a slaughter house located on the east bank of Oyster Creek. Part of the second floor was occupied by the printing plant which published the *Texas Commercial News* and did contract printing. The rest of the second floor was devoted to storage and manufacture of all kinds of materials for maintenance of the townsite, the company houses and buildings. Occasionally other small enterprises would appear in its cavernous recesses, to be moved elsewhere if successful, or abandoned if not.

As the growing of sugar cane on the Sugar Land and surrounding farms continued to decline, Eldridge experimented with new crops, particularly vegetables, and increased the acreage devoted to beef and dairy cattle. In 1922 Sugarland Industries reported owning 1,400 head of fine Herford cattle. Sugar Land became a large supplier of beef to the Houston market.

By 1920, it seemed that all the business enterprises in Sugar Land were doing well. There had been some very good farm years; the Imperial Sugar Company was prospering and had made as much as $2,000,000 in that year; most of the smaller businesses in the town, while not big money makers, were at least breaking even. The program of capitalizing a town in order to provide the best facilities for building a profitable industrial and farming base was paying off. And Eldridge knew that the Kempners were justly proud of their ownership of the clean, bustling and productive small town, which at this time was receiving quite a bit of publicity as a model community, and they were understanding of the talent and effort Eldridge was putting into his part of the partnership. To Eldridge, this seemed to be a good time to try for a bigger slice of the pie.

He and his "associates" (one of whom was S. E. Kempner, Mr. I. H.'s brother) desired to enter a three year contract to furnish 3,000,000 cwt. of raw sugar per year to the refinery (this was the maximum annual requirement of the plant at that time), to market the resulting refined sugar, and to pay the refinery ninety cents per cwt. for refining. They also wished to take a three year lease on all lands owned by Industries, for the purpose of drilling for oil. They were to pay Industries $300,000 for the lease and agreed to spend $50,000 per year to drill at least two wells per year. In addition, they asked permission to sell certificates of beneficial interest in Sugarland Industries for a commission of twelve percent of the proceeds. The trustees agreed to all three proposals. However, in 1922, two years later, Eldridge appeared before the trustees to ask that he and his associates be relieved of their obligations. The sugar markets had gone against them, they had had no luck finding oil, and they were unable to sell any

Industries' certificates. The trustees promptly relieved them of their commitments.

By then, however, Eldridge's ownership of the Sugar Land Rail Road, which he had kept in excellent shape, was paying off handsomely. Although the line was only 14 miles long, he was collecting the originating rate on a considerable volume of freight. Most of it came from the 1,000,000 pounds per day of refined sugar being shipped outbound. He also received a portion of the freight on the inbound tonnage of raw sugar each day from Galveston. In addition, the town was originating quite a bit of freight from its farming and miscellaneous manufacturing activities. There was a good deal of lading from the paper mill, the acid plant, the cotton gin, the feed mill, the meat packing plant, the potato dehydrating plant, and the mattress company, plus the output of the cattle ranch, the corn, celery, spinach, and various other farm products. The railroad was also picking up outbound freight from other growers and cotton ginners in the area. Shipments were going as far as Minneapolis, Chicago, Kansas City, Denver, and St. Louis. In the early 1920's, the Sugar Land Railroad was handling over 250,000,000 pounds of freight annually or over 8,000 carloads per year. This amounted to a trainload of miscellaneous freight originating in Sugar Land each day, possibly more than the rest of Fort Bend County combined. Not bad for a relatively new small town. Few towns in Texas with a population of less than 1,500 were as well organized or as productive.

However, as government regulations and management requirements became more complex, the operation of a short line railroad became increasingly difficult, and in 1926, Eldridge sold the Sugar Land Railroad to the Missouri Pacific, which also took over the operation of the switching facilities in the yards of the Imperial Sugar Company. The price paid for the fourteen mile system was rumored to be over $1,000,000.

As part owner and president of a short line railroad which was originating large tonnages of freight, the long haul railroads had allowed Eldridge the use of private cars for his travels. After the Sugar Land Railroad was sold to the Missouri Pacific, Sugarland Industries provided him with a gasoline powered private car to be driven from Sugar Land to the juncture of one of the main lines and hooked onto whatever passenger train he chose.

By the early 1920's, the Sugarland Industries had indeed become a small town conglomerate. In 1925 an advertisement in the *Texas Industrial News* listed the following activities in the company town of Sugar Land:

The Imperial Sugar Company, Manufacturers of the Famous Imperial Brand of Pure Cane Granulated Sugar.

The Sugar Land Manufacturing Company, Manufacturers and Refiners of Sulfuric Acid, Vinegar, and Pickling Products.

Ice Plant and Cold Storage Warehouse.

The Sealy Mattress Company, Manufacturers of the Famous Sealy mattress, known in almost every home in the country.

Feed Manufacturing Company, Manufacturers of the Famous Eldridge Mxtrite Stock Feed.

The Sugar Land Cotton Seed Oil Mill, Manufacturing Raw Oil from Cotton Seed and Peanuts.

The Sugar Land Cotton Gins and Cotton Seed Storage Warehouses.
The Imperial Mercantile Company, among the large retail Mercantile Companies
    of Texas.
General Offices of the Sugar Land Railway.
The Imperial Bank & Trust Company.
The Imperial Furniture Company
The Imperial Poultry Farm.
The Imperial Squab Farm.
The Imperial Creamery.
The Imperial Drug Company.
New $25,000 High School.
Modern Telephone Exchange.
New Imperial Hotel. (i.e., The Imperial Inn)
Churches.
Dairy, Hog, and Chicken industries being developed.

In 1928, the *Southern Pacific Farm News* reported that in 1927 Industries had 3,500 acres in cotton which yielded 2,500 bales, 60 acres of spinach with an average yield of 300 bushels per acre, 200 acres of Irish potatoes producing 57 carloads, and 100 acres of cabbage producing 5 to 12 tons per acre. There were forty acres in strawberries, 10 in celery, 25 in cucumbers. Three thousand, five hundred rhubarb plants were set out, along with onions, asparagus, fall tomatoes, and fall artichokes. It was planned to increase the potato acreage to 1,500 in 1928, to be followed by sweet potatoes on the same land after the Irish potatoes had been harvested. A five acre experimental farm, under the supervision of a trained agronomist, was established to determine what additional crops were best adapted to the area.

Most of the cotton and some of the other crops were grown by tenant farmers. Sugarland Industries furnished farm houses and outbuildings, animals, seed and equipment. The tenant furnished the labor and received from one fourth to one half of the proceeds, depending on the nature of the crop. In 1923, the company reported that they were using seventy-five tenant farmers on the farms and planned to increase that number the following year. They let it be known that they would prefer to let the land lie idle than to employ a "shiftless tenant." Some of the crops were farmed by day labor, and a good many of the vegetables were grown on Industries' land, leased to contract farmers, some on shares.

With all these activities going on in Sugar Land, one would think that the owners had their hands full. But by then they had a well-deserved entrepreneurial reputation, and opportunities were coming their way, not only in Sugar Land, but elsewhere.

In 1927, Industries acquired the Brazos Valley Irrigation Company in Grimes County. This enterprise had a charter to construct, maintain, and operate reservoirs, lakes, and dams for the sale of water and the development of power in the Navasota area. It also had a permit to appropriate 99,000 acre feet of water annually from the Brazos River. This water was used to irrigate rice crops north of Sugar Land; later this system was merged with the pumping station and canals on the Brazos River which furnished the water through Oyster Creek to the Sugar Land activities. It also supplied water to the rice farms southeast of Sugar Land. The Brazos Valley Irrigation Company for some obscure reason owned the Navasota Country Club. In the 1930's the entire system was sold to the American Rice Growers Association, which changed the name to the "American Canal Company." The system was later sold to a group of investors and named "The American Canal Company of Texas," and in 1967 it was sold to a major state agency, the Brazos River Authority.

Both Kempner and Eldridge had previously been involved in various short haul railroads, particularly where there was rapid growth in local products. Eldridge had had a very profitable experience in the building and selling of the Cane Belt Railroad at Eagle Lake in the 1880's; Kempner had also had a successful experience in developing and selling the Wichita Falls and Southern Railway to the Missouri-Kansas and Texas Railway Company.

In the 1920's, the Rio Grande Valley area was showing promise in increased production of fruits and vegetables, and large deposits of a species of limestone containing liquid asphalt, which was in demand for paving. Industries either acquired or contracted and built several rail lines in the Valley. They acquired the Asherton and Gulf Railway Company, the Rio Grande City Railway Company, the Port Isabel and Rio Grande Valley Railway, and the Uvalde and Northern Railroad. They also contracted and built the Asphalt Belt Railway Company.

But as large and small railroads proliferated in Texas, there was a great deal of buying and selling, receiverships, acquisitions, etc., taking place. Long haul lines began competing for the smaller originating lines. There was a rapid increase in Federal and State regulations of railroads. In 1926, when Eldridge sold his Sugar Land Railroad to the Missouri Pacific, the Sugarland Industries also began to dispose of their railroad interests. Industries sold the Rio Grande City Railway and the Asherton and Gulf Railway to the Missouri Pacific for $500,000. They also sold the Port Isabel and Rio Grande Valley Railway and their interests in the Asphalt Belt Railway in 1931. The Uvalde and Northern was abandoned due to a wash-out of the tracks by flood waters and the prohibitive cost of repairs.

Industries also bought and sold land at various times. In 1925 they acquired 8,809 acres in Dimmit County. This land was used for ranching and growing vegetables for some twenty years until it was sold in 1946. In 1926, they bought 2,272 acres adjoining the Sugar Land farms on the southeast and at one time owned as many as 21,000 acres in Fort Bend County. They also had 15,000 acres in Brooks County and 14,000 acres in Dimmit County. In 1926 they bought a 4,811 acre farm 15 miles northwest of Sugar Land on the banks of the Brazos River. This property was named Foster Farms and is still owned by the Kempner family in 1990.

In 1927, Sugarland Industries bought from Eldridge his 4,700 acre Eldridge farm on the Colorado River next to Bonus, about twelve miles south of Eagle Lake. The purchase included the company town of Eldridge and the Faber Mercantile Company, and was finally disposed of in 1946 after Industries had spent a great deal of money in vain attempts to control the persistent flooding from the river.

In the days when communications were slow and manual, it was a tribute to the management skills of Eldridge that he not only kept a close watch on all the details at Sugar Land but also saw to it that these additional activities elsewhere in the state were properly supervised. He was also a beneficiary of the Kempner management style which gave him free rein once the merits of a project had been determined by the partnership.

On occasion, Eldridge would embark on a new venture on his own if Kempner preferred not to involve the Sugarland Industries. On at least two occasions, Eldridge personally entered into projects which Kempner had vetoed as too uncertain for participation by Industries. Each was indicative of the wide range of investments which could captivate Eldridge's interest. One was the Norfleet story; another was the Austin car.

In 1925, Eldridge became interested in the saga of a west Texas rancher named J. Frank Norfleet. This man, in his fifty's, a typical booted and big-hatted picture of a cowboy with an iron grey mustache, had been bilked of a fortune by a gang of five confidence men. Unable to get the law enforcement agencies satisfactorily active in his case, he had himself deputized, and, armed with the necessary warrants, set out alone to bring the culprits to justice. In three years, after tracking them down one by one all over the United States and abroad, he had managed to put each one behind bars.

On two occasions in 1926, Eldridge had Norfleet come to Sugar Land in person and relate his story to the citizens and school children, from the stage of the school auditorium. Sugarland Industries had a ghost writer compose a book of the Norfleet story, printed in hard cover. Eldridge even took a trip to Hollywood with the intention of having the book made into a movie. He returned to Sugar Land when he discovered that, although Douglas Fairbanks and Mary Pickford were available for the starring roles, they demanded a larger investment in the proposed film than even he could afford to risk. Unfortunately, the general public did not share Eldridge's enthusiasm for the Norfleet story, and a large inventory of the books languished in Sugar Land until 1968 when they were bought by a distant relative of Norfleet.

In 1930, Eldridge was offered the statewide distributorship for the Austin automobile, the first of the subcompacts and far ahead of its time. Mr. Kempner preferred that the Sugarland Industries not get involved in this, so Eldridge entered on his own. He was quite successful in selling dealerships generally throughout the state, probably with little or no investment of his own, as the dealers were required to set up retail showrooms and repair shops, and to maintain an inventory of cars; Eldridge received the distributor's commission. Unfortunately, the Austin car never captured the public fancy, and many of the dealers lost substantial sums of money.

But these sideline ventures by Eldridge were minor events. By the end of the 1920's, Sugarland Industries was well established as a productive farming and cattle enterprise, a managing entity of several diversified and profitable businesses, as well as a supplier of necessary goods and services to the community.

Meanwhile, the core of the Kempner-Eldridge plans at Sugar Land, the Imperial Sugar Company, after extensive infusions of capital and personnel, was developing along its own lines into a major Texas industry.

THE IMPERIAL SUGAR COMPANY
1906-1930

From the beginning, it was to be the operation and future growth of the sugar refinery which would justify all background expenditures for the company town. Kempner and Eldridge could envision a modernized and efficient cane sugar refinery operating 12 months each year, processing raw sugar not only from the plantations in eastern Fort Bend County, but from offshore.

Growing and harvesting seasons throughout the world occurred at different times of the year, and once the cane was run through the raw sugar mill and made into raw sugar, the brownish yellow-colored, large grained, sticky raw sugar could be stored and shipped to refiners to be processed into sparkling white, free flowing refined sugar when convenient. Cheaper raw sugar from foreign shores became more and more attractive to United States cane sugar refiners, particularly since it was available on a year-round basis.

Although there was an abundance of competition from beet sugar processors and cane sugar refiners for the mid-western and western refined sugar markets, Kempner and Eldridge recognized an opportunity to turn the sugar refinery at Sugar Land into a growing and profitable enterprise. Population growth meant increased demand for refined sugar, and the Cunningham plant was the only cane sugar refinery between Louisiana and San Francisco. Rail freight rates gave Sugar Land an advantage as far north as Kansas City.

This refinery, later well known as the Imperial Sugar Company, provided the basic payrolls for the town and performed as the crown jewel in the Sugar Land program. Although the farming operations, the railroad, the stores and various other businesses which were being established in the town were potential sources of income, for the next eighty years it was to be the steady and profitable operation of the sugar company which produced the core employment for the community, as well as the income and cash flow necessary to keep the overall enterprise healthy and growing.

In 1908, when Kempner and Eldridge had acquired both the Ellis and Cunningham properties, they were operating two raw sugar mills, the Imperial mill on the Ellis Plantation and the Cunningham raw sugar mill at Sugar Land, as well as the Cunningham refinery at Sugar Land. The mills were grinding and processing sugar cane grown on the Ellis and Cunningham lands, and on other plantations in a radius of about fifteen miles. Most of the harvested cane stalks were hauled into the mill by rail, although some came by wagon. Both mills usually ran day and night from the beginning of the harvest through December, then shut down until the following September. This left the huge sugar refinery idle and unproductive for some 200 days per year.

Unfortunately, under Cunningham, the cleaning and maintenance work which should have been done after the mills and the refinery finished the crop had been inadequate for years. The buildings were on solid concrete foundations and the heavy timber construction was in good condition, as was the outside of the corrugated iron buildings, but the equipment and machinery were badly run down.

In 1908 at the same time that Kempner and Eldridge began building the town, Eldridge hired a number of experienced and capable sugar technologists, mechanics, managers, and foremen, mostly from the Louisiana mills and refineries. Just as the original group of people brought to Sugar Land from Schulenburg had been Germans and Czechs, these sugar men from Louisiana were mostly of French background—the Varnaus, Laperouses, Trahans, Andres, Le Bourgs, Le Normans.

In 1910, they were able to run the refinery ten and a half months, and in future years it generally operated over eleven months per year, with an annual two week period for cleaning and repairs. In 1907, the capacity of the refinery had been 500,000 pounds per day. By 1910 they had increased this to 750,000 pounds; and most of the annual raw sugar requirements of the refinery were coming from Cuba by ocean freighter to Galveston, stored in dockside warehouses and then shipped by rail to Sugar Land for refining-in-transit. The raw sugar was shipped from the islands in burlap bags weighing 100 to 300 pounds. Once it was able to operate year round, the sugar refinery became quite profitable, although profits varied considerably from year to year due to the constraints of the markets, competition and sugar legislation.

In 1911, the refinery, which was still under the Cunningham name, was leased to the Imperial Sugar Company for a period of ten years. The brand name was changed to Imperial, with a logotype containing the royal crown, similar to that which Mr. Kempner had seen on the stationary of the Imperial Hotel in New York.

Since about 1910, the impending removal of the cheap field labor provided by convict leasing was forcing a reevaluation of farming practices in the Sugar Bowl of Texas. This was at a time when the production of raw sugar throughout the United States was on the decline. For years the federal government had been playing politics with the tariffs on imported raw sugar, at times eliminating tariffs entirely and forcing United States growers of cane and beet sugars to compete with the cheaper labor and cheaper raw sugar available to refiners from the off-shore growers, particularly from Cuba at that time. Sugar bounties had been put into effect to protect United States sugar growers, only to be removed capriciously before expiration of the legislation. The result was that the United States was increasingly open to the cheaper off-shore raw sugar of good quality, and even to cheaper off-shore refined sugar.

At the same time, infestation of sugar crops in Louisiana and in the Sugar Bowl of Texas was becoming a serious problem. Other crops, particularly cotton, were beginning to be more attractive to growers. The result was that, with the exception of the World War I and the immediate post war years, Imperial found itself progressively processing less and less locally grown cane through its raw sugar mill and the refinery, and at the same time importing more and more raw sugar in bags from foreign sources. And this was to be an unrelenting progression until 1928, when the last locally grown sugar cane was processed at Sugar Land.

In the Rio Grande Valley, the growing and processing of raw cane sugar was also on the decline, as other crops became more attractive. During the Mexican Revolution, cane fields on the border were burned and one raw sugar mill was destroyed. After World War I, when raw sugar prices fell from $20.00 to less than $2.00 per hundredweight [cwt.], other crops replaced the growing of sugar cane and the last of the Rio Grande Valley mills was closed in 1922.

When the partners sold the Ellis plantation to the state of Texas, the Imperial raw sugar mill had been excluded from the sale and remained the property of the Imperial Sugar Company. Under the terms of the sale, the state was to use the plantation as a prison farm, with the convict population growing sugar cane for delivery to the nearby raw sugar mills at Sugar Land. The state was to pay for the land by the cane deliveries over a period of ten years. After four years, the State defaulted, and although Eldridge sued, the State was successful in claiming an immunity. Eldridge became so incensed over the failure of the State to carry out its agreement that he entered into a back and forth front page newspaper battle with the then Governor Colquit, a battle which lasted several months and one which he was destined to lose.

As a part of his castigation of Colquit's management of Texas prison affairs, Eldridge made a public offer to take over the entire management of the Texas prison system, putting up a one million dollar bond which would be forfeited if he failed to make a profit for the state of five million dollars in five years. As a part of his program he proposed better living facilities and more humane treatment of convicts, pre-release education and training to enable ex-convicts to enter the labor market, production of goods by convict labor to be sold to pay the operating expense of the system, and several other improvements. Although he managed to pick up noticeable backing for his program, he was unable to get it past the bureaucracy.

While battling with the State, Eldridge was simultaneously using the newspapers to help him confront the nation-wide sugar trust. This trust was a group of cane sugar and beet sugar processing companies which had come to control the pricing and marketing of refined sugar generally from the East Coast to the West Coast. Eldridge, ever the rugged individualist, refused to be told by the trust how to price and where to market his refined sugar. The trust responded by an open attack in which they reduced the price of refined sugar in the Southwest while maintaining a higher price elsewhere in the country. Since this predated the antitrust laws, Eldridge took his battle to the public in the newspapers. The trust finally withdrew its assault.

In May 1914, D. W. (Dan) Kempner resigned as president of the Imperial Sugar Company. Dan had not only been actively guiding the rebuilding of the sugar refinery, but had supervised the leveling and drainage program for the farm lands. But now the family needed his expertise in the expanding world-wide cotton business and in other farming and cattle activities in which they were engaged. Dan's lifetime interest in farming and ranching was to be of great value to the family investments in these areas. I. H. Kempner then took over the presidency of the Imperial Sugar Company, a position he would hold for over thirty years, to be succeeded in 1947 by his son Herbert.

During the grinding season in late 1914, the Imperial raw sugar mill burned to the ground and was never replaced. By then, the remaining mill at Sugar Land was adequate to process the declining sugar cane crops grown in the area.

Although in 1915 the capacity of the Cunningham refinery had increased to 850,000 pounds per day, they were easily able to schedule sufficient off-shore raw sugar shipments to keep the refinery in steady year-round operation, despite the continuing decline in locally grown raw sugar.

In 1917, with four years remaining on the Cunningham lease, ownership of the Cunningham raw sugar mills and the refinery was officially transferred to the Imperial Sugar Company. Then in 1919, when the Sugarland Industries was formed as a trust estate, the Imperial Sugar Company was dissolved as a corporation and it became a separate department of the Sugarland Industries, with G. D. Ulrich as general manager of Industries. In effect, he was general manager of everything in the then 13,000 acre property, including all the businesses, the farms and the company town, all of which was owned by Kempner and Eldridge through their joint ownership of the Sugarland Industries.

During World War I the call to arms depleted the farms and mills on the European Continent of their labor; the beet fields in Europe became battlegrounds; sugar became scarce, and what there was of it was husbanded. Ocean shipping was diverted to war tonnage. Sugar became a scarce commodity, and in 1918 the Allies began buying up Caribbean and Pacific crops at a fixed price. The raw sugar crops were carefully apportioned among the United States refiners, the price paid by consumers in the United States was fixed, and the consumption in the various other allied countries was regulated. Soon after the close of the war, the various governments removed their restrictions. The fixing of prices ceased. A mad scramble for the commodity ensued, and the price of sugar in the United States began to rise rapidly from the $9.00 per cwt., at which it had been fixed, to $22.50 per cwt. in May 1920.

But Cuba and other countries such as the Philippines and Hawaii had been increasing their production, shipping again became available, and it turned out that the rapid run up had been fueled to a large extent by speculation. In just six months, in November 1920, the bubble burst, prices began to weaken, then fall rapidly, and by December the price was $3.75 per cwt. By 1921, it had fallen to $2.00. It was one of the wilder pricing periods in Imperial's long history, but with a combination of shrewd discretion in the markets and providential good luck, the company managed to make nearly $2,000,000, a lot of money in those days.

As the importation of raw sugar from various world sources replaced more and more of the locally grown and milled supplies, the growing and milling of raw sugar in Texas gradually came to an end, and in 1928 the remaining raw sugar mills in the area, including the one at Sugar Land were closed and dismantled. The waving fields of sugar cane which had flourished through the days of the Texas revolution, through the pre Civil War plantation era, through the good and bad years of the early 1920's were gone for good.

The Imperial sugar refinery, then the only sugar manufacturing entity left in Texas, was operating entirely on raw sugar imported by ocean shipping through Galveston, plus a relatively small amount received by rail from Louisiana. In later years, government subsidies or protections of one type or another would again encourage the growing of raw cane sugar in Louisiana, Florida, Hawaii and the Rio Grand Valley of Texas, and Imperial has relied on those sources as well as raw sugar imported through Galveston for its raw material.

In the early 1920's, the Imperial Sugar Company was recognized as a factor in the manufacturing and sale of refined sugar throughout the central part of the country. It was a big business, with a capacity of 1,000,000 pounds of refined sugar per day, which meant that it was bringing some thirty-five carloads of ninety-six percent pure raw sugar from Galveston to Sugar Land every day, and shipping out some thirty-five carloads of almost 100 percent pure refined sugar per day. In those days a carload of sugar weighed about 30,000 pounds. Considering the capacities of railroad tracks and engine equipment, at that time, thirty-five carloads still amounted to a trainload per day.

The population in Texas was growing and the Imperial sales force was successfully taking most of the business in the state, which at that point had a strong loyalty to Texas products. The outlook for the future was encouraging, and Kempner and Eldridge were faced with a decision as to whether to make another substantial investment in increasing Imperial's plant capacity. It wasn't an easy decision at that time.

They were well aware that a group of eastern investors was seriously looking into the advisability of building a competing cane sugar refinery at Texas City, Texas, just sixty miles from Sugar Land. There were already plenty of competitive cane and beet sugar sellers soliciting business aggressively in the Midwest, including Imperial's primary market in Texas. Nevertheless, the backers of the proposed refinery at Texas City pushed forward with their program, and for the first time in history Imperial was faced with the competition of another sugar refinery in Texas, practically in its back yard. Competition between the two sugar refiners would be fierce, particularly for the Texas and Oklahoma markets.

Under the circumstances, it took quite a bit of entrepreneurial courage and faith in the future of the Imperial Sugar Company, but the decision was made to go ahead with the program to increase the plant capacity at Sugar Land and then battle it out with the Texas City plant.

Had they decided just to rock along as they were, the chances are good that the Imperial Sugar Company would not be here today, but in 1924 they drew up an ambitious plan to increase refined sugar production by fifty percent from 1,000,000 pounds per day to 1,500,000 pounds per day. That necessitated enlargement of almost every station in the plant, as well as the construction of three new buildings. The largest new building was to be the bone char filter house, an eight story brick building. The increased capacity also required a large, fireproof, brick warehouse for storing refined sugar, and a new five story building for additional boiling pans. Together, these improvements were estimated to cost $1,500,000 over the next three years. In addition, experiments were being made in the sugar refining industry looking forward to changes in the packaging of sugar, which, if successful, would require another $1,000,000 worth of conveyers and packing machines.

This program for a fifty percent increase in production also necessitated a substantial increase, in working capital. Raw sugar inventories at Galveston and Sugar Land had to be increased, as did the refined sugar inventories at Sugar Land and outside warehouses. Raw sugar had to be paid for within ten days after arrival at Galveston. It was then stored in a Galveston dockside warehouse, from which it was shipped by rail to Sugar Land, run through the refinery, possibly stored again and then shipped to the customer to be paid for ten days later. The whole inventory and marketing process tied up a great deal of money for as much as four to six weeks. The willingness of the Kempner family to finance this expansion and improvement program in the face of increasing competition in their basic trade territory was impressive.

Since the enlargement program would involve rather large capital expenditures, it was felt necessary to change the financial structure of Imperial. On September 11, 1924, Imperial, which had been operating as a department of Sugarland Industries since 1919, was reorganized as a separate five million dollar corporation, with 300,000 shares of no par value common stock authorized, 100,000 shares outstanding. The outstanding shares were still owned by Sugarland Industries, which in turn was owned jointly by Kempner and Eldridge. The sugar company had no funded debt and was conservatively valued at $3,500,000.

In addition to the common stock, Imperial's directors authorized the issuance of seven percent Cumulative Convertible Participating Preferred, $100 par value, $2,500,000 authorized, and $885,000 outstanding. This issue was to provide capital during the planned improvements to the refinery. Some of the preferred shares were bought by the families of the owners, some by investors, and some by customers. Kempner felt that customers owning even a small interest in the company would tend to have a certain loyalty toward Imperial. This seven percent preferred was convertible to common stock in 1930, and by 1933 about half was converted, leaving $442,000 preferred outstanding, and for the first time dispensing to the outside public some shares of Imperial common stock.

By the end of 1924, the company had completed the 75,000 square foot refined sugar warehouse. The 100 pound bags of sugar, packed in cotton or cotton-lined burlap bags, were delivered into the building on a system of conveyor belts which could stack the bags forty-two layers high, thus storing a seven day output. This provided a great deal of flexibility in both the refinery operations and in marketing and shipping. It was a much more efficient and less costly method of handling the heavy bags of sugar. The same system of conveyors, in reverse, took the bags from the storage stacks into box cars for shipping. This warehouse is still operating in 1990, using automatic palletizing equipment to stack the bags and cases for storage or shipment on wooden pallets.

In 1926, they completed the new "char house," a large filtration plant to remove certain colors and impurities from the raw sugar. Replacing an older and less efficient unit built by Cunningham in 1900, this would be an eight story steel and brick building containing thirty-two vertical cylindrical cast iron tanks,

Imperial Sugar Company

1926 The Texas Sugar Refining Corporation of Texas City, the only other cane sugar refinery ever built in Texas, operated sporadically in competition with Imperial from 1925 to 1932. The buildings and machinery were sold at auction in 1935. This entire area was destroyed in 1947 when the cargo vessel "Grandcamp" exploded at this slip.

each larger than a railroad tank car, to be filled with burned, ground and screened animal bone. Colored sugar syrups, filtered slowly through the bone char, came out pure crystal white. The lower floors of the building contained furnaces to reburn the bone char for further use. This process would provide a much higher quality of refined sugar and reductions in cost, as well as a fifty percent increase in capacity. It was a large eight story building, the largest building in Fort Bend County for the next fifty years, and a landmark which could be seen from miles away. In 1990 it is still in operation, with a throughput of 4,000,000 pounds per day, and its design is the equal of any char house operating in the United States. Its cost in 1926 was $1,000,000, and represented a measure of the determination and faith of Kempner and Eldridge in the future of the company.

In 1925, before Imperial had finished its expansion program, the new Texas Sugar Refining Company was completed and in operation in Texas City, Texas. It had its own slip and dock, and could accommodate ships bringing raw sugar at the very door of the plant, which gave it a distinct cost advantage over Imperial. However the refinery was not well designed, made use of some inefficient and antiquated processes, and had serious problems with its fresh water supply wells. Also, it had started off with a burdensome long term debt liability and was only marginally financed in a capital intensive business. Its refining capacity was 1,300,000 pounds per day, as compared to Imperial's planned 1,500,000 pounds. In Imperial, it was up against a long established competitor, and Imperial made it tough for them to get started. The new "Diamond Star" brand created no particular excitement in the market.

The new Texas Sugar Refining Company's first year of operation resulted in a loss of $959,000. The owners then executed a tolling contract with the American Sugar Refining Company, packing both the Texas City's Diamond Star and American's Domino brand sugars. They managed to make a profit of $218,000 in 1926, $326,000 in 1927, $215,000 in 1928. Then it was reported that the owners began withdrawing capital in 1929 for other investments. The company fell in arrears in dividends on its cumulative preferred stock and was defaulting on bond payments.

The plant closed for two months in 1929 and was reopened by a bondholders protective committee incorporated as the Texas Sugar Refining Company. They lost $17,000 in 1929, made a profit of $207,000 in 1930 but lost $200,000 in 1932. In 1932 the plant was again closed and the properties fell into the hands of a receiver. The bondholders made futile efforts to revive the company, but the refinery, land and docks were sold at auction in 1935. The buildings and docks were bought by the Monsanto Chemical Company. Imperial bought such refining equipment as it could use. The Texas Sugar Refining Company was history.

In an epilogue to the short history of this refinery, it was at this old sugar dock in Texas City that the vessel Grandcamp exploded in 1947, killing 573 people and demolishing the dock and several of the old buildings which had housed the Texas Sugar Refining Company.

Meanwhile a far-reaching and important change in the packaging and marketing of refined sugar to the consumer was taking place. Historically,

120

refined sugar had first been packaged at the refinery in barrels, then in 100 pound cotton bags or in cotton-lined burlap bags for shipment in carload lots to wholesalers. The wholesalers then delivered the barrels or bags to retail grocers in less-than-carload quantities. There were no retail chain stores, no super-markets, only relatively small neighborhood grocery stores, many owned by a family and known as "mom and pop" stores. They handled relatively few pre-packaged items, since most food preparation in those days took place in the home, using bulk ingredients. The retail grocer usually dumped his 100 pound bag of sugar into an open metal drum and then laboriously weighed out whatever the customer wanted; one pound, five pounds, or twenty-five cents worth into small paper bags. There was no brand identity to the sugar.

Then, as retail stores grew larger, and weighing small packages of sugar became an inconvenience, a demand arose for pre-packaged sugar from the refinery. In 1926, Imperial, like other refiners, responded and began packaging sugar at the refinery in two, five, ten, twenty-five, fifty, and one hundred pound cotton bags. The retail grocer was then able to stack small bags of sugar on his shelf for the housewife to pick up whatever size she chose. Each of these small bags had the Imperial logo prominently displayed, and for the first time, brand selling of sugar to the consumer had arrived.

In 1927, then, Imperial embarked on a brand advertising campaign which has continued unbroken for over 60 years. In that year, Imperial placed its advertising account with the Dallas firm of Tracy-Locke-Dawson and entered into what was in those days an intensive program of brand advertising, using newspaper ads, billboards, and radio. In the late 1920's, newspapers were smaller, there were far fewer advertisers, and Imperial's ads in Texas news-papers, large and small, across the state, attracted attention. The same thing was true of Imperial's radio coverage in almost every station in Texas. The billboard advertising was probably the most noticeable. In the days when there were not so many billboards in the towns and cities, Imperial had 22 billboards in Dallas, 14 in Fort Worth, 16 in Houston, 12 in Beaumont, 10 in Abilene and numerous others in scattered smaller towns. Competing sugars simply could not or would not concentrate their sales efforts in Texas to the same extent. Imperial probably had a larger sales force active in Texas than all its competitors combined. It was an effective program, and it is interesting to record that although the advertising and merchandising activities of the company have changed with the times, in 1990 Imperial still uses the successor to its original advertising agency, now known as Tracy-Locke Company.

In 1927, Imperial completed the major part of its planned expansion program with the construction of an additional pan house for boiling sugar syrups to a grain. This was a five story steel and concrete structure and cost $250,000. In addition to the increased output of 1,500,000 pounds per day, it was an important contribution to the program of cost reduction.

A two-lane paved road replaced the old gravel, crushed shell and mud roads between Sugar Land and Houston and Richmond. This improved road trans-portation diminished the isolation of Sugar Land. Some of the businesses which had been necessary in a self-sufficient community were no longer required, and in the 1930's there was a gradual decrease in the number and types of businesses operated by Industries. The abattoir and the meat packing plant were closed, the printing and publishing business was sold and moved to Houston. The paper mill had been closed when the cane stalk fibers were no longer available in the late 1920's, and the acid plant was shut down at the same time.

In 1928, Mr. Kempner's second son, I. H. Kempner, Jr. (known as Herbert) graduated from Harvard and came to Sugar Land to learn the various local businesses, the sugar business in particular. He had worked in the refinery and the refinery offices during his summer vacations. In 1930, he was married and shortly afterward moved into a company owned house in Sugar Land. He was made treasurer and a director of Imperial, and in 1932 his first son was born. Named I. H. Kempner, III, this young man was nicknamed "Denny" and some thirty years later would follow his father's footsteps into the Imperial Sugar Company; and in 1971 would be elected chairman of the board, first of the Imperial Sugar Company, and later of the expanded Imperial Holly Corporation. Herbert's second son, James C. "Jim" Kempner who had also worked at Imperial during the summers of his school years, would in 1988 become executive vice president, a director and chief financial officer of the Imperial Holly Corporation.

Additional working capital for the sugar company was needed again in 1929. There was another issue, this time seven dollar Cumulative Convertible Preferred, no par value, 35,000 shares authorized, 9,267 shares outstanding. This stock was convertible into common in 1935, but only a few shares were converted, and in 1935 there were 13,333 shares outstanding.

At this point in its history, Imperial Sugar Company was in excellent condition. Its physical plant was modern and well maintained, its raw supplies were adequate from many offshore sources, its financial condition sound, and its products well established in the market place.

In 1929, Imperial had a total plant investment of $6,533,000, a net worth of $5,084,000 and working capital of approximately $400,000, plus excellent lines of credit with several banks in Houston, Dallas, and New York. Since 1924, regular dividends had been paid on both the common and preferred shares. In 1929, Sugarland Industries properties were appraised at $7,480,219.56, of which $967,284 was for the town of Sugar Land and $6,188,777.00 was for the local farm lands.

Thus, the combined value of the Imperial Sugar Company and Sugarland Industries at the end of 1929 were in the neighborhood of $12,500,000. Since the partnership had paid less than $2,000,000 for the Ellis and Cunningham Plantations in 1908, they had obviously plowed a considerable fortune into their original investment. In today's aura of high finance and billion dollar buyouts, $12,500,000 may not seem particularly remarkable, but in those days of 25 cents an hour wage rates and 5 cent loaves of bread, it was impressive indeed.

Considering the condition of the Sugar Land properties when they took it over in 1906, Eldridge and Kempner had accomplished a great deal in those twenty-four years. By 1930, they had built up a modern sugar refinery in excellent condition, a fine staff of experienced workers living within a stones throw of the plant, an excellent standing in a growing trade territory, and a world-wide source of raw sugar . . . and they had recently overcome the threat of a major competitor in south Texas.

The diversified farming and cattle raising activities as well as the various other enterprises established in Sugar Land in that period were, in the aggregate, profitable. At times, the Kempner family had arranged credit for the Sugar Land activities to the detriment of the family's ability to enter or conduct other enterprises which might have been more lucrative at the time. Eldridge had completed the partnership with his own personal management and entrepreneurial skills. The program envisioned by Kempner and Eldridge for their company town had possibly exceeded their expectations. The capital devoted to building a model community on top of the old "hell hole of the Brazos" had turned out to be a sound investment.

I. H., Dan, Lee and Stanley Kempner. The wall painting is of their father, Harris Kempner.

THE DEPRESSION YEARS — 1930-1940

This was the decade which was to mark the beginning of the active full-time Kempner Family management of the Sugar Land enterprises, a management which would endure for over half a century and into the present. It was also to be one of the more difficult decades in the history of the company town, its people and its enterprises.

Neither the Imperial Sugar Company or the Sugarland Industries was burdened with long term debt at this time. However, Imperial was a capital intensive business and depended upon regular and substantial borrowings to finance its growing purchases of raw sugar from abroad. The money received from the sale of preferred stocks as well as a good part of its retained earnings continued to be plowed back into enlarging and modernizing the refinery. Sugarland Industries had been a consistent borrower to finance its crops and its forays into new enterprises. Occasionally Imperial had financed an adventure by Sugarland Industries into still another new project. As a consequence both companies lacked liquidity; but neither Kempner or Eldridge, caught up like many other businessmen in the euphoria of the late 1920's, were overly concerned—things had been going too well.

Despite the stock market decline in the fall of 1929 and early 1930, no one could foresee the problems looming just around the corner. By the end of 1930, it was apparent that the economy in the United States was in a serious depression. Businesses throughout the country were retrenching or closing, employees were being laid off or their wages reduced. There were few if any unemployment, health or retirement benefits available at that time, either from the government or from employers. People reduced expenses, reduced spending, cut back on buying. Volume of business declined to bring about still further reductions in incomes and purchases and still further pay cuts and layoffs. Sales of refined sugar declined and competition increased. Prices for farm products fell. Sugarland Industries' cotton crop, once a source of considerable income, hardly paid for the planting and ginning as cotton prices had declined dramatically.

In 1931, the model school plant built in 1918 in Sugar Land was still in excellent condition, but inadequate to house the number of youngsters growing into the higher grades. In spite of the looming depression, the two companies built a second group of school buildings, duplicating the first group, but with a gymnasium and a heated indoor swimming pool. Few small towns in Texas enjoyed such excellent school facilities.

Then in 1931, the Imperial Sugar Company suffered its first loss in a decade, its cash position was dangerously low and banks everywhere were tightening

125

their lines of credit. It was becoming increasingly obvious that, one of their enterprises, the Texas Fig Company, was in serious and expensive trouble.

In the late 1920's, Sugarland Industries had entered into a venture which very nearly proved disastrous to both Industries and the Imperial Sugar Company, the processing and marketing of preserved figs. Fig trees had become a popular and potentially profitable venture in the areas around Dickinson, Webster, Texas City, Pearland, and Friendswood, Texas. Packaged in glass jars, preserved figs, which were very sweet and used large quantities of sugar, suddenly became much in demand by consumers, and the business started growing rapidly. The large quantities of sugar being ordered by the fig packaging plants attracted the attention of the sales department at Imperial, and a good friend of Eldridge, named R. J. Clymer, prevailed upon Eldridge and Kempner to form the Texas Fig Company as an investment of Sugarland Industries. The records of this company are not available, but its investments seemed to be concentrated in the manufacturing, packaging and sale of the preserves, and not in the orchards. They converted the old Sealy Mattress Company plant into a fig-processing facility; and apparently tried to corner the market in the south Texas area by buying and building several other processing plants and contracting for vast amounts of figs from the growers.

At just about the time when the fig company had expanded its ownership and its production to a high level, the market for the product collapsed. The public, which had at first seemed to have an almost insatiable demand for the processed figs, suddenly found them too sweet for a steady diet. Business dropped precipitously, and in 1932 Sugarland Industries was forced to pay off some $1,800,000 to creditors. One piece of correspondence places the loss at well over $2,000,000, a shockingly large loss for that time. Industries had to turn to Imperial for a loan.

In 1932, Imperial suffered its second loss year in a row and in advancing over $1,500,000 to Sugarland Industries had reduced its working capital and endangered its credit to the point that it could not finance the purchases of raw sugar so necessary to the continued operation of the refinery. Neither Imperial nor Industries was able to pay dividends on their common stocks, and Imperial was obliged to discontinue payments on its two issues of cumulative preferred stock. Both Imperial and Sugarland Industries were but a step away from receivership. By late 1932, the Kempner family was faced with a decision as to how far they could go to save the Imperial Sugar Company, the Sugarland Industries and the company town. They decided to face the crisis and do what had to be done.

Mr. Kempner spent a month in Washington negotiating with the Reconstruction Finance Corporation, which was headed by his Houston friend, Jesse Jones. He was applying for a loan of $1,800,000, to be repaid within eight years, with installments to begin in two years. Jones finally approved a loan of $1,200,000 to be made to Sugarland Industries from a group of several banks. Installment payments were to begin in six months. The RFC guaranteed the bank loans. Jones was a cautious guardian of RFC money, and required that the loans be secured by a mortgage on the Imperial Sugar Company, Sugarland Industries, and all properties in the company town; in addition that the four

W. T. Eldridge

Kempner brothers execute a personal guarantee for the entire amount of the loan. Few people ever knew of this personal involvement of Mr. I. H., R. Lee, Dan, and Stanley Kempner, and the H. Kempner family trust until some 35 years later when Homer Bruce, an Imperial director and the Kempner lawyer, presented a resolution to the board of directors expressing the appreciation of other members of the Kempner family.

The RFC loan agreement also contained the stipulation that no dividends or interest could be paid on the common and preferred stocks of Imperial or the certificates of Sugarland Industries. Upon receipt of the loan money from the various banks, Sugarland Industries repaid the money which had been advanced by Imperial to aid in liquidating the Texas Fig Company. The crisis had been averted, at least for the moment.

In 1932, at age 69, Eldridge was still actively engaged in all phases of the various Sugar Land activities. However, he became quite ill in the early summer of that year and died in August. Eldridge had spent the last few years of his life with his third wife, Mildred, and his young son, Randle, in their attractive new home on Lakeview Drive. His death was a severe blow to the Kempners and to the citizens of Sugar Land who had worked under his leadership for so many years. He had taken such a deep personal interest in everything that went on in the community, and in the welfare of the employees and their families that he would be sorely missed.

At the time of Eldridge's death, his estate was estimated by one of his daughters at over $5,000,000. He had various investments in lands in Harris, Fort Bend, and several other counties, stocks, bonds, and cash accounts. About a year and a half before his death, he had created a new will, leaving all his assets, with the exception of his fifty percent ownership in Sugarland Industries, to his wife, Mildred, and his young son, William Randle. His stock in Sugarland Industries was divided mostly among Mrs. Eldridge and the two Eldridge daughters, Mrs. R. J. (Ivy Eldridge) Bauereisen and Mrs. Walter F. (Ethel Eldridge) Woodul, with smaller amounts left to grandchildren, the local hospital and the school district. At that point, all the properties at Sugar Land were owned fifty percent by the Kempner family, forty-nine percent by the Eldridge heirs and one percent by the Laura Eldridge Hospital Association and the Sugar Land Independent School District.

The burden placed on the Kempners by the death of Mr. Eldridge was made even more pronounced by the fact that none of the Eldridge heirs had any experience with or knowledge of the complexity of the many enterprises at Sugar Land. The only heir who had the background to understand the businesses was Walter F. Woodul, the husband of Ivy Eldridge.

Woodul was a partner in the Houston law firm of Woodul, Atterbury, and Folk, and was active in local and State politics. He was willing to act as a representative of the Eldridge family in their part ownership of the activities at Sugar Land, but was far too busy with legal and political affairs to devote any sustained effort toward the management at Sugar Land. In 1934 he was elected lieutenant governor of the state of Texas for one term. He was helpful in many ways during the next fourteen years, although his business philosophies were not always the same as those of the Kempner family.

I. H. "Herbert" Kempner, Jr.

It was timely indeed that Herbert Kempner, second son of I. H. Kempner, had become quite active in the management of the Imperial Sugar Company and knowledgeable in the various enterprises of the Sugarland Industries. It was also fortunate that the Kempners had the services of Gus Ulrich. Mr. I. H., Herbert, and Ulrich brought the companies through the depression of the 1930's.

In 1932, there was a great deal of belt tightening to be done by management and by employees. The major financial problems of the companies had been solved, at least for the moment, by the RFC loan, but the problems being created by the depression were growing and both companies showed losses throughout the next six years. Consumption of sugar continued to decline, competition for the remaining sugar business increased, and even with the RFC money, there were times when the refinery was unable to secure credit for raw sugar purchases in time to avoid shutdowns at the plant. There were even times when the refinery was forced to ask its larger customers for payment of refined sugar in advance of the purchase of raw sugar, in return for a reduction in the price of refined. There were many three-day work weeks, and occasionally the refinery would be unable to operate for as much as two weeks. Even with the emergency measures instituted by the Kempners to keep the Sugar Land employees housed and fed, there were several years of difficult times for all.

But the Kempners were determined to keep the Imperial Sugar Company, which had the largest payroll and most of the employees in the town, operating at a level which would keep the town functioning, the stores open, and the houses occupied. Sugarland Industries continued to plant their cotton, vegetable and feed crops, kept their cattle herds, and in spite of reduced business, kept the company stores operating.

Although both companies reduced salaries and wages, they attempted to give each hourly employee enough work so that he could pay his rent and buy food for his family. When the refinery was shut down or did not have enough work for all the men, they were assigned to work on the farms, picking cotton, picking and sorting potatoes, strawberries, watermelons, or whatever crop was in season, or perhaps working on some of the city services. The companies arranged a Works Progress Administration program for the Sugar Land area in which local people were employed in various local projects such as cleaning ditches, or repairing roads and city facilities.

Wages for general labor were only twenty cents per hour and skilled workers drew thirty cents per hour. But rents were low, from $5 to $20 per month depending on the size and location of the house; a loaf of bread cost five cents, beans were four cents a pound, and beef was six cents a pound. Only a few executives had cars. People got by on small wardrobes. There were no expensive appliances.

Complete medical care continued to be provided at Eldridge Memorial Hospital for employees of the local companies at a cost of $1.50 per month deducted from paychecks, and during the depression even this charge was discontinued at times. Families of employees were treated by the medical staff and by the hospital at minimum charges, and again, in hardship cases, these charges were either delayed or cancelled.

Many families had enough land around their company home to grow vegetables, raise chickens, possibly keep a cow. Those who needed more were allowed free use of additional plots of company land near their houses. Jim Guyer, the one-legged labor boss and local constable, was given authority to issue staples such as flour, beans, surplus vegetables, sugar, etc. to those Sugar Land families who were in real need.

Even so, some were unable to keep current, and in those cases, the companies allowed the men to fall as much as six months behind in their rent, to draw coupons as advance wages, and in some cases extended extra time on grocery bills. The Kempners instructed Gus Ulrich, who, along with his department heads, knew the financial and personal circumstances of every family in Sugar Land and on the farms, to be sure that those in real need received help. It has been said by some of the older employees who were in Sugar Land at the time that there was not a single vacant company house during the depression. Both companies made every effort to keep every employee, and they did it.

Recent interviews with many of those still in Sugar Land who experienced the depression there indicate that the times did not seem so bad, at least in retrospect. They speak with pride of the spirit of cooperation in which management and employees worked together to get through their difficulties. The chances are good that the people in Sugar Land were better cared for than those in most Texas towns from 1932 to 1938.

During these difficult years, the owners also attempted to create more jobs in Sugar Land by bringing in outside companies. In 1930, Imperial Sugar Company made land available for a building to house the Visco Products Company. A local chemist in the Imperial Sugar laboratory had, along with two outside chemists, patented a process to use sodium aluminate in the manufacture of oil well drilling mud and proposed to set up a manufacturing plant in Sugar Land. They originally hired only ten people, but over the years grew steadily and in 1956 the company was acquired by Nalco Corporation. Nalco increased the size of this operation until in 1990 the plant was spread out over forty acres and regularly employed 460 people.

In 1936, Sugarland Industries persuaded the Marshall Canning Company of Marshalltown, Iowa, to move one of its food processing plants to Sugar Land. This plant processed fruits, meats, and vegetables, and was attracted by the opportunity of contracting for locally grown produce, the availability of the unoccupied Texas Fig plant (formerly the Sealy Mattress Company), and the access by rail and truck to the Southwest market.

Marshall contracted with Sugarland Industries and with farmers generally throughout Fort Bend and nearby counties for the growing of such vegetables as beans, cabbage, corn, sweet potatoes, spinach, and similar crops. The canning plant ran year round, packing fresh vegetables in season and running on dried beans and dried peas in the off season months. It had a fleet of its own trucks and vans, ran twenty-four hours per day, five to seven days per week most of the year, and provided employment for well over 100 workers. Its arrival required that the Sugarland Industries build a few more houses, but most of the employees came from people already residing in Sugar Land company houses. It was a welcome payroll and a fine addition to the community.

The various retail establishments, such as the general store, the bakery and the restaurants, the bank, the drug store, trucking company, the feed mill, farm implement company, the automobile agency and gas stations, the small hotels, the telephone company, all remained essentially unchanged. After the death of Eldridge, the experimenting in new ventures and new crops came to a halt. For one thing the Kempners were trying too hard to maintain what they had built; for another, Gus Ulrich was a conservative manager and not as absorbed in fostering new enterprises as Eldridge had been.

The farms remained the same. A few crops were added and a few abandoned. There was an increase in the acreage devoted to cattle. The original 18,000 acres which Kempner and Eldridge had purchased in the Ellis and Cunningham Plantations had varied considerably over the years as the Sugarland Industries occasionally bought and sold lands both adjacent to Sugar Land and in distant counties. During the 1930's, even though it was a poor time to be disposing of land, Industries was forced to do so. They sold various tracts adjoining Sugar Land, all on the periphery and particularly in that southern part of the properties which were outside the levee system, much of it wooded. By the end of the decade, they had retained approximately 11,000 contiguous acres around the town of Sugar Land, most of it to the south and east of the town.

In the aggregate, earnings of the Industries were not impressive. Most years, the operations of the several retail and service stores produced limited profits, some operated at a loss which was subsidized by those which were profitable; the rationale being that the community needed to be self-sustaining without overcharging the employees. The farming operations, like most agricultural enterprises, had good and bad years. The long range potential for the stockholders was in the future value of the land owned by Sugarland Industries and the profitable operation of the Imperial Sugar Company.

Meanwhile, the 1930's had seen a marked increase in the influence of the United States Government on the sugar industry, with the passage of the Jones Costigan Amendment to the Agriculture Adjustment Act in 1934. This marked the beginning of a progression of legislation, controls, and proclamations from Washington which would have, for over fifty years and until the present, a basic impact on the operations of the United States sugar industry.

Planned to protect the income of domestic beet and cane sugar growers, ensuing legislation over the years would make various use of tariffs, excise taxes, processing taxes, quota systems, benefit payments, acreage controls, loan provisions and price floors to accomplish its purposes. From the growers' standpoint, the program was generally a success, but it introduced complications in the operations of cane sugar refiners which eventually, by the 1980's would help bring about the demise of several refiners. Imperial's survival could be attributed to its long-term program of efficiencies in plant operations and marketing programs.

It was a surprise when, in 1938, notwithstanding the efforts of the two companies in Sugar Land to keep the townspeople and employees working, the union movement in the United States came to Sugar Land, and enough of the employees of Imperial Sugar Company were swayed by their promises to support a local election. While not particularly entranced by the idea, the owners did not take a strong stance against it. Herbert Kempner is known to have felt that there might be a need for better communications between employees and managers. Upon hearing about a "secret" organization meeting to be held in Stafford by a group of employees, Herbert invited the group to hold the meeting in one of the refinery buildings in Sugar Land. While ambivalent about the real need for a union, he saw no reason to place obstacles in their path if the employees wanted one.

The election resulted in the formation of a local union, named the United Sugar Workers Local Union #917 of the Congress for United Organizations. Through the years, the union changed its affiliation with various national organizations, most often those which represented other sugar refiners.

Separate union contracts were later signed with Sugarland Industries, and this was a much more difficult set of regulations because of the complexity of the varied operations of that company. It covered the employees of the local grocery, appliance, filling station, garage, general store, truck line, feed mill, cotton gin, and various other enterprises in which it was difficult to coordinate general job descriptions, work rules, and pay scales. It placed the local stores at a disadvantage with competitors in Houston, but nevertheless, remained in effect until the final liquidation of Sugarland Industries in 1973.

Since the establishment of the unions in Sugar Land in 1939 and the successive one, two, or three year contracts which were negotiated until 1973 in the case of Sugarland Industries, and until the present with Imperial Sugar Company, relations with employees of both companies have been good. There has never been a strike or even a serious threat of one. Turnover of employees at Imperial has averaged only three to five percent per year for fifty years, and amounted to five percent in 1989, which may be something of a continuing record among manufacturing companies.

By 1938, in spite of the cliff-hanging rescue by the RFC loan in 1932, and the desperate efforts by the Kempners to stave off the disasters which overtook so many companies during the depression, the companies were still undergoing difficult times. During that period, Sugarland Industries appeared to do little more than break even at best. Although Imperial returned a healthy profit in 1937 after six straight loss years, by early 1938 it was by no means clear that the depression was coming to a close, and the company was again in financial difficulties.

The companies were unable to continue the required payments on the RFC loan. The $125,000 in annual unpaid dividends on Imperial's preferred stock issues was in arrears in the amount of over $750,000, and the company was again experiencing increasing difficulty in borrowing to finance the necessary raw sugar purchases. In 1938, large customers were again being solicited to pay several weeks in advance of receipt of refined sugar to enable the company to purchase raw supplies.

The Kempners worked out a program for refinancing, with the help of the Bank of New York and the approval of the RFC, and this proved to be the last substantial financial assistance the companies would need. The program offered holders of the two issues of Imperial Sugar Company preferred stock an exchange whereby the stockholder would surrender his preferred stock by the end of 1939 and receive in exchange a $100, four percent, twenty-five year debenture, plus $4 in cash for each share of preferred stock and one share of Imperial common stock in lieu of the back dividends. The common stock would come from the Imperial stock owned by Sugarland Industries; thus there would be no dilution of the stock.

At that time there were 17,643 shares of the preferred stocks outstanding, worth a face value of $1,764,300. The program necessitated the transfer of 17,643 shares of Imperial common to the 435 holders of the preferred stock residing in several states, but mostly in Texas.

In 1938 the holders of the preferred stock who perforce exchanged their shares for the new debentures, the $4 and the share of common stock were not enchanted. They had far less faith in the future of Imperial than did the Kempners; some were offering their new $100 debentures for as little as $30 each, with the shares of common stock thrown in free as an incentive.

The RFC agreed to an extension of their loan balance to December 31, 1942. Once again there was a breathing spell in the financial affairs of the Imperial Sugar Company and the Sugarland Industries. And the timing was fortunate, because the end of the depression appeared to be in sight and the two companies were then in position to make the most of the improving economic conditions in the country.

WORLD WAR II AND THE
POST WAR YEARS — 1940-1950

By September 1941, all the remaining shares of Imperial's preferred stock had been retired, and the company's capitalization was 300,000 shares of common stock authorized, 100,000 outstanding. Thirteen thousand shares of common stock were still in the hands of former holders of the preferred stocks, and the balance of the 100,000 shares was owned by Sugarland Industries, which in turn was still owned entirely by the Kempner family and the Eldridge heirs. Also outstanding was the $1,764,000 in four percent debentures due in 1963. Payment of dividends to holders of stock in Imperial and Sugarland Industries were resumed for the first time in eleven years, and interest payments on the debentures were made regularly. Once again both companies were back in the good graces of the financial community.

Management of the affairs of the Imperial Sugar Company, the various Sugarland Industries activities and the company town was headed by Mr. I. H. Kempner, Herbert Kempner and Gus Ulrich, with the overall accord of Walter Woodul, representing the Eldridge heirs. The Kempner brothers, R. Lee, Dan and Stanley continued their activities in assisting Mr. I. H. particularly with the bank, the farms and the various cotton factoring, compressing, marketing and trading enterprises of the Kempner family.

At the onset of World War II in September of 1939, there had been a buying and hoarding spree on the part of consumers and industrial users of sugar which caused a great deal of speculation in the sugar market. This was short-lived, however, as the early months of the war in Europe were followed by a "sit-down war" in which there was relatively little military activity by either side.

But as the war in Europe intensified and the conflict spread to the Pacific in 1941, the public in the United States again became concerned over a possible shortage of sugar and began another round of hoarding. Beet sugar fields in Europe were being destroyed and increasing amounts of raw cane sugar acreage were being lost or had become inaccessible in various Pacific Ocean areas. German submarines were beginning to threaten ocean traffic in the Atlantic and the Caribbean. A serious shortage in ocean shipping was impending. Clearly, it was becoming increasingly necessary to impose controls in sugar usage and prices.

Early in 1942, marketing and import quotas of raw cane sugar under the Sugar Act were suspended and unlimited imports were invited. Limitations on production of beet and cane sugar farms in the United States were removed, and incentives in the form of subsidies to U.S. beet and cane growers were expanded.

I. H. Kempner

For the first time in history, formal rationing of sugar by coupons and certificates to all users including the householder were established. This required the registration of practically every person in the United States as well as every wholesaler and retailer, industrial user, hotel, restaurant, and institution using or dealing in sugar. A vast organization under the OPA (Office of Price Administration) and the Department of Agriculture was set up to administer the rationing and price program.

A brief description of the sugar rationing program might be of interest. Each consumer was registered and given books of ration stamps to be presented to the grocer for sugar. The number of pounds authorized by each stamp was changed from time to time as the supply situation varied, as was the length of time for which each stamp was valid; the government might announce that certain stamps were good for two pounds or five pounds and for a period of two to eight weeks, for example. The housewife, who had received ration books for her family depending upon the number of family members registered, presented her stamps to the grocer and received the authorized amount of sugar. The grocer accumulated stamps, which he pasted in a book. The book was presented to a wholesale grocer authorizing the wholesaler to deliver a corresponding amount of sugar to the retailer. The wholesale grocer accumulated books from his many retail grocer customers. He then deposited the books in his "sugar ration account" at his bank. He could then write a sugar check on that account for a carload of sugar to be purchased from the refiner, providing of course that he had an adequate balance in his bank account. The refiner deposited the check in the refiners "sugar" bank account and kept a permanent record of all transactions.

Manufacturers of sugar-containing products were provided with opening allotments of sugar based on their historical use. These allotments were used to establish a "sugar" bank account at the manufacturer's bank. The manufacturer then wrote sugar checks made out to the refiner in order to receive sugar. Additional manufacturer's allotments were given at intervals, the size and timing of the allotments depending upon the supply situation.

It was a cumbersome arrangement, but it worked surprisingly well, and the public seemed to accept the patriotic need to comply with this and with all the other wartime regulations covering shoes, tires, gasoline, etc., as well as the many shortages of all sorts. Sugar rationing was continued in the United States for two years after the cessation of hostilities, as it was necessary to make supplies of sugar available to those nations whose crops had been destroyed or which had been unable to receive sugar under wartime conditions.

The Defense Supplies Corporation, and subsequently the Commodities Credit Corporation, were established to purchase raw sugars from Cuba and other offshore suppliers and to ration these supplies out to the cane refiners. Prices of raw sugar to the refiner and refined sugar to the users were set by the OPA, thus fixing the refiners margin of profit. Also, to avoid profiteering, a World War II excess profits tax was in effect between December 1939 and 1946. The rates were 90% in 1942 and 1943, and 95% in 1944 and 1945, applied to adjusted excess profit net income of corporations.

One wartime regulation that played an important part in the future of the Imperial Sugar Company was the "zoning" restrictions which were placed on United States refiners of cane sugar and processors of beet sugar. In the United States, one of the problems encountered in wartime was a shortage of rail cars. Early on, to reduce the cross-hauling of sugar (for example shipping refined sugar from California to Texas at the same time Texas sugar was being shipped to Chicago) the government seriously considered closing all but the larger refineries and processors, thus concentrating the rail traffic more efficiently. Imperial was listed as one of the refineries to be closed, but frantic efforts on the part of Imperial and others slated for closure resulted in a different plan.

The new plan involved "zoning" regulations, under which Imperial was assigned as exclusive sugar supplier for the state of Texas, with the exception of far west Texas, which was assigned to the California and Hawaiian Sugar Refining Corporation, Ltd., a co-op owned by the Hawaiian sugar growers, with its refinery located at Crockett, California. Imperial was also assigned Oklahoma along with certain Louisiana refiners. In return, Imperial was not allowed to ship outside its assigned territory. Similar territorial zoning was applied to other areas of the United States.

The result was that for five years, from 1942 to 1947, Imperial sugar was featured exclusively on the grocery shelves and in the food processing plants in most of Texas and Oklahoma. This was to have a far reaching effect on Imperial's post-war marketing program.

Meanwhile, in 1942, Herbert Kempner and his brother, Harris, volunteered to serve in the U.S. Navy. Both served in Washington, D.C., for three years, until the end of the war, and were discharged as lieutenant commanders. During Herbert's absence, Mr. I. H. Kempner once again became more active in the affairs at Sugar Land, assisted by Ulrich in the Sugarland Industries, and by H. G. Thompson as executive vice president and by O. R. Armstrong as vice president and sales manager of Imperial. Mr. I. H. and Herbert corresponded extensively about the affairs of the Sugar Land enterprises throughout the war.

The year 1942 marked a significant change in the packaging of sugar as the industry converted from cotton to paper bags. Although more subject to breakage during handling and shipping, paper bags lent themselves to high-speed mechanical filling and sealing and thus were particularly advantageous during the developing wartime shortage of labor. Paper was less expensive, and cotton was much in demand for military supplies, so the transition was fairly rapid.

For the citizens of Sugar Land, the war brought about dramatic changes in life styles. Many of the younger men and women had joined the armed forces, and suddenly, from the short work weeks of the 1930's, the remaining men and women were working twelve and sixteen hour days. For example, men might work eight hours at a regular laboratory or maintenance job, then help out in the packaging department for an additional four to eight hours; and it was not unusual for the refinery to run for six consecutive weeks, seven days per week. At times it ran until maintenance requirements forced a shut-down for repairs.

More women were employed, and almost any transient passer-by was hauled into the plant and put to work. Jim Guyer, the constable and labor boss for both companies, visited the nearby prison compound every morning to corral any convict who had served his time or been paroled. In this way a good many ex-convicts were hired. Even before the war, newly released or paroled convicts, turned out on the highway only two miles from Sugar Land, often headed straight for the refinery or Sugarland Industries headquarters to ask for a job. Many of them were hired, given a house in the town, brought their families to Sugar Land and became model and productive citizens. Guyer stated that he would not hire an ex-convict who had been a thief—he preferred those whose crime had been committed in a single burst of passion, such as violence or even murder. He felt that after the experience of life on a prison farm in those days, such an unfortunate could be rehabilitated, and it appeared that he was right, because quite a few ex-convicts remained in Sugar Land, became valuable long-time employees and raised families who also became employees of Imperial or of Sugarland Industries.

It seemed strange that so much sugar production would be needed while sugar was being rationed, but early on it was apparent that America would have to become a sugar bowl for many allied countries whose sugar production would be reduced or whose sugar supplies would be cut off by the war. America's 11,000,000 man armed forces appeared to be consuming more sugar per capita than these same men and women had been accustomed to consume as civilians before the war. It was speculated that civilians were using the entire amount of their ration even if that ration represented more sugar than they were previously accustomed to consume.

It was fortunate that adequate raw sugar supplies were available. Early in the war, the government had relaxed acreage restrictions on United States grown beet and cane sugars. In spite of a shortage of ocean shipping, there seemed to be enough vessels available in the Caribbean to deliver raw sugar from Cuba and other island growers. The government program of allocating raw sugars seemed to be generally well administered, and Imperial managed to keep operating at an unusually high level.

Maintenance of the refinery buildings and equipment was a very serious problem during the war. Running as it did twenty-four hours per day, seven days per week, sometimes continuously for as much as six weeks, maintenance could be done only on an emergency basis. Machinery and parts, copper and steel, rubber and leather, even concrete and lumber, could only be bought on a priority issued by the government, a time-consuming process. This difficulty continued into 1947, as the United States attempted to feed the war-ravaged countries and to rebuild their buildings. As a consequence, 1947 found the sugar company in substandard shape mechanically, and badly in need of a general rebuilding.

Sugarland Industries was also plagued by shortages of personnel to man the stores and manufacturing operations, to farm the fields and to look after the cattle. This company did a noteworthy job of supplying food, and fiber from its farms and in serving the needs for services in the hard-working local community. The price of cotton had risen from the depressed levels of the 1930's, and the company was able to return to profitability, although it, like the sugar company, had to resort to exceptional means to hire workers.

During World War II, so much labor had left the farms that they were relying heavily on transient labor, mostly Hispanic, for harvesting, particularly the cotton and corn crops. Nearly half the 11,000 acres then owned by Sugarland Industries had been converted to pasture land for herds of Hereford cattle. But after the war, the increasing availability of new and improved farm machinery such as cotton picking machines, tillers, gang plows, land movers, etc., soon began to solve the labor problem as less transient labor was needed during the harvesting seasons.

At the end of the war, the veterans and those who had left to engage in wartime work soon returned to Sugar Land and took up where they had left off. The labor shortage in the town was over, the refinery was operating steadily, and the town was back to normal. Once again, life in Sugar Land was good, and the feeling in the town was that under the continuing Kempner management it would carry on that way.

In the fall of 1945, both Harris and Herbert Kempner were discharged from the navy. Harris returned to Galveston to resume his activities in the various Kempner interests. Herbert moved his family to Houston and commuted daily to Sugar Land. He was vice president, treasurer and a director of Imperial and had been kept closely posted on events in the company by his father and by Harry Thompson, and thus was able to take over where he had left off to go into the navy. He returned in time to oversee the reconstruction of the badly run-down refinery and to assist his father in some of the problems which had arisen over the years.

At the end of 1945, quarterly dividend payments were resumed on Imperial's common stock and have continued to the present, into 1990. Sugarland Industries resumed payment of annual dividends in 1944.

The terms of Imperial's debenture issue enabled the company to call at will by drawing by lot the particular debentures to be purchased. In 1944, $50,000 worth were called; in 1945, $50,000 in 1946, $50,000 and in 1947, $75,000. These annual calls continued until all the debentures were liquidated in 1962, at which time Imperial's capitalization was represented only by the shares of common stock outstanding, the majority of which were owned by the Kempner family.

In 1946, one continuing problem was the lack of complete accord between the Kempners and the Eldridge heirs as to the future plans for the Imperial Sugar Company and the Sugarland Industries. Both companies were in such shape that decisions needed to be made.

Since the death of Eldridge in 1932, the Eldridge heirs had taken little active interest in the daily management of the properties at Sugar Land. Walter Woodul had become a trustee of Sugarland Industries and a director of Imperial Sugar, and in these capacities was kept well informed about both companies. At times he was in disagreement with the Kempners. As early as the mid-1930's, when it appeared that both Imperial and Sugarland Industries were in danger of foreclosure and were paying no dividends, the disenchantment of the Eldridge heirs had become apparent in lengthy correspondence between Woodul, Mr. Kempner, and Herbert. In the early 1940's, Woodul made several unsuccessful attempts to have the Sugarland Industries trust agreement either changed or terminated. He felt strongly that capital expenditures for improvements and efficiencies in the plants and on the farms were being given too great a priority by the Kempners, at the expense of dividends.

When he proposed that the sugar refinery be put up for sale, Mr. Kempner suggested that the entire Sugar Land operations be sold as a unit. Kempner felt that the family did not wish to continue ownership and management of the rather cumbersome Sugarland Industries and the company town without the refinery, which employed the most people and held the most promise for growth and profit. Nevertheless, they proposed that Woodul see what sort of sale could be arranged.

In the early 1940's Woodul was able to secure an offer from National Sugar Refining Company of New York, but only for the refinery. Woodul met numerous times with Mr. Kempner and with Herbert, who was then in Washington in the Navy. Mr. Kempner and Herbert corresponded frequently and at length, making every attempt to keep the partnership intact, at least until an equitable disposition could be worked out. Finally, in 1945, when Woodul objected strenuously to a Kempner program of expensive long term rehabilitation of the Sugar Land activities, particularly the sugar refinery, Mr. Kempner and Herbert decided to make an offer to the Eldridge heirs to either buy or sell the entire Sugar land enterprises.

Realizing that a great deal of money would have to be devoted to modernizing the refinery, and having no desire to take over the properties in the run-down shape they were in at the end of the war, the Eldridges chose to sell to the Kempners for $2,500,000 in cash and on May 11, 1946, the sale was finalized. Sugarland Industries bought the 39,000 shares of Industries stock held by the Eldridges. The Imperial Sugar Company was included in the purchase, since Sugarland Industries owned 86,350 of the 100,000 outstanding shares of Imperial common stock. Industries also bought the 500 shares of Industries stock left to the Laura Eldridge Hospital Association, and the 500 shares left to the Sugar Land Independent School District by Eldridge. The 40,000 shares thus bought by the Industries was retired, leaving ownership of Sugarland Industries vested in the 40,000 shares originally owned by the Kempner family. Sugarland Industries financed the purchase of the Eldridge family shares by selling land holdings in Cameron, Starr, Colorado, Fort Bend, and Harris Counties. The Colorado County property which was sold at that time was the 4,700 acre farm and company town of Eldridge, which Mr. Eldridge sold to Sugarland Industries in 1927.

Finally, for the first time, the Kempners were totally in charge of policies at Sugar Land, and this was a dynasty which has continued at Imperial for over forty years until the present time; under the successive leadership of I. H. Kempner, his two sons, Herbert and Harris, and Herbert's two sons, Denny and James. The Kempner family was then sole owner (except for the small number of shares of Imperial stock held by the public) of nearly everything in the company owned town of Sugar Land and some 11,000 acres around the town. Visco Products had a small plant on the west side of the town, Marshall Canning Company was operating in a leased building known as the old Sealy Mattress Building. The Southern Pacific and Missouri Pacific had rail lines through the town; there were some Houston Light & Power lines and some gas lines through the properties; but everything else in the 11,000 acre holding was owned by the Imperial Sugar Company or the Sugarland Industries.

Physically, the old company town had remained basically unchanged since about 1925. The population was just over 2,000, and the companies were occasionally hiring workers who commuted from surrounding communities. There had been a few new homes built, some streets paved, the school plant had doubled and the hospital improved, the paved road to Houston had been widened, but the town itself, the stores and the services were much the same.

Prior to the end of World War II Herbert had instructed Imperial's staff to prepare plans for a complete overhaul of the refinery properties. Anticipating similar programs from the many United States factories which had been unable to secure parts and materials, he had the staff file for the necessary priorities for the most critical requirements as quickly as possible. By the time the Kempner family bought out the Eldridge interests Herbert was ready to present his plan to the family, along with his preliminary estimate of $1,577,000 as the cost of the program for the first three years. He hired W. H. Louviere, an experienced sugar engineer, to develop and manage the reconstruction program.

It would have been just an ordinary building program, except for the complication that a train load of raw sugar was coming into Sugar Land from Galveston each day, and a 2,500,000 pound train load of refined sugar was being shipped to customers each day. The building program had to be done in such a manner that the routine was not interrupted while the refinery was in operation sixteen hours per day from five to seven days a week. This meant that some processes had to be temporarily rerouted around new building construction and then replaced back in the new building when it was completed. This program of bypassing, tearing down, and rebuilding continued for almost 6 years, but in the end Imperial could boast of a new, modern, and efficient cane sugar refinery.

While planning and initiating the capital rehabilitation program for the refinery, Herbert was also recasting the sugar sales program with a goal of holding the remarkable distribution of Imperial Sugar in Texas and Oklahoma which had been brought about by the wartime zoning regulations. These regulations had guaranteed the Imperial brand 100% distribution in most of the Texas and Oklahoma markets, and were expected to remain in effect well into 1947 until some semblance of normal world wide distribution of this commodity was resumed. Texas represented the second largest market for sugar in the west, next to California. The state was growing rapidly after World War II, and almost every sugar sales manager in the industry wanted a toehold. There was a huge perennial oversupply of refined cane and beet sugar west of the Mississippi compared to the sugar consumption in the area.

Anticipating that when the war time zoning restrictions were lifted at least a dozen aggressive competitors would return to the Texas and Oklahoma markets with a vengeance, Herbert decided to concentrate Imperial's sales effort in those two states. He brought R. M. Armstrong, who had been marketing Imperial Sugar in the north half of Texas, to Sugar Land to implement the program, enlarge the sales force and increase the advertising and promotional activities. He set up a plan of sugar quality control to insure that Imperial sugar was at least equal to the best competitive sugar available, and that the service from the refinery was everything any customer wanted it to be. In a series of meetings with company personnel he explained his programs in detail and asked for enthusiastic cooperation between departments to implement them.

Herbert emphasized that Imperial was planning to ask each customer to continue to give Imperial all its sugar business—which meant that Imperial would have to bend over backward to give each customer the very best in quality and service. "The customer is always right—never argue with a customer. Do what he asks and if it turns out that he was too demanding, one of our executives will talk to him later." Few customers ever took advantage of this; and when it was an obvious departure from the norm, it was seldom difficult to arbitrate.

Customer service became a common goal throughout the company. If a customer truck showed up at the plant on a day when the refinery was closed on a week end or holiday, the gatemen were instructed to call one of the shipping department managers to round up a loading crew. When the Missouri Pacific trainmen who handled the switching of raw sugar into the plant and refined sugar outbound went on a strike, threatening customer service, an amateur crew of Imperial junior executives and a Missouri Pacific supervisor managed to switch trainloads of sugar in and out of the refinery for several days until the strike was over. Of the six Imperial psuedo-railroad men, one, Bob Hanna, is now Imperial Holly's president and CEO; two more, Jim Skiles and Bill Coker are vice presidents.

One valuable byproduct of Herbert's program was the enhanced pride of the employees—pride in being part of a company which made the best sugar and gave the best service, a pride which resulted in people wanting to see things done right, the plant kept clean, the Imperial trucks sparkling on the highways.

Television was still just a gleam in the eye of the electrical manufacturers. Imperial enlarged its consistent advertising schedules in Texas newspapers, large and small, and in the local radio stations. Offering a series of Imperial Sugar cookbooks, free with a cutout of the red "pure cane" block from an Imperial package, and participating in all sorts of grocery promotions and industry activities, the company promoted its brand intensively—much more heavily than its competitors. It had several advantages in its proximity to its Texas market. One was a Texas loyalty to Texas products, and Imperial was the only sugar refinery in the state, a point which it emphasized. Its proximity to the market gave it an advantage freight-wise, and an ability to meet customers' needs more quickly. Competitors, all of whom historically spread their sales activities over several states, of which Texas was only one, still fell far short of Imperial's concentrated Texas effort. Customers often expressed surprise at the intensity of Imperial's sales effort. Territorial and headquarters sales representatives and brokers were told that, "You folks from Imperial go after the sugar business as though you didn't already have all of it." All this, taken in conjunction with the headstart given the company by the wartime zoning regulations and its long history of statewide activity going back to the early days of the Kempner-Eldridge partnership, resulted in Imperial's continuing domination of the rapidly growing Texas market. The company went after the smaller Oklahoma market as well as the bordering cities in New Mexico and

Louisiana with the same intensity, but with not quite the same success. It continued to market some twenty percent of its output in the Midwest; in Kansas City, Milwaukee, Minneapolis, Chicago, but with a far less intensive sales program.

Imperial was manufacturing a complete line of grocery packages. Granulated sugar was available in two, five, ten, twenty-five and fifty pound paper bags; powdered and brown sugars in one pound boxes and cube sugar in one and two pound boxes. For the food processing industries it supplied hundred pound, fifty and twenty-five pound bags of granulated sugar, powered sugar and brown sugar. It also produced special grain sizes for some manufacturers, such as the large, oblong crystals used on gum drop candies. Shipments to customers were mostly by rail, as rail rates were reasonably low, and the freeways and highways which later brought trucks into the plant were not yet in place.

Two new products were added to the sugars available to the industrial food processors: liquid and bulk sugars delivered from the refinery in specially designed tank trucks and tank rail cars to large users of sugar for the processing of food products—soft drinks, candies, dairy products, bakeries, canners, etc. These innovations eliminated the need for manhandling of the heavy 100 pound bags in food processing plants and resulted in considerable reductions in handling costs both in the refinery and in the customer's plant. Imperial engineers assisted the customers in designing and building the necessary liquid and bulk sugar handling systems in customers' plants and even financed the equipment if requested. Since the storage tanks in customers' plants which received bulk or liquid sugars were not large enough to store extensive inventories of these products, Imperial's fleet of bulk and liquid trucks and rail cars were able to provide better and more reliable service than its competitors.

The sales program was begun at once, in mid-1946. The zoning restrictions and rationing regulations were lifted at the end of 1947, and competition did indeed return with a vengeance. But the sales program was effective, and Imperial managed to keep over ninety percent of the grocery sugar business in Texas and a satisfactorily high share of the food processing business, a success which was aided in no small degree by the continuing insistence on quality of product and service to the customers. The combined capital improvement and sales programs were profitable to the company and to its employees, as well as to the town of Sugar Land, in regular operations with quite a bit of overtime pay, no layoffs, and steadily increasing wage rates and fringe benefits.

The company's policy was to pay rates generally comparable to those paid by other competitive cane sugar refiners. Sugar company wage rates, which, during the depression of the 1930's had reached a low of 15 cents per hour for basic labor, burgeoned during the World War II years to $1.00 per hour. By 1960, the base wage would have risen to $2.22, in 1970 to $3.17, in 1980 to $7.47 in 1986 to $10.18 and in 1990 to $11.00. Skilled wages were generally about 25% to 40% above the base rate. In spite of the 400% increase in wages, the companies had not increased the rental on company houses in twenty years. The owners, appreciative of the work force they had built up, were simply not interested in pressing for a few dollars more in rent or services—their company town was working out too well.

After a short illness, Gus Ulrich passed away on January 22, 1947. He had been vice president and manager of nearly everything in Sugar Land for almost forty years. Next to Mr. Kempner and Mr. Eldridge, Ulrich had been the man most responsible for the building and operating of the many business enterprises of the Sugarland Industries, the Imperial Sugar Company, and the company town. He had been "Mr. Sugar Land."

Industries was fortunate to have the service of Thomas L. James, who had come to Sugar Land in 1929 as a stenographer to Ulrich. In that capacity, James had been in a position to observe and take part in the wide range of activities which Ulrich managed, and in later years, Ulrich entrusted James with more and more responsibility. James had also attended the meetings of the trustees of Industries as secretary. He was thoroughly familiar with the activities of the company. Mr. I. H. Kempner, president of Sugarland Industries, a position he had held since its formation, made James vice president and general manager, and later promoted him to the office of president when Mr. Kempner was elected chairman. James would oversee the management of this complex of farms, real estate and variegated small businesses for the next twenty-six years.

By 1948 the refinery capacity at Sugar Land had been increased to 2,500,000 pounds per day, and the new modernization program was adding to the daily output slowly but surely. It was interesting that as a bottleneck developed at one station, for example the evaporators, the addition of evaporator capacity provided some increase in refinery output, but also moved the bottleneck to another overloaded station, such as the centrifugals. Development of increased capacity at the refinery has progressed as a series of bottleneck crackings to this day.

Sugar Land still had a population of about 2,000, little changed in the past two decades. The daily output of the refinery had almost doubled in that period, but automation and increased efficiencies had made it unnecessary to bring in additional employees. Employees who retired or passed on seemed to be replaced when necessary by members of the younger generations who had grown up in Sugar Land. It was a community which raised its own replacement work force.

As the decade of the 1940's came to an end it was evident that Herbert Kempner's long range plans were working out. Over $4,000,000 had been spent on the plant improvement program, with dramatic results in improved output and efficiencies, although the rising costs of labor and materials was becoming worrisome. Herbert expected that it would require another $1,000,000 on capital expenditures to complete the major requirements at the plant.

In 1949, both Imperial and the Sugarland Industries were operating profitably. Under the Kempner ownership the town was again prospering.

THE END OF THE COMPANY TOWN
1950-1960

In 1950, it was still a sleepy little country company town, with the homes and buildings clustered near the large sugar refinery which dominated the flat coastal landscape. It was bounded on the west by state prison farms, and on the other three sides by the company's vast expanse of cattle ranges, cotton fields, corn, rice, alfalfa and other crops. With its company stores, food processing plants, fuel and machine distributorships, bank, telephone company, its power plant, water wells, truck gardens, meat and vegetable markets and the many other local enterprises, it was still almost self-sufficient.

In the early 1950's, the original semicircular school complex on Lakeview had become impractical. It was crowded, the central heating systems for the individual buildings had become costly to operate, and all the flat roofs needed replacement. The individual buildings did not lend themselves to the new air conditioning systems. A new high school building was built along Lakeview and several new buildings were constructed inside the semicircles. The old semi-circular groups of class rooms were then torn down. The old auditorium, built in 1918, and the gymnasium, built in 1932, are still in service as part of what is now the Lakeview Elementary School.

In 1950, sugar sales passed 5,000,000 hundredweight for the first time in history. Almost all the sales increase was in Texas and the border states, and in its basic trade territory, Imperial was by far the largest supplier of refined sugar. Competition was keen. In the minds of most users and buyers, sugar was sugar; competitive pricing kept the prices of various brands pretty much the same. But Imperial's long time consistency in brand advertising, its superior service, proximity to the market, its larger sales force in that territory—not to overlook its long time mystique as the oldest business in Texas—combined to give Imperial the large share of the market. Particularly in Texas, where the company had enjoyed such as enviable reputation for so long, at times the Imperial brand occupied over 90% of the grocery shelf space, and maintained an enviable share of the industrial food processor business.

The capacity of the Imperial refinery had been increased to 2,800,000 pounds per day. The plant was operating sixteen hours per day on two eight hour shifts and employed 420 people, almost all of whom lived in Sugar Land. But Imperial's sales had increased to the point that they were exceeding the plant's capacity to produce. In addition, overtime operation was costly, as was the practice of shutting down the plant for eight hours out of each twenty-four.

The obvious solution was to run the refinery on three eight hour shifts daily, but that would necessitate an additional 100 workers for the third shift, and there were no empty houses in Sugar Land. Herbert Kempner felt that it was preferable that refinery shift workers live in the town, rather than commute to Sugar Land; but he was still committed to a capital program of modernizing and enlarging the refinery on a scale that made the building of new houses undesirable.

His solution was, for the first time, to make property ownership in the town available to employees for homesites. Lots were offered on Cleveland and Alkire Lakes and elsewhere to those employees occupying company owned houses who would be willing to start immediately on the construction of their private dwellings. Prices for the sites were low, from $500 to $2,500 per lot, with the added incentive that twenty-five percent of the cost of the lot would be refunded to all employees who could move out of their company houses and into their new homes by December 31, 1950.

This sparked a local housing boom of no mean proportions, and by the end of the year the company was able to offer vacated low-rental company houses to enough additional people to provide the work force necessary for a three-shift operation of the refinery. Imperial had no difficulty in attracting new employees of whatever skills were needed, because rentals in company houses were low, they were maintained in excellent condition and were close enough to the refinery that people could walk to work. Wages were comparable to those in Houston, the work was steady, and it was widely known in the area that Sugar Land had an excellent school system and was a good place in which to live and raise a family.

This small step toward individual home ownership in the company town was, although not realized at the time, the first phase of a process which would result in the incorporation of Sugar Land in less than ten years; probably inevitable anyway, given the impending rapid growth of Houston toward Sugar Land in the 1960's and 1970's.

The Kempners then turned their attention to the offices and the retail stores. Since the early 1900's, the office buildings, the huge general store and the various other retail establishments had been located in a number of one, two and three story corrugated iron buildings on the north side of what is now Highway 90-A. The office spaces were crowded, and the retail businesses were unable to accommodate the many new products and services which were coming into the market after World War II.

In 1950 the grocery department of the general store still operated as it had thirty years before. A housewife brought her grocery shopping list to the long counter and gave it to one of the clerks. The clerk laboriously assembled the items from a long line of shelves behind him, some of the shelves fifteen feet above the floor. The higher shelves were reached by a long ladder mounted on rollers at the top and bottom of the ladder; the intermediate shelves by a plier-like arrangement on the end of a long handle. It was slow and costly, difficult to maintain inventories, and the store simply could no longer compete with the new supermarkets which were becoming the vogue in Houston and Richmond. The old appliance department did not have room for all the new appliances. In fact, all the retail departments except the farm implement sections were sadly lacking in space.

The Kempners decided to present the town with a new and modern shopping center, the first in Fort Bend County. In December of 1950, Sugarland Industries let a contract for the construction of an $800,000 office and shopping center to be built on the south side of Highway 90-A. The new center was to be housed in a two story brick and glass building, about a block long, with a large paved parking area at the front. The upper story was planned to provide modern office space for both the Imperial Sugar Company and Sugarland Industries. The lower floor accommodated a grocery supermarket, a Western Auto appliance center, a dry goods store, a new bank with a modern vault, a barber shop, beauty parlor, a drug store with a gift shop, a small restaurant with soda fountain, a post office and an insurance office. The offices and all the stores moved into the new center in the summer of 1952 and were a source of much pride and convenience to the community. The old general store building remained where it was, but with more space available for its farm equipment, heavy hardware and furniture. The old vacated corrugated iron store buildings were torn down to make way for further expansion of the sugar refinery.

The old Imperial Bank & Trust Company, which had been formed in 1908 as the Imperial State Bank, moved into modern quarters in the new shopping center. In 1955, it received a new charter as the Sugar Land State Bank, in which the majority of the stock was sold to local businessmen and citizens of the community. T. L. James was elected president of the Sugar Land State Bank, and brought in L. J. "Jack" Merrigan as vice-president and cashier.

The Sugar Land Telephone Company, growing as the population of eastern Fort Bend county increased, needed new quarters and was moved to the second floor of Imperial's new engineering building. The telephone company then accommodated 948 customers in a five mile circle around Sugar Land. Robert Hill was named vice-president and general manager, as well as a director of the company and later became president. He was probably one of the few presidents in the telephone industry with practical experience in pole climbing.

In February of 1953, it was discovered that Herbert Kempner had a malignant growth on his lung, and after an operation by Dr. DeBakey, he soon learned that he had only a few months to live. He continued to come to his office in Sugar Land until just a few days before his death on October 20, 1953, and in the interim planned for his family and for the Sugar Land operations.

In the months preceding his death, Herbert wrote a detailed manual, planning the policies of the Imperial Sugar Company and Sugarland Industries, and describing the abilities and duties of the department heads of both companies. His detailed insight into the operations and possible future problems of each department, as well as his instinctive evaluation of each of the executives was perceptive and has proven to be correct. The pattern of capital improvements and growth which he set out has been appropriate to the sugar company for the thirty-seven years since his death and is in great measure responsible for the continued success of the company.

Three of his recommendations were to be particularly important to the sugar company's future. First, he urged that the program for quality of product and customer service be constantly monitored by management; second, that at least half the annual cash flow be plowed back into increased productivity, efficiency and capacity of the refinery, even if, when necessary, at the expense of dividend payments; and third, that the company promote top executives from within. He encouraged each department head to make certain he had an assistant well qualified to move up in case a promotion came the way of that department head, a program which naturally contributed to morale. Thirty years later, in the 1980's, Imperial was to survive a debacle among cane sugar refiners at least partly because of its adherence to Herbert's recommendations.

Sugar Land people had felt that he was one of them. The Kempner family came very close to disposing of the Sugar Land properties after Herbert's death, but in the end decided to continue. They contributed funds for a concrete stadium and an athletic field on Wood Street in Sugar Land, as well as $30,000 for accessories, in Herbert's memory. They also established three I. H. Kempner, Jr., scholarships to be awarded annually by the Imperial Sugar Company to graduates of the local high schools, the recipients to be chosen by the faculties. These awards continue to be much sought after by the students.

After Herbert's death, his brother Harris L. Kempner was elected to the board of directors of Imperial. W. H. Louviere who had been executive vice-president was promoted to president and R. M. Armstrong to executive vice-president. Ken Laird became sales manager. Louviere was the first president of Imperial who was not a member of the Kempner family.

Herbert Kempner's death was also a severe blow to the Industries. After concentrating his efforts in the late 1940's and early 1950's in renovating and reorganizing the Imperial Sugar Company, he had, after the death of Ulrich, devoted an increasing amount of his time to working with T. L. James on the affairs of the Sugarland Industries. The burden of overseeing the Sugar Land activities again fell heavily on Mr. I. H. Kempner, Sr., and his brothers, Dan, R. Lee and Stanley, as it had so many times in the past.

Included in the several recommendations made by Herbert Kempner before his death was the rebuilding of a number of houses. Among the 500 company-owned houses, there were some 200 substandard dwellings owned by Imperial and occupied predominantly by black and Hispanic employees and their families. The Kempners felt that those loyal employees deserved a better standard of living than had been available up to that time. Before his death, Herbert had recommended a program for improving the living conditions in this area, and in the late 1950's the work was begun. The plan was to provide new two and three bedroom houses and to tear down the old ones as they were vacated. Occupants of the old company houses would be given the opportunity to purchase the new dwellings on attractive terms—attractive enough that not a single employee failed to take advantage of the offer.

The new houses were priced at cost, in the range of $7,000 to $10,000, and could be bought with five percent down, the balance financed on FHA loans guaranteed by the company and paid back by payroll deductions over a negotiated period of time. Within fifteen years, all the mortgages were paid out, without a single foreclosure. Older, retired employees who did not feel that they could buy a house were moved into some nicer company owned dwellings which were left after so many employees moved into the new houses. This program, of course, was one more step away from company ownership of homes in Sugar Land. At this point, almost half the homes in the company owned town were privately owned, almost all by employees of the Imperial Sugar Company or Sugar Land Industries.

By the mid-1950's, one could stand on the top floor of the refinery and watch the approach of the four to six lane Southwest Freeway from Houston toward Sugar Land. The rapid expansion of Houston, one of the country's fastest growing cities at that time, was forcing that city's limits ever closer to Sugar Land; stores, huge shopping centers, office buildings, and residential subdivisions were following the completion of each mile of the freeway. The view from the refinery was a forerunner of complete change in the company town and the lifestyle of the area.

On a trial basis, anticipating the movement of Houston families into the Sugar Land area as the freeway approached, Sugarland Industries formed the Belknap Corporation and began the development of several subdivisions around the periphery of the town. Lots were sold on both sides of Oyster Creek, and a new subdivision named Imperial Estates was established north of town; to be followed by other developments such as Brookside, Belknap, Alkire Lake, Horseshoe Lake and others south and east of town. Movement of families into these areas was slow but steady, and most of the newcomers were from Houston. More and more Houstonians would begin looking to Sugar Land as a bedroom community. The town was no longer populated exclusively by the employees of the local industries, farms and stores.

Next, Sugarland Industries dredged out a system of interconnecting lakes and waterways around which they would lay out some 300 waterfront lots. Located just south of Highway 90-A on the east side of town, the development was named Venetian Estates. Lot sales were slow for the first few years, but as the area grew more accessible to Houston workers, it became a growing bedroom community, one of the more attractive home areas in Fort Bend County.

Industries also opened a 1,000 acre industrial subdivision for office buildings and light industry. The acreage was just north of the Southern Pacific tracks, one mile east of Sugar Land. Streets, utilities and landscaping were installed, and several new industries moved in. Among the early arrivals were Johnson Testers and Vector Cable, both subsidiaries of the Schlumberger Corporation. They were followed by Sperry Sun and the Baylor Company, along with several smaller entities. These companies brought hundreds of employees with them, many of whom bought or built houses in Sugar Land.

In 1958, Dr. L. A. Wheeler, a much-respected Sugar Land dentist and president of the Sugar Land school board, managed to persuade the Missouri City-Stafford group to join in the formation of the consolidated Fort Bend Independent School District. The new district purchased an eighty acre tract on the east side of the Sugarland Industries farm lands. It began construction of the John Foster Dulles High School and an administration building, the new facility opening in September, 1959. This plant grew rapidly with the addition of several high school and junior high school facilities, athletic fields, an auditorium and auxiliary structures. This was the initial campus from which the Fort Bend

Independent School District would grow to be one of the largest and most respected districts in the state in the 1980's.

All these changes—the new homes, the rapidly increasing population around the edges of 'old Sugar Land'—brought the old Harris-Fort Bend Telephone Company, whose franchise territory included most of Eastern Fort Bend County, into the modern era. Anticipating more rapid growth than its current facilities could handle, the company began construction of a complete new telephone exchange and office building to be opened the following year, located on a wooded one acre tract just east of the Sugar Land business district on Highway 90-A. The building was designed to house the newest and most sophisticated electronic equipment which was becoming available and which would permit conversion to a fully automated dial system. The headquarters would also allow for future expansion of the system. In 1959, the conversion was made to an all dial system, and the company was proud that it had finished its changeover ahead of the Southwestern Bell Company in Houston. At this point the company changed its name back to the Sugar Land Telephone Company.

The older citizens, while appreciative of the new dial system, were nevertheless disappointed to leave the era of the telephone operator. People had become accustomed to calling the operator for everything from weather predictions to the whereabouts of a spouse. A man might call his home phone number and be told by the operator, "Sorry, but your wife is playing bridge at Mrs. Thompson's. Do you want to call her there?"

The old Laura Eldridge Memorial Hospital, built at Wood and Lakeview in 1923, was badly in need of expansion and modernization. The original $165,000 endowments from Sugarland Industries and the Missouri Pacific Railroad had not only been preserved but had grown to over $450,000. This was largely because the Sugarland Industries and the Imperial Sugar Company had followed a practice of underwriting all losses of the hospital association and at times had made further contributions to the fund. Under the guidance of G. D. Ulrich and T. L. James over the years, the money had been invested wisely. Medical care had been excellent, but by 1956 the old facilities were outmoded.

The Association authorized the construction of a new, modern thirty-one bed hospital on Eldridge Road at Lakeview, to be enlarged to one hundred beds if needed in the future. The building was completed in 1957 at a cost of $350,000. As usual, it had the best facilities and equipment available at the time and was an important benefaction to the community. Although most of its patients were local employees, it was open to the Sugar Land newcomers who worked in Houston and elsewhere, as well as to people from nearby communities.

The original employee medical and hospital program, initiated in 1923 by the Laura Eldridge Hospital Association, continued to provide generous health care benefits to employees of the local companies at a cost of $1.50 per month deducted from their paychecks. The community and the hospital were fortunate to have the services of Dr. Carlos Slaughter from 1925 until his death in 1981. Although assisted at various times by other doctors, he was the "medicine man" of Sugar Land. Dr. Slaughter often said in his later years that he had delivered most of the population of Sugar Land into this world.

By the mid 1950's the Sugarland Industries was, at least temporarily, benefitting from the increasing population of the Sugar Land area and was then managing a diversified assortment of activities, much as it had in the past, as shown in the following charts:

ORGANIZATION CHART
SUGARLAND INDUSTRIES, INC.

	Wholly Owned Subsidiaries		Affiliated Companies
Sugarland Motor Co.	Sugar Land Truck Lines, Inc.	Texas National Warehouse Co.	Alcorn Farms Inc.
New Cars			Belknap Realty Company
Used Cars			Fort Bend Cattle Co.
Parts			Foster Farms Inc.
Service			Sugar Land Telephone Co.
Humble Station			
Texaco Station			
Truck Leasing			

Departments

Retail Departments	General Departments	Agricultural Departments	Miscellaneous Departments
Super Market	Feed Mill	Blacksmith Shop	General Office and Accounting
Drug Store	Dehydrating Plant	Alfalfa	Credit and Collection
Fountain	Cotton Gin	Johnsongrass	Engineering
Hardware	Cotton Buying	Corn	Electrical
Dry Goods	Cottonseed	Cotton Day Labor	
Appliance	Certified Cottonseed	Cotton 1/2 Tenant	
Lumber Yard	John Deere Farm Equipment Agency	Cotton 1/4 Tenant	
7-11 Drive In	Humble Bulk Agency	Feedlot Calves	
	Shipping Center Building	Pecan Orchard	
	Miscellaneous Rental Property		

Along with all the changes which were taking place in the community, the Imperial Sugar Company was continuing to keep pace with the growth in its trade area, and with developments in the industry. Until the mid-1950's, Imperial had been conducting its raw sugar receiving and storage operation in leased space on the docks at Galveston. Raw sugar in 300 pound bags were manhandled from the holds of ocean going vessels, across the docks and into the warehouses, then from the warehouse into box cars for transshipment to Sugar Land—about a trainload per day.

This cumbersome and difficult system changed in the early 1950's, as, all over the world, shippers of raw sugar were discovering the many advantages of handling this product in bulk form instead of in the heavy and cumbersome bags. There were equal advantages to refiners in receiving raw sugars in bulk, but, in order to do so, Imperial had to construct an entire new plant on the docks at Galveston.

The new facility covered five acres, featuring an automated warehouse capable of storing 60 million pounds of raw sugar. An enormous dock-side crane with a capacity of 10,000 pounds per scoop, moved along the docks from one ship's hold to another, depositing the raw sugar onto a system of conveyor belts by which it was transported into the warehouse. From the warehouse it could be transferred, again on a system of belts, into box cars for transshipment to Sugar Land. Later, a second crane was added to increase the speed of unloading, and to provide a backup in case of breakdown. Rail shipments from Galveston to Sugar Land still amounted to about a trainload per day, and represented almost 75% of the incoming dry cargoes received by ship into Galveston.

To accommodate the new bulk shipments from Galveston, Imperial, of necessity, had to construct an identical handling and warehousing system at the refinery in Sugar Land. The two systems represented a cost of some $3,000,000, but brought the company into the modern world of more efficient handling of its raw material.

One of the largest suppliers of bulk raw cane sugar to the United States at that time was the Hawaiian Islands, which produced about 1,000,000 tons annually. Of this, two thirds was shipped to the California & Hawaiian Sugar Refining Corporation, a cooperative owned by the Hawaiian sugar growers. The other one third was normally shipped to East Coast and Gulf Coast refiners. In 1956, Imperial entered into a ten year contract with C&H to buy approximately 200,000 tons of bulk raw sugar per year from Hawaii. This amount represented approximately twenty percent of the Hawaiian crop and about sixty percent of Imperial's projected annual requirements. The balance of Imperial's bulk raw sugar needs could be obtained by rail direct from several raw sugar mills in Eastern Louisiana, and by boat from Caribbean suppliers as well as other cane sugar-producing countries.

An interesting sidelight to the Hawaiian contract was that it led indirectly to the sale by the Kempner family of 25,000 shares of the common stock of the Imperial Sugar Company to C&H. This was twenty-five percent of the 100,000 shares then outstanding. The reason for the sale of the Imperial stock to C&H was Mr. I. H. Kempner's concern about the liquidity of the family investments, and the possible impact of inheritance taxes on some members of the Kempner

Imperial's raw sugar handling facilities at Galveston. The two cranes are unloading barges from Florida.

Imperial Sugar Company

1987   25,000 tones of Hawaiian raw sugar being unloaded at Imperial's facility at Galveston, to be stored and shipped to Sugar Land by rail.

family. At that time he welcomed the opportunity of raising a substantial cash fund for the stock while still retaining control of the company.

Shortly after the sale, Imperial split the stock two for one, which resulted in there being 300,000 shares outstanding of which C&H owned 75,000 shares, the Kempner family 180,000, with the balance of 45,000 in the hands of the public. The percentages then were Kempners sixty percent, C&H twenty-five percent, and the public fifteen percent.

In order to render better service to liquid sugar customers in North Texas, Imperial had been operating a liquid sugar distribution system in the Dallas area, and by 1950 the volume of business was large enough to justify the construction of a new and modern plant in Arlington, between Dallas and Fort Worth. This new plant received liquid sugar in tank cars from Sugar Land, then shipped tank truck loads to North Texas and Southern Oklahoma customers.

For some time the city of Houston had been active in extending its city limits to take in several nearby communities near its perimeters, and it appeared that Sugar Land might possibly be among some of its future acquisitions. There were even rumors that Stafford and Missouri City, also in the path of the growth of Houston, were looking into the advisability of annexing Sugar Land for its growing tax base.

By then, it was becoming increasingly impractical for the companies to extend the type of subsidized city services provided for their employees to the growing number of citizens who had no connection with the companies—the expanding need for more police and fire protection, and garbage pickup for example. Also some of the new citizens, having no association with the companies which were managing the community and its services, were expressing a need to have a voice in the government of the community. A convincing case could be made that Sugar Land as a company town was fast becoming an anachronism.

There was really only one course open to the Imperial Sugar Company and the Sugarland Industries, and that was to move toward incorporation of the community. Early in 1958, the two companies joined in petitioning the state for a city charter. In anticipation of its approval, they began the procedure for turning the city over to its public.

Imperial offered its 200 remaining company houses for sale to those employees who were occupying them at the time. The two, three, and four bedroom houses, some with two baths, were sold to the employees occupying them for a minimum of $3,000 and a maximum of $8,000, which in some cases was little more than the value of the land. The Company required ten percent down and agreed to arrange ten or fifteen year financing through the local bank. The response, of course, was immediate, and before the end of 1958, all the houses were individually owned.

The Sugarland Industries elected to continue to own and rent out its 65 company houses, and for the time being, to continue their operation of most of the various businesses which had served the community for so long, and to carry on their farming, cattle, and real estate activities as in the past.

In 1959, the city was officially granted its charter, which was accepted by a vote of the new property owners. Elections for a mayor and five city councilmen followed shortly, and a planning commission was appointed to assure the orderly growth of the city.

Employees, who were overjoyed at the prospect of owning their own homes, particularly at such attractive prices and financing, also discovered the joys of paying taxes to the city, the county, and the school district. Heretofore, the two companies had taken care of the management of the community; now the citizens had a voice in the election of their own officials. Services previously provided by the Imperial Sugar Company and the Sugarland Industries, such as fire, police, some utilities, garbage collection, street maintenance and upkeep of the townsite, now became public matters. The Kempners instructed the executives of Imperial and Sugarland Industries to respect the management of elected officials and to refrain from exercising undue influence on city policies. They felt that the citizens here, as in other communities, could be trusted to govern fairly and that the local companies were better off relieved of the responsibilities of a growing community.

The first mayor of the incorporated city of Sugar Land was T. E. Harmon, the retired manager of the dry goods store. Five aldermen were also elected; W. A. Little, C. E. McFadden, Melvin Pomikal, J. R. Pirtle and Mrs. Minnie Ulrich. None were to receive any compensation for the first year, but thereafter the mayor was to receive $40 per month and the aldermen each received $20 per month. Harmon served as mayor until 1961; he was followed by W. A. Little, merchandise manager for Sugarland Industries, 1962-1964; T. E. Harmon again, 1965-1967, then C. E. McFadden, manager of the Marshall Canning Company, 1968-1972; Roy Cordes, owner of the local dry cleaning plant, 1973-1981; Walter McMeans, a Houston lawyer who lived in Sugar Land, 1981-1986; then Lee Duggan, a local businessman and investor, 1987 to the present.

For the first few years as a city, most of the elected officials were employees of either the Sugarland Industries or the Imperial Sugar Company; not through any coercion by the companies, but simply because the majority of the voters at that time worked for one of the companies and preferred to vote for their long-time neighbors and fellow employees. However, as the city grew, the majority of the voters became what the old Sugar Landers would call "newcomers," who worked elsewhere but lived in Sugar Land, and by the mid-1980's none of the elected officials were in the employ of either of the original companies.

The transition from a company town to a chartered city government posed a number of problems, but the Imperial Sugar Company and Sugarland Industries worked closely with the Mayor and the City Council to effect the change as smoothly as possible. Initially, the newly incorporated city of Sugar Land had no money in its coffers, so the Imperial Sugar Company advanced funds when needed to carry the community over until the first tax funds were available. The city passed a revenue bond issue to buy the water and sewer system from the companies. Some of the streets and roads in Sugar Land had long since been dedicated to the county, some were still owned by the companies; all were dedicated back to the city. The companies gradually turned over to the city the other services such as garbage collection, fire and police protection. For example, after the incorporation, the city took over the control of the volunteer fire department, but the employees of the Imperial Sugar Company and Sugarland Industries, who made up almost all the volunteer personnel, were still allowed to leave their jobs when the fire whistle blew and to return when the emergency was over.

At this point, the old closed structure of the company town had become a thing of the past, and the community, although separately incorporated, was beginning to function as an outlying suburb of Houston, instead of a separate and isolated small town with its own tradition and ways. Now only those who grew up in the area before the 1960's can remember when Sugar Land, Stafford, Missouri City, Alief, Addicks, and Katy and many another community were really isolated small towns, rather than just names of different areas on the suburban map of Houston. From then on, local churches started to fill up with as many newcomers as old 'Sugar Landers.' Workers and executives in the sugar company and the many new businesses which located in the Sugar Land area were often commuters from other communities.

Curtis Hall, who previously served as labor boss and town constable for thirty years, was interviewed in 1958 by a local newspaper about the absence of crime when Sugar Land was a company town. He was quoted as saying, "Busy people with good jobs, security and nice homes just don't get into much trouble. They don't have the time or the inclination. This was a family town. It's the loafers who commit crimes and we just don't have any of them and never have had."

The constable's words were remindful of the day in the 1950's when he was called and asked for the key to the old one room jail, which the company was planning to tear down because it needed the space for a new refinery adjunct. He replied that he didn't have the key to the jail, and when asked, "If the chief and only law enforcement official of the town doesn't have a key to the jail, who does?" He stated that, "The Lions Club has the key—that's where they keep their popcorn machine and their bingo stuff."

Thirty years after incorporation, the old timers, veterans of the old company town era, still viewed the new surroundings and changed patterns of everything from shopping to traffic with barely concealed nostalgia. They liked it better the way it had been.

1960   The company town of Sugar Land. The railroad tracks were the main line of the Southern Pacific from New Orleans to the West Coast. The highway was the road from Houston to San Antonio, originally an Indian and later a Spanish trail from the Gulf Coast to San Antonio.

EPILOGUE

Officially, the company town itself was a thing of the past, but the two major entities, the Imperial Sugar Company and the Sugarland Industries continued to operate much as they had in recent years. The sugar refinery continued to run from five to seven days per week, continued to expand its capacity and kept its systems modern and efficient by investment of retained earnings. Sugarland Industries continued to rent out its sixty-five company homes on the south side of town, almost all to employees of Industries or the sugar company, to operate its several small businesses and to farm most of its remaining 8,700 acres of land.

Most of the employees now lived in their own homes, either homes bought from the Imperial Sugar Company or in newer homes bought in one of the local subdivisions. During the 1960's and 1970's their daily routines would be little different from the days of the company town—same jobs, same local shopping center, same proximity to work, same churches, schools and hospital, usually the same neighbors.

In 1966, the Imperial Sugar Company bought back the 75,000 shares of its common stock which had been sold to the California and Hawaiian Sugar Company in 1956. This stock was retired to the treasury, leaving 225,000 shares of common stock outstanding, of which the Kempner family owned some 180,000.

On July 31, 1967, the companies and the community mourned the death of I. H. Kempner. Although he was 94 years old, he had maintained an active interest in events at Sugar Land and had continued to chair the board meetings of both the Imperial Sugar Company and Sugarland Industries until a few months before his death. More than any other person, he had been responsible for the quality of life and the quality of employment in Sugar Land, and for the successes of the many and varied enterprises he controlled. He had been a kind and concerned man, and he had set an example of devotion to his principles; qualities which were also manifest in the attitudes of the other members of the Kempner family toward the community and its people.

Harris Kempner, Mr. I. H. Kempner's oldest son, was elected chairman of the board of Sugarland Industries and of the Imperial Sugar Company. In the long history of both companies, he was the second board chairman.

A graduate of Harvard University, he had assumed the management of the family's worldwide cotton business as Mr. I. H. and Dan became less directly active; he had also become involved in the numerous other Kempner enterprises. In 1967, he was a trustee of H. Kempner, a trust association; chairman of the board of the United States National Bank of Galveston; vice president and

161

1961   Lee and I. H. Kempner at the celebration
of Mr. I. H.'s 88th birthday.

director of Sugarland Industries, Inc.; and chairman of the Harris and Eliza Kempner Fund. He was sixty-four years old. His business career had included active leadership in a number of industrial and civic organizations including the Galveston and New Orleans Cotton Exchanges, Texas Cotton Association, American Cotton Shippers Association, and the Galveston Chamber of Commerce. He had served all these organizations as director, vice president, or president. He was decorated with the Legion of Merit for his World War II service as a Commander in the United States navy, and served as a Commodore of the Galveston Yacht Club.

Following his election, Harris wished to reassure the employees and members of the community of the Kempner family's desire to continue their ownership of the activities in Sugar Land. In September 1967 he made the following statement to the editor of the *Imperial Crown*, which was widely distributed throughout the community.

"My selection as chairman of the board of Imperial Sugar Company—the position my father had filled so ably for so many years—brings to mind a good deal of Sugar Land history.

"I remember my first trip to Sugar Land in 1910 or 1911 when I first accompanied my father on one of his periodic visits. In those days the best way to get to Sugar Land was to take the train or interurban from Galveston to Houston, and then get on the Southern Pacific, which was not supposed to stop in Sugar Land; so it was necessary to let down the gate at the Sugar Land Junction, and we would hastily disembark at this unscheduled stop.

"We arrived in the evening and spent the night at the old Eldridge home in the shadow of the char house, but it took me quite a few trips before I could get very much sleep because the trains passing on the track just in front of this house sounded exactly as if they were coming into the room.

"It is almost impossible to imagine how far Sugar Land has come since those days when the streets were full of pot holes, mud was everywhere, the atmosphere was greatly influenced by the convicts who worked the sugar fields; there was no school system, no hospital; the relatively few houses were neatly kept but by no means show places!

"The sugar mill was antiquated and the refinery, like everything else, needed large infusions of money and planning.

"On these early trips I had the opportunity to observe how determined was my father to build up not only the industry at Sugar Land but also the community so that those who were working with us would not only be proud of the company for which they worked, but also of the community in which they lived, and would have facilities and amenities of living as the community grew and prospered.

"The project was undercapitalized at the start, and the pursuance of this ideal called for larger and larger infusions of capital. As a result, all the earnings were plowed back for many years while stockholders waited for the dividends on their investments.

"The ideal was also close to the heart of my brother Herbert, who from an early age was determined to devote his business energies to the Sugar Land project, and I am sure numbers of you remember with what intelligence and devotion he directed the affairs of the Company until his untimely death in 1953.

Harris L. Kempner

"My father, who tended to denigrate his own achievements, was immensely proud of what Herbert had done, and felt highly gratified that Denny followed in his father's footsteps at Sugar Land.

"I assume this position of the chairman of the board with great confidence in the fact that our associates in the management and operation of Imperial have proved their high capabilities in a very competitive industry, and share the family's continuing desire to bend every effort to improve both the Company and the community.

"As testimony to the continuing family determination, I point to the fact that the Board of Directors of the Imperial Sugar Company also includes my cousin, Mrs. Mary Kempner Thorne; my cousin, Dan Oppenheimer; my son, Harris L. Kempner, Jr.; and my nephew, I. H. Kempner, III, who is also active in the daily affairs of the Company as raw sugar manager, and secretary-treasurer."

Harris Kempner served as chairman of the board of Sugarland Industries and Imperial Sugar Company until 1971. In that year, following his long practice of encouraging younger family members to assume as much responsibility as they could manage, he voluntarily resigned both positions so that Denny Kempner could succeed him. Denny, more formally known as I. H. Kempner, III, was the son of Herbert Kempner, who had been Imperial's president until his death in 1953. Denny had been active in the daily management of both Industries and Imperial since 1964, and was eminently qualified to take over the reins.

Herbert Kempner's recommendations, made before his death in 1953 for the management of the Sugar Land companies, continued to set the pattern until the present. Quality of product and customer service continued to be the foremost criteria by which the performance of the plant and its employees were evaluated. Imperial was still determined to deserve its customers loyalty. Approximately half the annual cash flow of the Imperial Sugar Company and Sugarland Industries was regularly reinvested in capital improvements, at times to the detriment of dividend payments to the owners. Promotions to executive positions were made from within the companies. At Sugarland Industries, Tom James continued as president from 1950 to 1973 when the company was liquidated. At Imperial, the next four presidents, W. H. Louviere from 1953 to 1964, R. M. Armstrong from 1964 to 1973, H. L. Williams form 1973 to 1979 and R. C. Hanna from 1979 to the present, all had been department executives for many years and all had served several years as executive vice president prior to taking over the top management. Leon Anheiser, whose father, mother, brother and sister were also employed by Imperial, is now vice president, refinery operations. He had graduated from Sugar Land High School, then from the Audubon Sugar School of Louisiana State University on an I. H. Kempner, Jr., scholarship. A. M. Bartolo, now executive vice president and chief operations officer of Imperial Holly, also a graduate of Louisiana State University, has been with the Imperial Sugar Company since 1958. W. A. Little, whose title is Senior Vice President, Sales and Marketing, had held various executive titles both with Imperial and Sugarland Industries since 1957. J. R. Skiles, vice president, distribution, has been with Imperial since 1956; W. A. Coker, Jr. vice president, transportation and traffic, since 1966 and R. E. Henderson, vice president and

I. H. "Denny" Kempner, III

treasurer, since 1967—a well seasoned and proven staff of executives, all brought up through the ranks in the Kempner tradition.

Although Sugar Land was now a full-fledged incorporated community, it was to be several years, perhaps until the early 1970's, before the flavor of the old company town lifestyle was lost in the rapid growth of Houston toward the Southwest. But in increasing numbers, around the periphery of this cluster, more and more new houses and subdivisions were springing up, and more "outside" people were moving into Sugar Land.

When, in the late 1960's, the Southwest Freeway reached toward the center of the Sugarland Industries' farm lands and across the edge of Sugar Land itself, the process accelerated. The Kempners, led by Harris and Denny, anticipating even more explosive activity from the growing Houston economy, made plans to control the quality of the impending growth in residential and commercial development of the Sugarland Industries' remaining 8,700 acres of farm lands.

They had been impressed with the manner in which Jake Kamin of Houston and his associates had planned and developed a complete new community called Nassau Bay, to serve the NASA space center. Before construction they had prepared a display table depicting a miniature model of the suburban community as it would appear when complete, including houses, buildings, streets and facilities, even to the fire plugs and the sailboats on the bay. After the city was completed the developers had an aerial photograph taken—it matched every detail of the layout on the display table.

This display and the Kamin plans for a similar suburban program at Sugar Land were suitably impressive to Harris and Denny and they agreed to a tentative sale of 1,200 acres to be developed by Kamin and his associates, subject to the approval of Harris's brother-in-law, Dan Oppenheimer, who headed a private family-owned bank in San Antonio.

After Kamin had given Dan a thorough tour of the Nassau Bay properties the two men repaired to a coffee shop to debate the final terms of the sale. Following considerable discussion and before leaving the coffee shop, they wrote out and signed the details of their agreement on the back of a coffee stained paper napkin. The Kempners felt confident that this group could be depended upon to build a high quality residential suburb which would set the tone for the future development of the remaining 7,500 acres of Sugarland Industries' farm lands in the neighborhood.

They were correct in their assessment of the Nassau Bay developers. This group, headed by Jake Kamin, David Searls, Stuart Morris, Dan Arnold and Don Russell, embarked on a program to build a new and up-scale community of 3,500 new homes. They spared nothing to provide the best in planning and materials. The new area, named Sugar Creek, included a twenty-seven hole Robert Trent designed golf course, an elegant country club, tennis courts, shopping centers, office complexes, lakes and open spaces. By 1990, it had fulfilled all expectations, was ninety percent complete, and was indeed a prestigious and successful development. It also heralded the end of the old Sugarland Industries' conglomerate of small stores and service businesses which had served the community so well for so many years.

By 1970, each mile of new freeway continued to bring with it new stores, new and modern shopping centers, new service businesses. It also made it convenient for Sugar Land people to patronize these newer, more modern establishments with their greater choices of merchandise and facilities. The old retail stores in Sugar Land, handicapped by lack of size and by restrictions of their old union contracts, were simply unable to compete.

At the same time, all the activities along the freeway, and the rapid growth of the Sugar Creek community presaged new needs for expanded city, county and educational service, with predictable and resultant increases in land values and tax liabilities. The farm and cattle lands were already becoming unprofitable for these activities. In early 1972 the Kempners made a decision to enter into a program of complete and final liquidation of the Sugarland Industries within twelve months. The various businesses operated by the company, many of them for almost sixty years, were either sold or closed. The Kempner family insisted that Industries employees be taken care of one way or another. Some of the employees chose to work for the new owners of the stores, others were retired or offered jobs with the sugar company, the telephone company or the bank, all done in an orderly and compassionate manner.

Sugarland Industries' most valuable asset was the remaining 7,500 acres of farm and cattle land adjoining the town of Sugar Land and the new and prestigious Sugar Creek development. Land values were booming in the area which was obviously headed toward intense development. The Kempners felt that they had neither the expertise or the funds to enter into residential and commercial development of the properties on the scale which they envisioned.

They put the entire southern portion of the land, some 6,000 acres, up for bids and later included the 1,500 acre north tract. The successful bidder was the Gerald Hines interests, and the price for the 7,500 acres and the shopping center was $43,000,000; at that time one of the largest land sales in Texas' history. Hines formed a company named Sugar Land Properties to develop the land.

Shortly after this transaction was completed, the Imperial Sugar Company bought back the shopping center in Sugar Land. They remodeled this mostly into office space for the sugar company and built an adjoining office building for the Sugar Land Telephone Company.

Hines, an experienced and respected developer, encountered initial difficulties in flood control and other problems, but soon, with more than adequate financing, was able to proceed full speed on his elaborate plans for the area. And proceed he did. Suddenly the land was attacked by hordes of earth moving equipment. Levees sprang up around the property, the lands were leveled and drained by an elaborate network of drainage ditches; pumping stations were installed. Many miles of wide streets were created and attractively landscaped as they were finished.

A carefully designed golf course was sculpted, complete with lakes, streams, cart paths, and attractive plantings which included several thousand imported palm trees. The Sweetwater Country Club, which was to become the home of the Ladies Professional Golf Association, featured an enormous club house. In addition to the usual club facilities, it had indoor air-conditioned tennis courts as well as outdoor courts. There were indoor and outdoor swimming pools and indoor racquet ball courts. The three story club house itself towered over the surrounding developments.

Strategically located shopping centers appeared as more homes were built. The original plan included one huge shopping center so large it would require a tracked people-carrier to transport customers from one end to the other. Fort Bend Independent School District built an elementary school, a junior high school, and a senior high school in the area to take care of the growing family population.

Land in chosen areas was sold to carefully screened developers who would build in each area according to the Hines specifications. This was at the start of the Houston building boom, and it seemed that the expensive homes were being sold about as fast as they were completed. Several subdivisions were started at the same time, the most prestigious being Sweetwater in the golf course area. First Colony became a general development under which various subdivisions were formed, including Colony Bend, Williams Trace, Highlands, Sugar Lakes— by 1989 some 26 additional subdivisions had been added, with more being planned. There were open park areas, artificial lakes, some with attractive fountains. There were townhouse and condominium neighborhoods in various price ranges.

Hines set aside several large tracts for office buildings and various commercial activities, including the 1,500 acre north tract, north of the Southern Pacific tracks. Like the residential areas, they were beautifully landscaped and well kept. Each development featured wide streets and buildings designed to fit into the ambience of the area. Hines had been heard to say that he hoped that people who lived in his development could, if they wished, find business facilities or employment within the area. A diversified assortment of office and light industry activities, as well as shopping centers quickly moved in, followed by several large employers. Fluor Corporation constructed an international headquarters on a 300 acre tract, reportedly with office and laboratory facilities for 4,500 engineers and designers. Kaneb Corporation built an attractive building for its international headquarters. Reed Tool Company and Container Corporation both built large facilities on the north tract. Numerous office building and warehouse spaces sprang up.

Jake Kamin and his Sugar Creek development and Gerald Hines with his massive Sugar Land Properties project were driving the little town of Sugar Land toward the new and modern twenty-first century with a vengeance.

And it was all being done in an orderly manner, so that "old Sugar Land," itself a neatly arranged and planned town, was now surrounded on three sides by new, modern and well planned communities. On the west, south of Highway 90A, another large planned development, "New Territory" is under way. Also west of town, but north of Highway 90A, the prison farm lands of the Texas Department of Corrections will probably be sold some day, hopefully to a developer who will continue the pattern of quality facilities set by Kamin and Hines.

The local school system, which had graduated one student in 1918 and only 8 in 1926, is now a part of the Fort Bend Independent School District, with 20 elementary schools, seven junior high schools and four senior high schools.

The most recent high school opened with the appropriate name of the I. H. Kempner Senior High School. In 1990, the school population is 34,000 and growing rapidly. Plans are in the works for four new elementary schools, one new middle school and one more high school.

Twenty years after the incorporation of the city, the fire department was still a volunteer organization, and a good one, with a great deal of pride in its abilities. But as the town and its environs grew, it was no longer practical for the Imperial Sugar Company to supply enough volunteer firemen from its work force to help cover the entire community 24 hours per day, and there were not enough volunteers from the rest of the community. The town was simply getting too big to be completely protected by an all-volunteer fire department. In 1987, the first full-time paid fireman was hired, and Johnny Pokluda, an experienced volunteer, was hired as a full time fire chief. In 1989, Pokluda resigned and was replaced by Sugar Land's first lady fire chief, Diane Breedlove. By then the department had grown to include thirty-three full time paid firemen and provided twenty-four hour manning, seven days per week. There were now two modern fire stations with nine fire trucks and two Emergency Medical Service units.

After the town was incorporated in 1959, Curtis Hall continued to provide single handed police protection, while he was also the labor boss of the Imperial Sugar Company. In 1962, the city hired its first police chief, J. E. Fendley, who served until his retirement twenty years later, in 1982. By then he had a force of fifteen employees. Fendley was succeeded by Chief Larry Ross, who had grown up in Sugar Land. Since then, with the population growth in the area, the Sugar Land police force has increased to forty-five with nineteen police vehicles, with John W. Looper as chief.

The old Sugar Land Rail Road of the Cunningham and Eldridge days, sold by Eldridge to the Missouri Pacific in 1926, was finally abandoned and the tracks taken up to make way for development. The Missouri Pacific, now owned by the Union Pacific, still does the inplant switching of the raw and refined sugar cars. All the raw sugar for the Imperial refinery still arrives by rail from Galveston and Louisiana; most of the outbound refined sugar shipments are by truck instead of by rail. The new long distance freeways and higher rail freight rates have gradually forced the change-over to highway transportation for refined sugar to the Texas markets. Now, only 20% of Imperial's outbound shipments of refined sugar moves by rail—50% goes in customers' trucks, and the remaining 30% by company or common carrier vans.

In 1987, his many friends and co-workers were saddened by the accidental death of Harris Kempner in Galveston at age 84. Since his youth he had taken a personal interest in Sugar Land and its people, had served on the boards of directors as chairman, and had guided the affairs of the companies in the years following the death of his father, Mr. I. H. Kempner. He had been the second board chairman of the Imperial Sugar Company and the Sugarland Industries. Like his father and his brother, Herbert, Harris had personified the same warm and caring interest in the people of Sugar Land, and seldom endorsed a major decision without first inquiring as to the effect on the community.

The Sugar Land Telephone Company, now chaired by Denny Kempner and with R. C. Brown as president, continued its growth and by the late 1980's was serving some 25,000 customers, with a potential of perhaps 140,000. It had also diversified into a wide variety of modern communication services, part of an $85 million holding company formed by the stockholders of the telephone company— a far cry from its 1908 inception as a one line, two phone system from Eldridge to the refinery superintendent.

The Sugar Land State Bank, successor to the old Imperial Bank and Trust, had continued a steady growth, and in 1966, in answer to the need for more space, constructed a new and modern bank building banking facility on Highway 90-A about a half mile east of the shopping center, where it remains today, but with new owners and a new name. In 1972, the bank had merged with United States Bankshares of Galveston, (owned by the Kempner family) and the stockholders received stock in Bankshares. Jack Merrigan became president of the Sugar Land bank, a position he held until his retirement in 1981. He was succeeded by Charles Avery, who had been executive vice-president of the Galveston bank. In 1982, Bankshares was sold to the Cullen-Frost Bank of San Antonio and now operates in Sugar Land as Cullen Bank-Sugar Land.

At this point, the large Kempner holdings in Sugar Land, first established in 1906 and 1908 had been winnowed down by the march of progress in the area to the controlling ownership of the Imperial Sugar Company and the Sugar Land Telephone Company and its subsidiaries.

While these significant local changes were going on around it, the Imperial Sugar Company continued its pattern of strategic growth in its markets. Annual sales, which had been in the neighborhood of 2,000,000 cwt. in the 1940's, then 5,000,000 in the 1950's, had risen to 10,000,000 in the 1980's. Imperial was more than holding its own in the growing and highly competitive sugar market. Daily plant capacity was approaching 4,000,000 pounds per day, and Imperial continued its dominance of the refined sugar market in the Southwest. With most of its refined sugar moving outbound by trucks to its Southwestern market, Imperial's proximity to that market provided a distinct advantage in customer service; and the company was continuing its distinct predominance in sales and advertising efforts in the area.

In the 1970's, as the consumption of sugar continued to increase, Imperial bought 13 acres of land at Great Southwest industrial subdivision at Arlington, Texas, and built its own distribution plant, complete with tank storage and a blending system to blend sucrose and invert syrups, as well as various types of corn syrups to customers specifications. Part of the Imperial truck fleet for delivering liquid sugars was transferred to the Arlington plant. Later, in the 1980's, this Arlington plant was enlarged to receive bulk rail hopper cars of dry refined sugar. This bulk refined sugar was automatically unloaded into storage tanks, to be melted to make liquid sugar. In addition to its refinery at Sugar Land, Imperial was then operating a large installation at Galveston for raw sugar and another at Arlington for the manufacture and distribution of liquid sugar. And, along with the continuing growth of population in the Southwest, the per capita consumption of sugar, almost unbelievably, was growing. People find it hard to believe, but they are eating more sugar than ever—real sugar, too, not artificial sugar.

Epilogue

As the United States public was increasingly deluged with television, radio and newspaper advertising, as well as books and magazines, all bewailing the dire consequences of sugar consumption, many could envision the imminent demise of the sugar farming and processing industry. Quite to the contrary, it is alive and well and growing. Sugar industry figures, as well as statistics published by the Department of Agriculture show that the consumption of caloric sweeteners (cane, beet, corn sugar, and honey) in the United States during the thirty year period from 1930 to 1960 had remained fairly constant in the range of 100 to 115 pounds per person per year.[1] Just as a matter of human interest, or perhaps human frailty, it is startling to look at the same figures today. Now after decades of diets, "sugar free" advertising, weight watching, all sorts of sugar substitutes and adverse publicity, the per capita consumption of those same caloric sweeteners has risen—until in 1989 it had reached 134.2 pounds per person per year, and is still going up.[2] Our friends proudly tell us about their diets and how little sugar they eat; and it is probably true that they make reduced use of the sugar bowl; but the quantities of soft drinks, candy, ice cream, desserts, sweetened canned or bottled products consumed in the prosperous United States grows with each decade. An interesting independent survey of dry grocery sales in the Houston market for 52 weeks of 1988 shows sales of the five pound bag of Imperial sugar as the number one ranked seller in both pounds and dollars.[3] When one combines the population growth with the increasing per capita consumption of sugar, one can only conclude that it should continue to bode well for the United States sugar industry.

Imperial had managed to keep pace with the growth of the industry, and its program of concentrating its sales efforts in the growing Southwest had earned it an enviable competitive status in that area. Its profitable operation had enabled it to maintain its plants at Sugar Land, Galveston and Arlington, Texas, in peak condition and efficiency, and its financial condition was among the strongest in the industry.

In the mid-1980's, it was a good thing that the company's position was sound. In spite of the continuing growth in sugar consumption, a combination of circumstances brought about the downfall and closing of a number of long established cane sugar refineries in the United States; mainly refineries which had not been maintained at peak efficiency, or may have been in an unfavorable competitive situation, or poorly financed—or a combination of these factors. Beet sugar processors, enjoying certain advantages under sugar legislation, were not as exposed as the cane refiners.

A new liquid sweetener derived from corn, known as High Fructose Corn Syrup (HFCS) had come on the market at a substantially lower price than the established cane and beet liquid sugars. Not being controlled by the complexities of sugar legislation, as were the cane and beet sugar industries, the manufacturers of the new HFCS were able to price their products far under the high level of sugar prices maintained by the legislation, and as a consequence were able to take almost all the liquid sugar business in the United States away from the traditional suppliers. Within three years the cane and beet processors had lost some 20% of their total sugar sales to the newcomers. Most of this loss was felt by the cane sugar refiners because of their relatively vulnerable position

172

under current sugar legislation; and it was disastrous for some. In the seven year period between 1981 and 1988, nine long established East Coast and Gulf cane refineries had closed their doors and been dismantled.

In addition, the trend in sugar legislation and its application by government agencies was clearly creating a climate which might be threatening to some of the surviving cane sugar refineries. Once again, as had happened so many times in the past, the Kempner family, as majority stockholders, were forced to evaluate the options open to them in continuing the operation of the Imperial Sugar Company. And once again, they stepped into the breach. This time they took a step which was second in importance only to Mr. I. H. Kempner's founding of the Imperial Sugar Company in 1906.

In 1988, led by Chairman I. H. (Denny) Kempner, III and President R.C. Hanna, Imperial merged with Holly Sugar Corporation to form the Imperial Holly Corporation, combining Imperial's cane sugar refining activities with those of eight beet sugar processing plants operated by Holly in the western United States. The transaction was completed in April, 1989, when Imperial purchased, through a cash tender offer, two-thirds of the common stock of Holly; financed with an $81,000,000 loan, which was repaid during 1989 mainly with the funds realized through a $75,000,000 private placement. Imperial, in completing the acquisition, issued common shares in the new company in exchange for the remaining Holly shares. Ownership of the new Imperial Holly Company stock was then about 60% by Kempner family members, 10% by an Employee Stock Ownership Plan (ESOP), and 30% by public stockholders. The stock was initially listed on the "Over-the-Counter" market, but in August, 1989, the listing was changed to the American Stock Exchange, with the appropriate stock symbol of IHK.

Imperial Holly thereby became one of the nation's largest producers and marketers of refined sugar, producing a balanced combination of cane and beet sugar. Imperial continues to process raw cane sugar, as it had since 1906. Its Holly Sugar subsidiary continues to produce refined beet sugar by processing sugar beets at eight processing plants located in California, Wyoming, Montana and Texas. Holly also sells by-products (beet pulp and molasses) resulting from the manufacturing and refining procedures for use as livestock feed, carries on beet seed research and produces and markets beet seed. Shortly after the merger, the Imperial Holly bought the Brookfield Terminal, a distribution center for liquid and bulk sugars located near Chicago.

The ability of the merged companies to produce near-equal volumes of refined cane and beet sugar, totalling in the neighborhood of 25,000,000 hundredweight of product annually, is unique in the industry. This balance and diversity gives Imperial Holly the flexibility and ability to smooth out the peaks and valleys that may occur because of the uncertainties of nature as they affect agriculture. Further, it gives Imperial Holly a balanced position from which to deal with the uncertainties of farm legislation and government regulation.

The new company became the second largest publicly owned sugar processing company in the United States, with sales in fiscal 1990 of over $717,000,000, placing it among the prestigious Fortune 500's leading United States companies.

HOLLY SUGAR CORPORATION
Map of Facilities

Sidney

MONTANA

Sheridan

Worland

WYOMING

Torrington

Hamilton City

Tracy

COLORADO

Colorado Springs

CALIFORNIA

Betteravia
(Union Sugar)

TEXAS

Brawley
(Imperial Valley)

Hereford

▲ Factories
● Research
■ Offices Maintained

Holly Sugar Building, Colorado Springs, Colorado

Holly Sugar Corporation, Hereford, Texas

176

Holly Sugar Corporation, Worland, Wyoming

Holly Sugar Corporation, Torrington, Wyoming

Holly Sugar Corporation, Tracy, California

Holly Sugar Corporation, Hamilton, California

Holly Sugar Corporation, Brawley, California

181

Holly Sugar Corporation, Betteravia, California

182

1988   *The Imperial Sugar Refinery at Sugar Land. Buildings at the top are at the Hull Field Airport.*

It was a new experience in moving from a privately controlled to a public corporation, and involved the financing of a sizeable long term debt, something which Imperial had been without for over 20 years. James C. Kempner, Denny's younger brother, with many years of experience as an investment banker and finance officer, was brought into the Imperial Holly management team as executive vice-president and chief financial officer to handle the financial affairs of the merged company and to introduce management to the relative complexities of public ownership.

The principal product of the merged company, refined sugar, accounted for 92% of consolidated sales in fiscal 1989. The company produces and sells granulated white, brown and powdered, as well as liquid sugar to wholesalers, retail grocers and food manufacturers. Grocery product sales (1/3 of sugar sales) are made under the Imperial and Holly labels and increasingly, over the past fifteen years, under various private labels. Although Imperial Holly sales are generally concentrated in the western and mid-western states, sales were recorded in each of the 48 contiguous states in fiscal 1989.

The Sugar Land cane sugar refinery processes over four million pounds of raw sugar daily with 85% of the raw material provided by domestic producers (mainly Louisiana, Florida and Hawaii) and 15% from foreign sources. The beet sugar plants have a combined capacity of processing over 40,000 tons of sugar beets daily. About 1,500 independent growers are under contract, supplying the factories from more than 225,000 acres planted. The by-products of beet sugar processing (beet pulp and molasses) are sold as beef and dairy cattle feed to the domestic and foreign markets.

So, the old Imperial Sugar Company, the oldest business in Texas still operating on the same site, once the centerpiece of an 18,500 acre empire and company owned town, with its long history of ups and downs, had finally joined the big leagues.

But time and the march of progress had caught up with the little isolated, self-sufficient company town of the early 1900's, surrounded by its farm lands. Gone was all but a memory of a most unusual Texas company town. Gone also were the many conglomerated enterprises and small stores, the town services and finally the extensive farming and cattle lands of the Sugarland Industries.

In 1989, as air conditioned cars on concrete streets and freeways connect Sugar Land citizens with their air conditioned homes and offices, supermarkets, department stores, and country clubs, it is difficult even for the old-timers to visualize the area when the Karankawas probed in the swamps for clams—or the movement of Spanish troops as they crossed the creek between their missions and forts—or the plodding progress of the first settlers in their ox carts toward their promised leagues of land—or the Dilue Rose family and their neighbors fleeing across Oyster Creek during the "Runaway Scrape"—Santa Anna's army pillaging his way through Sugar Land—the first primitive raw sugar mill on the banks of the creek—the extensive pre-Civil War plantations in the Sugar Land area, or the deplorable episodes of slavery and convict exploitation at the "hell hole of the Brazos." However, they were all real enough in the dimming past of the area in which we live so comfortably.

184

Epilogue

Now, in 1990, it seems that the rapid growth experienced in the Sugar Land area in the early 1980's is again on the rise. Large new subdivisions are springing up south and west of the city, some of which will probably be annexed when the time comes. The day seems not too far off when the 4,400 acre lands of the Texas Department of Corrections on the western edge of Sugar Land will be more suitable for development than for prison activities. The miles between the Sugar Land city limits and the Brazos River to the south and west are wide open to development, and already plans are being discussed for providing the necessary drainage, highway and utility facilities in preparation for future residential and commercial enterprise.

And the story of the Imperial Sugar Company is far from over. The business, first started as a primitive family wooden cane crusher in 1830, then enlarged into a commercial raw sugar mill in 1843; then into a sugar refinery on the same site in 1900; continually enlarged and improved by the Kempner-Eldridge partnership, later by the Kempner family—then merged into the present Imperial Holly Corporation, is still vigorous and growing.

In spite of the many extraordinary expenses associated with the merger procedure and the ensuing reorganization, the new company turned in excellent earnings records in each of its first two years of operation. And following the Kempner tradition, the first two years of the merged company saw almost half the large cash flow reinvested back in the form of expenditures for enlarging and improving plant and distribution facilities. It appears that the merger may well signal a continuation of solid growth, under the same conservative, experienced and enlightened Kempner family management that had characterized the old Imperial Sugar Company for over 84 years.

[1]U. S. Department of Agriculture Economic Research Service. Agricultural Economic Report No. 138, July, 1968, p. 84.

[2]*Sugar and Sweetener*, U. S. Department of Agriculture, Economic Research Service, September, 1979, p. 74.

[3]SAMI Top 500 Report, 541 Fairbanks Court, Chicago, IL 60611, Dry Groceries, Houston Market, Issue 288-290, p. 1.

SOURCES

Anheiser, Betty, *Texas Oldest Sugar Refinery.*

Carter, Robert F., *History of Missouri City.*

Colorado County Historical Commission; *Colorado County Chronicles.*

Cronholm, Barbara, *History of the Kempner Family.*

Day, James, et al, *Soldier of Texas.*

Eagle Lake Historical Association, *A History of Eagle Lake.*

Eldridge, W. T.; *Trial Transcripts.*

Farr Company, N.Y.; *A Manual of Sugar Companies.*

Fehrenbach, T. R.; *Lone Star, A History of Texas and the Texans.*

Henson, Margaret Swett, *Samuel May Williams.*

Johnson, W. R., *A Short History of the Sugar Industry in Texas.*

Johnson, W. R., *Imperial of Texas.*

I. H. Kempner, *Recalled Recollections.*

Lasater, Dale; *Falfurrias, Ed C. Lasater and the Development of South Texas.*

Michner, James A., *Texas.*

Mintz, Sidney; *Sweetness and Power.*

Minute Books and files of Cunningham Sugar Company, Imperial Sugar Company and Sugarland Industries.

Nathan, R. J. Associates, Inc.; *Cane Sugar Refining in the United States.*

Recollections of the writer and numerous other vintage citizens of Sugar Land.

Reed, S. G., *History of Texas Railroads.*

Richardson, R. N.; *Texas, the Lone Star State.*

Sibley, Marilyn McAdams, *The Port of Houston.*

Silverthorn, Elizabeth, *Plantation Life in Texas.*

Sitterson, J. C.; *Sugar Country.*

Sowell, A. J.; *History of Fort Bend County.*

Steen, Ralph, *The Texas Story.*

Sugar Land Sesquicentennial Committee; *Sugar Land, A Pictorial Tribute.*

Taylor, Fred G.; *A Saga of Sugar.*

Texas Almanac, 1986-87.

Texas Commercial News.

Texas State Historical Association, *Memoirs of Dilue Harris.*

Texas State Historical Association Commission, *The Handbook of Texas.*

Texas Coaster; *Sesquicentennial Edition,* June 1972.

Turner, Jack T.; *The Marketing of Sugar.*

U.S. Cane Refiners Association, *Sugar Economics.*

U.S. Department of Agriculture, A History of Sugar Marketing.

Wharton, Clarence, *History of Fort Bend County.*

Whisenhunt, David; *Texas, A Centennial Celebration.*

Yelderman, Pauline; *The Jay Birds of Fort Bend County.*

Zeigler, Jesse; *Wave of the Gulf.*

THE AUTHOR

Born in April 1908, Robert M. Armstrong was destined to write the history of Sugar Land and the Imperial Sugar Company. Five hours after his birth in Oklahoma City, his father, O. R. Armstrong, went to work for the Meinrath Brokerage Company, selling Cunningham Sugar. In the same month, Kempner and Eldridge purchased the Sugar Land properties which included the Imperial Sugar Company.

O. R. Armstrong was to spend the remaining 53 years of his life in the marketing of sugar in Texas and the Southwest. He retired as vice president of sales for Imperial in 1947 and was a director of the company until his death in 1961.

So, following his father, Robert was raised in the business. He worked in the summers in the Imperial plant and in the short lived Texas City Sugar Refining Company plant in Texas City. Graduating from high school in Sugar Land in 1926, and from Texas A&M in 1930, and following an eight year stint as a Westinghouse sales engineer in the East, he returned to Dallas in 1938 as a junior partner in the W. W. Overton Company, a sugar brokerage firm, marketing Imperial sugar in the north half of Texas. After service in the Pacific during World War II, he moved to Sugar Land as Assistant Sales Manager of Imperial, progressed to vice president, director, executive vice president and finally president of the company from 1964 until his retirement in 1973. He remains a director emeritus of the company, now known as the Imperial Holly Corporation.

INDEX